# Border-Regional Economics

# Contributions to Economics

Peter R. Haiss
**Cultural Influences on
Strategic Planning**
1990. ISBN 3-7908-0481-9

Manfred Kremer/Marion Weber (Eds.)
**Transforming Economic Systems:
The Case of Poland**
1992. ISBN 3-7908-0585-8

Marcel F. van Marion
**Liberal Trade and Japan**
1993. ISBN 3-7908-0699-4

Hans Schneeweiß/
Klaus F. Zimmermann (Eds.)
**Studies in Applied Econometrics**
1993. ISBN 3-7908-0716-8

Gerhard Gehrig/
Wladyslaw Welfe (Eds.)
**Economies in Transition**
1993. ISBN 3-7908-0721-4

Christoph M. Schneider
**Research and Development
Management:
From the Soviet Union to Russia**
1994. ISBN 3-7908-0757-5

Bernhard Böhm/
Lionello F. Punzo (Eds.)
**Economic Performance**
1994. ISBN 3-7908-0811-3

Michael Reiter
**The Dynamics of Business Cycles**
1995. ISBN 3-7908-0823-7

Michael Carlberg
**Sustainability and Optimality
of Public Debt**
1995. ISBN 3-7908-0834-2

Lars Olof Persson/Ulf Wiberg
**Microregional Fragmentation**
1995. ISBN 3-7908-0855-5

Andreas Foerster
**Institutional Analysis
of Development Administration**
1995. ISBN 3-7908-0853-9

Ernesto Felli/Furio C. Rosati/
Giovanni Tria (Eds.)
**The Service Sector: Productivity
and Growth**
1995. ISBN 3-7908-0875-X

Giuseppe Munda
**Multicriteria Evaluation in
Fuzzy Environment**
1995. ISBN 3-7908-0892-X

Boris Maurer
**R & D, Innovation and Industrial
Structure**
1996. ISBN 3-7908-0900-4

Giovanni Galizzi/Luciano Venturini
(Eds.)
**Economics of Innovation:
The Case of Food Industry**
1996. ISBN 3-7908-0911-X

David T. Johnson
**Poverty, Inequality and Social
Welfare in Australia**
1996. ISBN 3-7908-0942-X

Rongxing Guo

# Border-Regional Economics

With 19 Figures

Physica-Verlag

A Springer-Verlag Company

**Series Editors**
Werner A. Müller
Peter Schuster

**Author**
Professor Dr. Rongxing Guo
Senior Research Fellow
Fondazione Eni Enrico Mattei (FEEM)
Via S. Sofia 27
I-20122 Milano, Italy
and
Beijing Graduate School of
China Univ. of Min. & Techn. (CUMT)
The College Road No. T-11
Mail Box 22
Beijing 100083, China

ISBN 3-7908-0943-8 Physica-Verlag Heidelberg

Die Deutsche Bibliothek – CIP-Einheitsaufnahme
Guo, Rongxing:
Border regional economics/Rongxing Guo. – Heidelberg: Physica-Verl., 1996
  (Contributions to economics)
  ISBN 3-7908-0943-8

The use of general descriptive names, registered names, trademarks, etc. in this publication does not imply, even in the absence of a specific statement, that such names are exempt from the relevant protective laws and regulations and therefore free for general use.

SPIN 10538178        88/2202-5 4 3 2 1 0 – Printed on acid-free paper

# ACKNOWLEDGEMENTS

This manuscript was prepared mainly while I was with the ENI Foundation (FEEM) in Italy.

Some preliminary ideas of border-regional economics in the first chapters of this book were presented at an International Colloquium on Border Economics held in Faculty of Economics and Research Institute of Oriental Studies, Gakushiun University, Tokyo, Japan, where I served as an invited speaker and received many valuable ideas from Professor Tatsuhiko Kawashima. I especially benefited from many thoughtful discussions with Professor Eui-Gak Hwang when I was lecturing at Korea University during March to June, 1994. I should acknowledge Professor Hyun Sik Chung and other participants for their important suggestions in a seminar held in Department of Economics, Sung Kyun Kwan University, Seoul, South Korea.

One year research activities in FEEM would have not gone smoothly had they not been helped by Professor Domenico Siniscalco. Dr. Alessandra Lanza, Patrizia Lughezzani, Marcella Pavan and other FEEM researchers and staff extended me much assistance, Marcella Fantinito also helped me to correct many structural and linguistic points of the draft, to whom I am very grateful. During my past researches on border-regions, many helps and constructive ideas have been also received from Professors Chen Baoshu, Gu Jirui, Zhao Renwei, Shen Liren, and Yang Kaizhong. I am also very grateful to Professor John Friedmann at UCLA, who suggested me many useful ideas and materials relating to border-regions.

My early research efforts on border-regional economics would not be possible without the financial grants from National Natural Science Foundation of China (NSFC #49301007) and National Social Science Foundation of China (NSSFC #90J.196). I would like to thank Professors Yang Wuyang of Peking University and Guo Tingbing, division Director of the NSFC for their research helps.

In addition, I should acknowledge all of my relatives and friends who have been supporting me through all and different aspects. My wife, Ms Liu Xiaohui, always understands me and bears most of the housework without any complaint. I am also indebted to my mother and my mother-in-law, both of whom have brought up their children dutifully and additionally helped to take loving cares to their grandchildren, including my son.

The last but not the least, I would like to acknowledge the FEEM, which financed me with an Annual Senior Research Fellowship and encourage me to publicize the manuscript. The views and errors produced in this book, however, are the author's sole responsibilities and should not be necessarily ascribed to the supporters.

Guo R. X.
Via S. Sofia, Milan
January 1996

# CONTENTS

# LIST OF TABLES

# LIST OF FIGURES

# NOTES FROM THE AUTHOR

1. The term 'political region' that appears in this book generally denotes an independent, dependent state, or any other form of administrative division.
2. Unless states otherwise, the term 'border-region' is defined in this book to geographically cover a cross-border scope, not just a single area in one side of a border.
3. The Chinese names are customarily written in the order of family name followed by given name. This is not always the case with Taiwan, Hong Kong and other overseas Chinese authors.

# INTRODUCTION

*This research work is*
*to commemorate all Guos' ancestor,*
*who guarded the border for his Majesty dutifully,*
*and who is the foremost supporter*
*in my academic career.*

For the past decades, economists and geographers from both developed and developing countries have studied the economic issues either within individual countries (regions), or between countries (regions). Only a relatively small part of these efforts has been focused on the economic affairs of those countries' (regions') peripheral areas and even less attention has been given to the structural analysis of economic mechanisms of the border-regions with different political levels and compositions.

My interest in border-regions more or less directly relates to some personal reasons of mine. The Chinese family name, Guo, means a guard for an outer city-wall (herein it used to be a political and military border in ancient China, e.g., the Chinese Great Wall). It is more interesting that Guo is written with a different Chinese character from that used for the like-sounding "Guo" (country). The Chinese writing of the latter is a square frame inside which lies a Chinese character, Wang (king), in the centre and a point in the corner. It might be simply supposed that the "point" was used by the inventor to necessarily represent the "border guard" probably because of its vital importance to the country. Nevertheless, according to the law of the origins of Chinese family names, Guo was ancestrally regarded as a border guard or at least had something to do with the border-regions.

Thousands of the Guo's descendants had devoted themselves to the Chinese (Zhonghua) nation, before I was born in a small village, Laojiu-zhuang, which is bordered by three counties in Central China's Henan province. In 1980, as a college student and later a university professor, I moved to Xuzhou, an ancient city bordering on four provinces of Jiangsu, Shandong, Henan and Anhui in East China, where I lived for more than 15 years.

\*    \*    \*    \*    \*    \*

Border-regions have been fortuitously involved in many of my living experiences. But the research interest of the economic mechanism of border-regions did not attract my first attention until the summer of 1987, when I attended a meeting on the economic development of Fengxian, a border county between Jiangsu, Shandong and Henan provinces in East China.

As the symbols used by adjacent political regimes to territorially identify their ruling divisions, borders are either visible or invisible on landscape. They have extension but usually no width, sometimes are marked only with stones or are fortified: the Roman *limes* against the barbarians to the North, the Great Wall (*Changcheng*) constructed by the Chinese to impede their northern enemies, the 38th Parallel which is still dividing the Korean peninsula into two antagonistic economies, and so on.

When a border serves as a division between two starkly different political and cultural systems, it might become totally an ideological watershed. On both sides of the border, there are two different lives but probably one single culture and tongue. Folks along the border share each other's sense of isolation and sad memory.

Located at the edges of political regions, border-regions are usually far away from their respective political and economic cores and hence have only relatively low efficient interactions and trade with their respective heartlands. Furthermore, cross-border separations have affected border-regions through all phases – political, social, cultural, and economic. The border-regions, however, may also be economically transformed under certain circumstances. Nevertheless, after the border-related barriers are removed, border-regions can substantially benefit from the cross-border trade and co-operation in terms of goods, capital, technology, information, etc. particularly when the adjacent political economies are structurally complementary. Some cross-border regions may also voluntarily form a single economic community so as to spatially overcome the internal diseconomies and benefit from the external economies of spatial sizes.

*    *    *    *    *    *

Compared with other regional economic studies, the major obstacle to analysing border-regions has been the difficulties in collecting sufficient and compatible cross-border data. Even worse, it is inconvenient, or even impossible sometimes, for border-regional scientists to visit the forbidden frontiers in order to explore in depth the natural and geographical features and socio-economic data due to the special physical and/or ideological environments in border-regions.

One important goal of this book is to establish a theoretical framework for border-regional economics which is closely related to but different from regional economics. Apart from the definition of some fundamental concepts relating to border-regional economics, another contribution of this book is that a series of case studies on border-regions with different natural, geographical features, and social and political structures have been done. I also develop some specific propositions and mathematical models in this study in order to analyse the spatial characteristics and operational mechanisms of border-regions. In addition to an introduction, the book has eight chapters, which are organised as below:

Chapter 1 focuses on the clarification of some fundamental concepts relating to political regions, regional borders, and border-regions. I analyse the forms and functions of regional borders between different political regions and develop some approaches to classify border-regions in terms of different analytical purposes. One of the interesting outcomes derived from this chapter is that the regional functions of different types of political borders and border-regions are economically compared. In addition, the natural and geographical facts and information concerning some typical political borders and border-regions between and within some independent countries of the world are also collected and analysed in this chapter.

Under the joint effects of such factors as nature, geography, social culture, and political economy, border-regions differing in fractional geometry in spatial organisation have posed challenges to regional scientists, economic geographers, and policy makers. After reviewing the recent literature on the socio-economic aspects of border-regions, Chapter 2 attempts to sketch a theoretical framework for border-regional economics which is defined as a new branch of regional economics in which the spatial organisations and economic developments in border-regions are studied. Three major objectives for border-regional economic research are proposed in accordance with the practical analyses of different border-regions. In addition, some basic theories and methodologies are also derived from economics, geography, system science, and history so as to contribute to the study of border-regional economics.

Being contradictory with each other and influencing border-regions simultaneously, the terms 'separation' and 'interdependence' plausibly characterize border-regional economics through two aspects. Starting with a simple comparison between the core and periphery in an autarkic economy, the geographical and political separations in border-regions are examined in Chapter 3. In practice, the adverse locational, economic, and social impacts of proximity to political borders are analysed respectively between North and South Korea, the western European nations, the United States and Canada, as well as mainland China's adjacent provinces. Using the data of 117 counties differing in nature, geography, resource, and spatial organization in China, we find that the average economic level in a border county is negatively related to both the number of provinces surrounding the border county and the number of villages and/or towns directly exposed to the outside province(s). After illustrating three basic propositions that are fundamentally important to serve as the theoretical bases for border-regional economics, Chapter 4 tries to explore more empirical evidences for the cross-border interdependence between adjacent political regions. We prove that the degree of cross-border interdependence in a border-region is positively related to the number of independent political authorities included in the border-region., which suggests that border-regions have more locational advantages to develop cross-border co-operation and trade rather than to maintain low-efficient economic ties with their respective remote heartlands. In addition, four different cases (Israeli–Palestinian co-operation, the Southwest U.S. border economic growth and the economic recovery in the inner-German border) are empirically analysed, which provides substantial evidences that border-regions can be economically transformed from the once-ever forbidden zones to the most dynamic poles (or triangles).

Due to the natural and artificial separations between different political regions, many border-regions have still been ineffectively developed. In Chapter 5, a $N$-dimensional static model of spatial economies is constructed to explain the spatial economic performances of $N$-dimensional border-regions ($N$=2, 3, 4, ...). Using the model, we conclude that, *ceteris paribus,* the largest economic output of a border-region is negatively related to the number of independent political regions involved in the spatial system. That is to say, the economic maximisation of a $N$-dimensional border-region will not exceed that of a $N$–1-dimensional border-region, *par analogie.* The model provides a practically valuable tool for border-regional scientists to estimate the economic impacts of political borders on the regional developments. As an application, a linear programming (LP) model is established for the spatial analysis of agricultural production in the border-region of Shanxi, Hebei, Shandong, and Henan provinces in Central China. Using this model, different scenarios of agricultural production under border and borderless conditions are derived respectively, from which we conclude that the agricultural production in this area has been decreased by approximately 10 per cent because of the border-related barriers between the four adjacent provinces.

The experiences and lessons of the regional development during the past decades have witnessed that border-regions might extricate themselves from the locational disadvantages under certain circumstances (such as the effective supports by the governments and the improvement of the cross-border relations). Based on the fundamental characteristics of border-regions, Chapter 6 proposes two basic approaches (i.e., the core-peripheral approach, or CPA and the cross-border approach, or CBA) for the border-regional development with an extensive examination of the spatial mechanisms and conditions of their applications in the first section. The rest sections of the chapter are three case studies. In order to solve part of its own national unemployment problem and achieve border development, the Mexican government established its border industrialisation programme (BIP) which was based on the workings of the U.S.–oriented "maquila" operations and has achieved a more rapid growth for its peripheral areas rather than the cores. China's frontier development strategy was put into effect by the central and local governments in the early 1990s when the coastal area's economic development had sustained for more than a decade. As an economic 'laboratory' of the mainland China's reform which concentrates on the *laissez-faire* and out-looking development, Shenzhen, a former frontier town *vis-à-vis* the Britain's New Territories in Hong Kong, had developed annually at an average GNP growth rate of about 38 per cent in the 1980s and perhaps been the fastest growing area in the world during the same period.

Among the factors contributing to the economic growth of the border-regions have been the increasing cross-border co-operation and mobility of persons, goods, services, and information. Chapter 7 introduces, *inter alia*, some ongoing cross-border co-operation programmes. The European cross-border co-operation programmes, which are aimed at the promotion of the cross-border development and ultimately a single political union, have been undertaken throughout many of West Europe's internal border-regions. The U.S.–Mexican border environment co-operation programme is a newly established joint venture by the governments of the United States and Mexico for the protection and improvement of the environment in their common border area. China's transprovincial border economic zones (BEZs) were established between two, three, four, or five adjacent provinces, autonomous regions, and autonomous cities in the 1980s as a result of the growing inter-provincial interdependence and the reconstruction of the inter-regional economic network in mainland China.

Cross-border interactions in border-regions have clearly generated economic benefits. However, they also have induced or intensified numerous problems that cannot be resolved by one side of the border alone. Since the early 1990s, the UNDP-sponsored Tumen River area development programme (TRADP), which was formally initiated by the three Tumen River riparian states (China, Russia, and North Korea) plus South Korea and Mongolia on May 30, 1995, has been one of the most promising possibilities for the multinational economic co-operation in Northeast Asian countries. Even though there have still been differences between the participating countries in some important aspects, it looks more and more possible, under the growing phenomenon of cross-border collaboration as well as the tendency towards the unanimity of political, social, especially economic points of views among the participants, to find an appropriate approach that can maximise the benefits, for all the parties connected, while also taking into account their respective articulated objectives.

Border-regional economic research has spurred rapidly since the end of the Cold War era. On December 27–30, 1993, an international conference entitled "Regional Development: The Challenges of the Frontier", co-hosted by the Negev Center for Regional Development, Ben-Gurion University of the Negev, and the Lewis Center for Regional Policy Studies, University of California at Los Angeles (UCLA), was held in the Dead Sea, Ein Bokek, Israel. This conference received as many as 180 papers and abstracts focusing on the natural, geographical, environmental, social, cultural and economic aspects of border-regions.[1]

---

[1]For more details of these papers, see (1) Keynotes and Abstracts of International Conference on *Regional Development: The Challenges of the Frontier*, the Dead Sea, Ein

From the standpoint of the heartlands, however, some border-regions have been still posing a series of social and political problems during the past years, as John Friedmann (1993) points out: "They are rife with 'native' uprising, drug mafias, war lords in brazen defiance of the state, guerrilla strongholds, and tribal warfare. There may be a danger of incursions from across the border, posing a threat to the heartland. Where political boundaries were never drawn with precision, frontier regions are often disputed with neighbouring states: precious resources or strategic advantage may be at stake. 'Surplus' population may need to be resettled from the heartland where land has become scarce in a periphery thought to be rich in forests, minerals and land."[2]

Based on a number of crucial assumptions for an isolated country, Chapter 8 develops a regional cost-benefit analysis (RCBA) framework that utilises the micro-economic approach to understanding the economies or diseconomies of spatial sizes for different political regions. Using the RCBA methodology, political regions (independent and dependent states, and other forms of administrative regions) in this chapter are categorised into three kinds of spatial status (i.e., I: the actual sizes of the political regions equal to their respective optimal ones; II: the actual sizes of the political regions are less than their respective optimal ones; and III: the actual sizes of the political regions are larger than their respective optimal ones). As an extension, the operational mechanisms of border-regions formed by political regions differing in spatial status are also compared, which provides a theoretical understanding for the political authorities to develop different patterns of inter-regional integration and cross-border co-operation so as to maximize their respective external economies and minimize their internal diseconomies.

\* \* \* \* \* \*

Of course, perhaps some political regions might be proliferated by new artificial borders, and some political regions might voluntarily unite or be

---

Bokek, Israel; (2) Yehuda Gradus (ed.): *Frontiers in Regional Development*, Rowman and Littlefield, forthcoming.

[2]John Friedmann: Keynote Address to the International Conference on *Regional Development: The Challenges of the Frontier*, the Dead Sea, Ein Bokek, Israel, December 27–30, 1993.

merged as a single economic or political community. Border-regions will therefore change their geographic scopes and be incorporated with new objectives along with the evolution of political regions. Perhaps some centuries later, the political regions will have become only a historical term, and we will never find the identical lines for the political boundaries in the landscapes and maps. Nevertheless, we should not be so disappointed after border-regions as our research interest disappear, because it is inevitably a historical tendency for border-regions to complete their life-cycle. Border-regions will thus get rid of all the disadvantageous locations and share the equal opportunity of economic development with the core regions along with the disappearance of political and economic borders. Ironically, Guos' ancestor, who had devoted himself to the border guarding, would have been more than happy had he known that his later generations would be able to live together with their former enemies peacefully in a borderless world.

# CHAPTER 1
# SOME BASIC CONCEPTS

Border-regions are never so strange for people who reside there, but they do have a special appeal to people who are far away from there. In a few of cases, border-regions are only referred as forbidden zones and strategically play an important role in political competition and/or military confrontation between the antagonistic regimes. While in many other cases, border-regions calmly exist in all and different landscapes: a border town or village under the jurisdiction of two or more authorities, a street dividing two districts, a zone between urban and rural areas, or even a province or autonomous region bordering on a foreign country, etc. Due to the border-regions' geographical complexities and political heterogeneities, a precise definition and classification of some related concepts should be carefully done before the framework of border-regional economics is fundamentally constructed. In this chapter, more efforts will be given to the theoretical and empirical clarifications of three basic concepts (i.e., political region, regional border, and border-region) with some functional extensions to their socio-economic implications.

## 1.1 Political Region

In the Oxford English dictionary, 'political' is concerned with the form, organization, and administration of a State or part of a State, and with the regulation of its relations with other States; 'region' refers to a definable portion of the earth's surface.[1] The political region I use here is specifically defined as a socio-economic entity necessarily with a certain area of territory in which a ruler (government or any other form of ruling power) and a number of residents exist. According to 1994's *World Atlas*, political regions may be classified into four major forms: (i) independent country, (ii) internally independent political entity under protection of other country(ies) in matter of defence and/or foreign affairs, (iii) colony and other dependent political units, and (iv) administrative subdivisions.[2]

---

[1]See Lesley Brown (ed.): *The New Shorter Oxford English Dictionary on Historical Principles*, pp. 2274 and 2527, Oxford: Clarendon Press, Vol. 2 (N–Z), 1993.
[2]Rand Mc. Nally & Company (1994): *World Atlas*, p. 2, USA.

## 1.11 Independent country

Independent countries are the highest form of political regions in the world. A country must have a territory. Since the disintegration of the former USSR into 15 independent states, the existing independent countries have territorially varied from as small as 0.2 square miles (i.e., Vatican City) to as large as 6,592,849 square miles (i.e., Russian Federation). There must also have citizens in the territory. As one of the largest countries in the world, China has already a population of 1.2 billions which are still expanding at the rate of more than 10 millions per year. Each sovereign country may also independently manage the socio-economic activities by means of laws and/or ruling regulations within its territorial area beyond which different political and economic scenarios may exist.

Independent countries are also diversified in form of organization. Until 1994, the world's 191 independent countries have been divided by 17 categories of political status in the forms of governments and ruling powers. (see Table 1–1.)

## 1.12 Internally independent political entity

Internally independent political entities can also be known as quasi-independent countries as they are independent in matter of internal affairs while under the protection of other independent countries in matter of defence and/or foreign affairs. For example, Andorra is a coprincipality under the joint protection of Spain and France; Bhutan is a monarchy under Indian protection; Cook Islands is a self-governing territory under the protection of New Zealand; Greenland is a self-governing territory under Danish protection; etc.

## 1.13 Colony and other dependent political units

These political units are generally regarded as the territories which are fully or partly subject to their respective mother states. For example, Hong Kong and Macao are Chinese territories under British and Portuguese administrations respectively; American Samoa, Guam, Midway Islands and Virgin Islands (U.S.) are unincorporated territories of U.S.A.; Cayman Islands, Bermuda, British Indian Ocean Territory, Gibraltar, Monsterrat,

Pitcairm (including dependencies), St. Helena (including dependencies), South Georgia (including dependencies), Turksand Caicos Islands and Virgin Islands (British) are dependent territories of U.K.; etc.

Table 1–1 Forms of Governments/Ruling Powers of the World's Independent Countries

| No. | Form of government or ruling power | Number of countries |
|-----|-------------------------------------|---------------------|
| 1. | Republic | 110 |
| 2. | Constitutional Monarchy | 18 |
| 3 | Parliamentary State | 13 |
| 4. | Provisional Military Government | 12 |
| 5. | Socialist Republic | 9 |
| 6. | Federal Republic | 8 |
| 7. | Monarchy | 6 |
| 8. | Federal Parliamentary State | 3 |
| 9. | Islamic Republic | 2 |
| 10. | Transitional Military Republic | 2 |
| 11. | Federal Islamic Republic | 2 |
| 12. | Transitional Government | 1 |
| 13. | Federal Constitutional Monarchy | 1 |
| 14. | Federation of Monarchy | 1 |
| 15. | Monarchical–Sacerdotal State | 1 |
| 16. | Constitutional Monarchy under Military Rule | 1 |
| 17. | None | 1 |

Source: *World Atlas* (1994), Rand Mc. Nally & Company, USA.
Calculations by the author.

## 1.14 Administrative subdivisions

Within the above political regions, there usually have administrative subdivisions differing in political status. The administrative subdivisions directly under the central government of a country are called first-class administrative regions, or province, dependent state, etc.; the second-class administrative subdivisions directly under the first class administrative regions are usually called municipality, county, etc.; ... Table 1–2 gives some facts on the first-class administrative regions for selected countries.

Table 1–2 The First-class Administrative Regions, Selected Countries

| Country | Name(s) | Number | Average territorial area ('000 sq. m) |
|---------|---------|--------|---------------------------------------|
| Russia | ARP, S, FR | 76 | 86.74 |
| Canada | P, T | 10 | 385.00 |
| U.S.A. | S, DC | 51 | 74.25 |
| China | P, AR, AC | 31 | 119.55 |
| Brazil | P | 25 | 131.44 |
| Australia | S, CT | 8 | 370.75 |
| Kazakhstan | S | 19 | 55.21 |
| Ukraine | S | 25 | 9.32 |
| Spain | P | 50 | 3.90 |
| Turkmenistan | S | 5 | 37.60 |
| Uzbekistan | AR, S | 13 | 13.31 |

Note: ARP=Autonomous Republic; AR=Autonomous Region; FR=Frontier Region; S= State; P=Province; T=Territory; AC=Autonomous City; CT=Capital Territory; DC=District of Colombia.
Source: Calculations by the author based on the maps of various countries.

In most rural areas of China, peasant household (*Nonghu*) may be known as the lowest form of administrative subdivisions. A number of peasant households which are in many cases bordered with each other in terms of farm land and/or resident yard usually constitute a *Zhu* (group), while the latter is under the jurisdiction of a village. A *Chunweihui* (committee for villagers) directly under a *Xiang* or *Zhen* government is usually composed of one or more adjacent village(s) and/or town(s). A county is divided into several *Xiang* and/or *Zhen* administrative units.

## 1.2 Regional Border

The English word, 'border' (or 'boundary'), which refers to a definition that delimits a political territory and life space, has wider meanings in political and economic geography than 'frontier', while the latter usually refers to a special case of border when it is used to divide the sovereign limits of adjacent independent states.[3] Border (or boundary) used here exists not only between independent nations but also between other forms of political regions as discussed in Section 1.1.

Intuitively, a political border exists wherever a political region is established. As both an ending and a starting point in landscape, borders can be viewed as a separation factor. A border cuts off two systems of political authorities. Each system can extend only up to the border. A political border also denotes a scope of territory where a government or ruling power can exercise its sovereignty and/or judicature. The governments in the political regions may manage the exportation and importation of goods using tariff and non-tariff instruments and supervise people who are crossing the borders by issuing visas and/or emigration permits. In conclusion, the border manifests itself in the following three functions: (a) a legal function, where the border line exactly delimits the territories subject to juridical standards and to the country's legislation; (b) a control function, where every crossing of the border line is submitted, in principle, to a state control; (c) a fiscal function, where the control function is accompanied by a perception of custom right assuring the adaptation of the fiscal rights in force in the country of entry.[4]

As the marginal lines of political regions, political borders are either visible or invisible on landscape: they have extension but no width. Sometimes they are marked only with stone, or they are fortified: the Roman *limes* against the barbarians to the North, the Magnet Line, the 38th Parallel, the Great Wall of China, etc. Political borders are also diversified. They can be generally classified by two approaches, i.e., (1) physical approach which divides political borders into natural and artificial borders; (2) geometric approach which divides political borders into linear and non-linear borders. The detailed classification and the socio-economic implications of different kinds of borders will be analysed below.

---

[3]In some other European languages 'frontier' is generally known as 'political border'.

[4]See P. Guichonnet and C. Raffestin (1974): *Géographie des Frontières* (Geography of Border Regions), Paris: Presses Universitaires de France.

## 1.21 Natural and artificial borders

This couple of borders are simply distinguished by the physical materials by which the borders are expressed.

## 1.211 Natural border

Natural borders are identified by different natural barriers or screens, such as mountains, rivers, lakes, seas, etc. Because their importance to military defences, mountains, rivers, lakes and seas have been usually adopted by territorial rulers to serve as political borders.

(1) *Mountain.* If a mountain exists between adjacent political regimes, it usually serves as a natural border. Mountains, when serving as political borders, have the military advantages of being easy to defend and hard to be attacked, while they have the economic disadvantages for the relevant countries or regions to develop cross-border exchange and co-operation due to the geographic barriers. Usually, the peak and/or watershed of a mountain between the adjacent political areas are/is selected by territorial rulers to determine their common border.

There are many mountains being used to serve as political borders: Switzerland, Italy and France jointly use the Alps to separate their territories; West Argentina has Andes Mts., between which and Pacific Ocean lies a geographically long and thin country, Chile; the Himalayas is now separating India, Nepal, Bhutan and China; the Pyrenees lies between Spain and France; the common borderland of Malaysia and Indonesia includes Upper Kapuas Mts. and Iran Mts.; etc. Tables 1–3 gives some principal mountains in the international borders.

(2) *River.* Because rivers have distinctive extensions, they are more suitable to serve as political borders. When demarcating a border along a river between two political regions, it has been commonly suggested that the border should be located in the central line either in the main channel of the river if it is open to navigation or between the two banks of the river if it is non-navigable.

Many rivers have been used to mark international border lines in the world. Oder River flows between Germany and Poland; Bulgaria, Romania, Yugoslavia, Czech Republic and Hungary meet at the River of Danube; Rio Grande River is the border of U.S.A. and Mexico; Amur (Heilong-jiang),

Ussuri and Argum Rivers cover three sections of Sino-Russian border; etc. Table 1–4 gives some principal rivers by which different countries are separated.

Table 1–3 The Principal Mountains in the International Borders

| Mountain | Country–country | Elevation (feet) |
| --- | --- | --- |
| Belukha, Gol'tsy | Kazakhstan–Russia | 14,783 |
| Blanc, mont | France–Italy | 15,771 |
| Elgon, Mt. | Kenya–Uganda | 14,178 |
| Everest, Mt. | China–Nepal | 29,028 |
| Fairweather, Mt. | Alaska–Canada | 15,300 |
| Gasherbrum | China–Pakistan | 26,470 |
| Haltiatunturi | Finland–Norway | 4,357 |
| K2 (Godwin Austen) | China–Pakistan | 28,250 |
| Kamet | China–India | 25,447 |
| Kanchenjunga | India–Nepal | 28,208 |
| Karisimbi, Volcan | Rwanda–Zaire | 14,787 |
| Korab | Albania–Macedonia | 9,026 |
| Llullaillaco, Volcan | Argentina–Chile | 22,057 |
| Makalu | China–Nepal | 27,825 |
| Margherita, Pk. | Zaire–Uganda | 16,763 |
| Matterhorn | Italy–Switzerland | 14,692 |
| Neblina, Pico da | Brazil–Venezuela | 9,888 |
| Ojos del Salado, Nevado | Argentina–Chile | 22,615 |
| Paektu-san | North Korea–China | 9,003 |
| Pobedy, pik | China–Russia | 24,406 |
| Rosa, Monte | Italy–Switzerland | 15,203 |
| St. Elias, Mt. | U.S.–Canada | 21,463 |
| Tupungato, Portezuelo de | Argentina–Chile | 22,310 |
| Zugspitze | Austria–Germany | 9,718 |

Source: *World Atlas (1994)*, Rand Mc. Nally & Company, USA.

Table 1–4 The Principal Rivers along the International Borders*

| River | Country–country |
| --- | --- |
| Abuna | Brizil–Bolivia |
| Amu Darya | Turkmenistan–Uzbekistan–Afghanistan–Tajkistan |
| Amur | China–Russia |
| Arauca | Venezuela–Colombia |
| Argun | China–Russia |
| Cassai | Angola–Zaire |
| Congo | Congo–Zaire |
| Courantvne | Guyana–Surirame |
| Cuando | Angola–Zambia |
| Cuango | Angola–Zaire |
| Danube | Hungary–Slovakia; Bulgaria–Romania–Yugoslavinia |
| Douro | Spain–Portugal |
| Drava | Hungary–Croatia |
| Drina | Yugoslavia–Bosnia and Herzegovinia |
| Faleme | Senegal–Mali |
| Gavalla | Liberia–Cote d'lvoire |
| Guapore | Brizil–Bolivia |
| Javari | Peru–Brazil |
| Lainoalven | Sweden–Finland |
| Limpopo | South Africa–Botswana |
| Logone | Chad–Cameroon |
| Maroni | Brazil–French Guiania |
| Mekong (Lancang) | China–Myanmar–Laos–Thailand |
| Meta | Venezuela–Colombia |
| Mloomou | Zaire–Central African Republic |
| Niger | Niger–Benin |
| Oder | Germany–Poland |
| Okavango | Angola–Namibia |
| Orange | Namibia–South Africa–Lesotho |
| Oued Drad | Morocco–Algeria |
| Oyapock | Brazil–French Guiania |

*to be contiuned*

Table 1–4 (*continued*)

| | |
|---|---|
| Prut | Moldova–Romania–Ukraine |
| Pupumayo | Peru–Colombia–Ecuador |
| Rhine | France–Germany–Switzerland |
| Rio Grande | U.S.–Mexico |
| Rio Orinoco | Venezuela–Colombia |
| Rio Paraguay | Brazil–Paraguay–Argentina |
| Rio Uruguay | Uruguay–Argentina–Brazil |
| Ruvuma | Tanzania–Mozambique |
| Sava | Croatia–Bosnia and Herzegovinia |
| Tumen | China–North Korea–Russia |
| Ubangi | Zaire–Congo |
| Ussuri | China–Russia |
| Yalu | China–North Korea |
| Zambezi | Namibia–Zambia–Zimbabwe |

\* Based on the maps of various countries.

Table 1–5 The Principal Rivers as the Inter-state Borders, USA\*

| River | State–state |
|---|---|
| Columbia R. | Washington–Oregon |
| Snake | Oregon–Idaho |
| Cololado | California–Arizona |
| Red | Texas–Oklahoma |
| Mississippi | Minnesta–Wisconsin–Iowa–Illinois–Missouri–Kentucky |
| | Missouri–Tennessee–Arkansas–Mississippi–Louisiana |
| Wabash | Indiana–Illinois–Kentucky |
| Ohio | Illinois–Kentucky–Indiana |
| | Kentucky–Ohio–West Virginia |
| Savannah | South Carolina–Georgia |
| Connecticut | Vermont–New Hampshire |
| Delaware | New York–Pennsylvania–New Jersey |

\* Based on the map of the United States of America.

Table 1–6 The Principal Rivers as Internal Borders, Brazil*

| River | Internal border(s) |
| --- | --- |
| Rio Parana | Parana–Mato Grosso Do sul–Sao Paulo |
| Paranpanema | Parana–Sao Paulo |
| Rio Grande | Sao Paulo–Minas Gerais |
| Paranaiba | Minas Gerais–Goias |
| Araguaia | Goias–Mato Grosso Do sul; Para–Tocantins |
| Braco Maior | Mato Grosso–Tocantins |
| Parnaiba | Maranhao–Piaui |
| Rio Sao Francisco | Bahia–Pernambuco; Alagoas–Sergipe |
| Gurupi | Maranhao–Para |
| Sao Manuel | Mato Grosso Do sul–Para |
| Jumunda | Amazonas Selvas–Para |
| Jari | Para–Amapa |

* Based on the map of Brazil.

Even inside the independent countries, there still have the administrative borders which are identified by rivers. For example, the United Sates uses the rivers in Table 1–5 as some of its inter-state borders. Under the topographical influence, Brazil is administratively divided by many internal rivers (listed in Table 1–6) between Atlantic Ocean and Andes Mts. Originating from Qinghai–Tibetan plateau in Southwest China, Yellow River (Huang-he) flows through Gansu, Ningxia Hui, Inner Mongolia, Shanxi, Shaanxi, Henan and Shandong provinces or autonomous regions before it finally converges into East China Sea. The river has ruptured about 1500–1600 times and changed about 26 waterways.[5] As the cradle of the Chinese culture, Yellow River used to separate Henan (south river) and Hebei (north river) provinces in Central China and is now representing some sections of the Shaanxi–Shanxi and Henan–Shandong inter-provincial borders.

(3) *Lake*. Characterized by clear segregations and convenient for water transportation, lakes are also regarded as suitable natural screens in which political borders may be established between adjacent regimes.

---

[5]See *Cihai*, p. 2058, Shanghai: Shanghai cishu Press, 1988.

A number of lakes are located in the international borders in the world. The Five Great Lakes (Superior, Michigan, Huron, Erie and Ontario), for example, are located between Canada and the United States; Khanka Lake (Xingkai-hu) lies on the Sino–Russian border; the Buir Nur Lake covers a section of the border between China and Mongolia; Victoria Lake separates Uganda, Kenya and Tanzania; Tanganyik Lake is the borders of Tanzania, Zambia, Zaire and Burundi; Switzerland meets France and Italy across the Geneva and Maggiore Lakes respectively; Lago Titicaca is located between Peru and Bolivia. Other lakes divided by international borders are Chad (between Niger, Chad, Nigeria and Cameroon), Albert (between Zaire and Uganda), Kanba (between Zambia and Zimbabwe), Mweru (between Zaire and Zambia), Rudoff (between Ethiopia and Kenya), Nyasa (between Malawi, Mozambique and Tanz), etc. In addition, lakes also serve as sub-political borders within independent states. Table 1–7, for instance, gives some principal lakes in the inter-provincial borders of China.

Cameroon and Nigeria are two central African countries. These two countries play a similar leading role within their adjacent sub-regional economies. They share an 1,600 kilometre long common border from the delta of the Rio del Rey in the South to Lake Chad in the North. Territorial ambitions on both sides often generated bloody incidents during the first two decades following their independence. The situation is a result of the historical circumstances leading to the creation, during the colonial era, of a poorly defined and highly contested border. In addition, economic issues like oil in the delta area, as well as hydraulic and fishery resources in the Lake Chad Basin, are some of the main reasons underlying the dispute.[6]

(4) *Sea.* Like lakes, seas have also a significant segregation and are suitable for water transportation. The international borders can be easily established between the territorial and international seas. For example, the Black Sea separates Romania, Turkey, Bulgaria and Russia; the Red Sea is surrounded by four nations of Egypt, Israel, Jordan and Saudi Arabia; The Aral Sea lies between Kazakhstan and Uzbekistan; etc. The scope of a country's territorial sea was generally known as three sea miles far away from the coastline under the lowest tide during the 18th Century, which was

---

[6]For more evidence, see D. Mouafo and J. Herrera (1993): "The Challenge of the Frontier in Central Africa: The Cameroon-Nigeria Border Case", unpublished paper, Univerite Laval, Canada.

also the largest range of gunfire during those times. The territorial seas of most of the 136 coastal countries have now ranged from 3 to 200 sea miles.[7]

Table 1–7 The Principal Lakes in the Inter-provincial Borders, China*

| Lake | Inter-provincial border |
| --- | --- |
| Chahan-diao | Hebei–Inner Mongolia |
| Danjiangkou-shuiku | Hubei–Henan |
| Dingshan-hu | Shanghai–Jiangsu |
| Dongting-hu | Hunan–Hubei |
| Erlongshan-shuiku | Jilin–Liaoning |
| Gaoyou-hu | Jiangsu–Anhui |
| Guanting-shuiku | Hebei–Beijing |
| Gucheng-hu | Jiangsu–Anhui |
| Hedi-shuiku | Guangdong–Guangxi Zhuang |
| Hong-hu | Hubei–Anhui |
| Hongjian-diao | Shaanxi–Inner Mongolia |
| Hongzhe-hu | Jiangsu–Anhui |
| Longgan-hu | Hubei–Anhui |
| Lugu-hu | Sichuan–Yunnan |
| Mitijiangzhanmu-cuo | Qinghai–Tibet |
| Nanshi-hu | Shandong–Jiangsu |
| Shijiu-hu | Anhui–Jiangsu |
| Tai-hu | Jiangsu–Zhejiang |
| Weishan-hu | Shandong–Jiangsu |
| Youyi-shuiku | Inner Mongolia–Hebei |
| Yuecheng-shuiku | Hebei–Henan |

* Based on the Map of China.

## 1.212 Artificial border

If no significant natural barrier is available or the natural screen is not suitable to serve as a border between two adjacent political regions, an

---

[7]More details may be found in Zhang Wenkui (ed.) (1991): *An Introduction to Human Geography*, p. 234, second edition, Changchun: Northeast Normal University Press.

artificial border should be jointly established by the adjacent political regions. Generally, artificial borders include three categories: (i) artificial barrier; (ii) latitude/longitude border; and (iii) cultural border. We analyse them as below.

(1) *Artificial barrier*. Among the artificial barriers serving as political borders, stone tablets and walls are most commonly constructed by one or both sides of the adjacent territorial rulers to identify its or their political divisions. Stemmed from the territorial division of the post-war Germany in the work of the European Advisory Commission (established jointly by the governments of USA, UK, and former USSR), the Berlin Wall, which separated Berlin into East and West Berlin cities under the jurisdiction of the former East and West Germany respectively during the period of the Cold War is a typical example. The border wall created many sad and tearful memories for the Germans of the both sides and was finally removed in 1989.[8]

Travelling 18 kilometers toward the east of Shenzhen city, South China, one may find a special town, Shatoujiao, which has been a typical standing point in the border between the British New Territories in Hong Kong and the mainland China. Shatoujiao town has an area of about four square kilometers which has been divided into two parts by a 200 meter long and two to three meter wide street, namely, *Zhongying-jie* (St. Sino–Britain). The eastern part of the town belongs to Bao'an county of Shenzhen municipality, while the western part of the town, together with the rest of Kowloon peninsula, has been colonially rented as the New Territories of Hong Kong by the British government for a period of 99 years since 1898 in accordance with Sino–British Treaty on the Extension of Hong Kong's Territories. On both sides of the street, there have been two different political systems, two citizens belonging to different nations but the same ethnical identity. In the middle of the street, seven stone tablets carved with "Sino–British Border, 1898" can still be seen clearly in both English and Chinese.

---

[8]More stories about the Wall may be found in (1) E. Pond (1990): *After the Wall: American Policy Toward Germany*, A 20th Century Fund Paper, New York: Priority Press Publication, and (2) P. Marcuse (1992): "The Goal of the Wall-less City: New York, Los Angeles and Berlin", Harvey S. Perloff Lecture, UCLA Graduate School of Architecture and Urban Planning.

As one of the greatest projects in the world's history, the Great Wall, or *Bianqiang* (border wall), was originally built during Spring and Autumn (770–476 BC) and Warring States (475–221 BC) Period in ancient China. After unifying the six states of Wei, Han, Zhao, Chu, Yan and Qitian, Qinshi-huang (258–210 BC), China's first emperor in Qin Dynasty, began to renovate and connect the northern sections of the border walls of Qin, Zhao, and Yan states in 214 BC in order to prevent the invasion from the Hunish aristocrats in the north. Extending from Linyao (located around Min-xian county of Gansu province) in the West, to Yin-shan in the North and Liao-dong in the East, the Great Wall has been generally called "*Wanli Changcheng*" (the ten thousand *li*[9] great wall). Almost all emperors in Han (206 BC–220 AD), North Wei (386–534 AD), North Qi (550–577 AD), North Zhou (557–581 AD) and Sui (581–618 AD) Dynasties invested a large amount of money and labour forces to rebuild the great wall in order to prevent their respective territories from being attacked by the North. During the Emperors Hongwu (reign 1368–1399) to Wanli (reign 1573–1619) in Ming Dynasty (1368–1644), the border wall was rebuilt as many as eighteen times. The latest wall – being 6700 kilometers long, 85 meters high and 5.7–6.5 meters thick – starts from Jiayu-guan in the west, ends at Shanhai-guan in the east and extends several sub-walls in the south of Xuanhua and Datong towns and between Shanxi and Hebei provinces.[10]

(2) *Latitude/Longitude border*. The longest latitude border is the U.S.–Canada border in the 49th Parallel of the north latitude. The international border of Egypt and Sudan is in the 22th Parallel of the north latitude. The

---

[9]*li* is a Chinese length unit. One *li* equals to 0.5 km.

[10]Source: *Cihai*, p. 69, Shanghai: Shanghai Cishu Press, 1988. In addition, the Great Wall project can still be found with complete facilities. The structure are solid and well laid out, good for both attack and defence. At each strategic point there is a fortress constructed for the garrison troops. They could go outside the wall to patrol, or when the situation required, to outflank the enemy from behind. At some main passes the double walls were constructed. The Wall was built in line with the terrain: where the terrain is flat, the wall is several meters thick and high; where the mountain is steep, the wall is only less than a half meter. On a mild slope between two steep points was cut sharp and stone blocks were laid. At the outer wall of the Great Wall buttresses and loopholes were distributed. In some strategic places three rows of holes were built for soldiers to shoot from three stances: standing, kneeling and prone. Protruding watchtowers were distributed in the wall at a different interval which was dependent on the strategic role. The watchtower is usually 10 meters in height, mostly with two stories.

longitude lines are used as the international borders between, among others, Canada and Alaska (U.S.A.) (the 14th Parallel of the west longitude), Egypt and Libya (the 25th Parallel of the east longitude), Indonesia and Papua New Guinea (the 14th Parallel of the east longitude). In addition, the 60°36'th Parallel of the west longitude is the border of Argentina and Chile in Greande de Tierra del Fuego Island.

(3) *Cultural border.* A cultural border is identified by two or more different cultures. In China, for example, four inter-provincial borders are currently characterized by different ethnic identities which include Uygur and Tibetan in the border of Xinjiang Uygur and Tibet, Uygur and Han in the border of Xinjiang Uygur and Gansu, Hui and Han in the border of Ningxia Hui and Shaanxi, and Hui and Mongolian in the border of Ningxia Hui and Inner Mongolia.

The disintegration of the former USSR caused serious aggravation of the inter-relation between Russia and Ukraine, especially at their common cross-border territories. This concerns the problems of culture and education as well. The area of the Ukraine, which is called Slobozhanskaya Ukraine, with its component part – Kharkov region – from the moment of its beginning is a good example for historic analysis of the origination of various cultural and educational trends. The multinationality of culture is represented by various geographical names in the contiguous regions, by types of relief, names of human settlements, rural areas, etc. Among a great variety of such problems, which are characterised for boundary territories, the most urgent one is that of what language should be spoken and used in the educational process at secondary and higher schools, in writing tuition plans and programmes and while preparing and passing entrance examinations at higher schools in the Ukraine, etc.[11]

The Israelis and Palestinians live together within a narrow territory along the eastern coast of Mediterranean Sea in the western side of Jordan River and Dead Sea. The cultural conflicts between the two different groups of peoples might be alleviated temporarily but never stopped during the past decades. It is expected that the peace process and economic co-operation between the two culturally different nations will be accelerated along with

---

[11]For more arguments, see A. Damasevich (1993): "Problems Concerning Cultural and Educational Development at the Transboundary Territories of the Ukraine and Russia", unpublished paper, Kharkov State University, Ukraine.

the successful delimitation of their joint geographic border even though the cultural separation between the two neighbours seems to last a long time.

However, there is another landscape in the heart of West Europe: one may find a special Alpine country – Switzerland – where four language groups live peacefully and talk in Swiss German, French, Italian, and Rhaeto-Romanic. As a neutral state, Switzerland combines almost all aspects of the heterogeneous European societies and plays an important role in the moderation of cultural separation between different parts of the West Europe.

## 1.22 Linear and non-linear borders

Political borders can also be geometrically classified. Consider a two dimensional co-ordinate system in which a successive border starts at point $(x_1, y_1)$ and ends at point $(x_2, y_2)$. For the sake of expositional ease, the geometric curve of the border is expressed by a non-turnpoint function, $y=f(x)$. By deriving the first order differential of $y$ with respect to $x$, we obtain

(1) if $f'(x)=dy/dx=$constant, it denotes a linear border;
(2) if $f'(x)=dy/dx\neq$constant, it denotes a non-linear border.

When the border is non-linear (i.e., $f'(x)\neq$constant), we may derive the second order differential of $y$ with respect to $x$ and obtain:

(2.1) if $f''(x)=d^2y/dx^2>0$, it denotes a concave border;
(2.2) if $f''(x)=d^2y/dx^2<0$, it denotes a convex border.

It is noteworthy that the convex and concave borders are converted to each other. For example, a border is viewed of convexity from one side and, simultaneously, of concavity from the other side (see Figure 1–1). The geometric properties of borders create different geographical locations in political regions. Obviously, it is not difficult to understand that the political regions with high degrees of convex borders have usually the geographical disadvantages of being hard to defend and easy to be attacked. On the other hand, however, the political regions with convex borders will benefit more from the cross-border co-operation with the outside world than those political regions with concave borders do.[12]

Many countries can be geographically identified in terms of convex and/or concave borders. The Bohai Bay, for example, creates a highly concave coastline for East China and strategically serves as a natural protection for much of its heartland where Beijing (Peking) has been the Chinese capital city for many centuries. Bordered by Egypt and Jordan, the State of Israel is just shaped as a dagger heading the Gulf of Arabia in the south. The convex border of this state sharply makes Negav (southern part of Israel) to be completely exposed to its outside world.

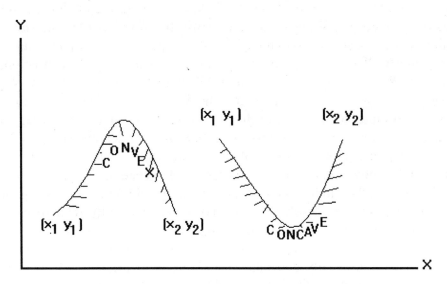

Figure 1–1 The Convex and Concave Borders

### 1.3 Border-Region

Being normally related to the political regions and regional borders, the concept of border-region, or interchangeably, cross-border region, largely refers to the spatial heterogeneities in terms of political and economic structures. Political borders divide different systems of political authorities,

---

[12]Furthermore, the spatial economic difference between a region with a convex border and one with a concave border may be quantitatively simulated by Equations (6–5)-(6–7) constructed in Chapter 6.

different ways of lives. A border-region *per se* combines the territories of two or more different political regions (such as independent and dependent states, provinces, municipalities, counties, etc.). More specifically, a border-region can be politically considered as a special geographic space comprising adjacent sub-regions which independently fall under the jurisdiction of two or more political regions respectively.

## 1.31 The demarcation

There still have not been consistent views on the demarcation of border-regions. From the traditional point of view, a border-region is generally known as a geographic space in proximity to a fixed border line inside which significant socio-economic effects due to the existence of a border are felt. *Cihai* (1988) defines that the geographic scope of the international border trade covers an area of as far as 15 kilometers from the border.[13] Li Qing (1991) argues that border-regions should be geographically determined in terms of either administrative divisions (i.e., to integrate all sub-regions which are connected at a successive section of a border line as a border-region) or inter-regional relations of social cultures.[14] Obviously, the former cannot inherently reflect the cross-border socio-economic relations, while the latter is rather indistinct and uncertain. In addition, Guo Rongxing (1992) suggests that a border-region may be economically demarcated in terms of administrative divisions and cross-border relations together.[15]

Nevertheless, the geographic demarcation of border-regions may not be rigidly fixed and usually depends on the objects of the research interests. The border-region along the U.S. side of the U.S.–Mexico border which was examined in James T. Peach (1985), for example, includes the 23 counties of the four states of California, Arizona, New Mexico, and Texas which share a border with Mexico plus Culberson and Dimmit counties of Texas which are located so close to the border as to be indistinguishable from the

---

[13]*Cihai*, p. 1035, Shanghai: Shanghai Cishu Press, 1988.

[14]See Li Qing (1991): "Pay More Attention to Border-Regions", p. 5, *Zhongguo Jingji Wenti* (Chinese Economic Issues), No. 4.

[15]Guo Rongxing (1992): "Some Theoretical Problems of Border-Regional Economics", in FAMY Organizing Committee (ed.): *Proceedings of the First Academic Meeting of Youths (FAMY), Chinese Association for Science and Technology*, pp. 1–6, Beijing: China Science and Technology Press, 1992.

others.[16] Other scholars, promoted by either the research interests or the availability of the data sources in the study of the border-region have defined the U.S. side border-region to include a much wider geographical scope.[17]

## 1.32 The classification

Largely stemmed from the diversification of political borders, border-regions which are functionally incorporated by different kinds of political status and economic structures will therefore create different operational mechanisms for their own. Usually, border-regions can be classified in terms of three different approaches (political level, political composition and spatial structure), which are analysed as below.

(1) *Political level.* When adjacent political regions meet together, a border-region will be formed between these political regions automatically. Political borders in general can be classified into different levels: first-class (or independent state) border, second-class (or dependent state, province, etc.) border, third-class (or municipality, county, etc.) border, etc. Thus, border-regions may also include different levels as below:

- first-class border-regions;
- second-class border-regions;
- third-class border-regions;
- etc.

Usually, the socio-economic complexity of a border-region is positively related to the political level of the border(s) involved in the border-region, i.e., the higher the border's political level, the more complicated structure the border-region will have. A striking difference of functions between first-class (or international) border-regions and the rest forms of border-regions is

---

[16]J. T. Peach (1985): "Income Distribution in the U.S.–Mexico Borderlands", in L. J. Gibson and A. C. Renteria (eds.): *The U.S. and Mexico: Borderland Development and the National Economies*, pp. 57–80, Boulder: Westview Press, 1985.

[17]Hansen, for example, used the Bureau of Economic Analysis Functional Economic Areas (FEAs) along the border which include such cities as San Antonio, Texas, and Palm Spring, California. See Niles Hansen (1981): *The Border Economy: Regional Development in the Southwest*, Austin: University of Texas Press.

this: unlike dependent political units and other administrative subdivisions, there is no obvious central authority that can enforce agreements among nations over the transnational issues. For example, the Tumen River Area Development Programme (TRADP), which was announced with much fanfare by the United Nations' Development Programme (UNDP) in 1992 as the answer to the development of the Northeast Asian border area, was ever in danger of foundering because of the existing political, cultural, and economic differences between the participating nations before an agreement of the programme was finally initiated by the three Tumen River riparian states (China, Russia, and North Korea) plus South Korea and Mongolia three years later on May 30, 1995.[18] One may simply image that, if this project is just located in a border-region between three dependent states or provinces of a sovereign country, it would not become so difficult to be set up by the "local" governments under the effective support from their central government.

(2) *Political composition.* In terms of the political diversification among the sub-regions of a border-region, border-regions can be basically classified into two forms:

- homogeneous border-regions (a homogeneous border-region is one in which there exists same form of government or ruling power);
- heterogeneous border-regions (a heterogeneous border-region is one in which there exists different forms of government(s) and/or ruling power(s)).

Consider $m$ categories of political forms (government(s) and/or ruling power(s)) that exist in a geographic space. Assuming that all the political regions can meet together, we may obtain the maximum number of forms of $n$-dimensional border-regions ($n=2$, 3, ...) between them by mathematical composition of any $n$  adjacent political regions in $m$ ($m{\geq}n$) forms of political regions, i.e.,

$$N=C_m^n$$

---

[18]More details about the Tumen River Area Development Programme (TRADP) may be found in Chapter 7.4.

where $N$ is the number of forms of border-regions by composition of $n$ ($n=2$, 3, ...) in $m$ forms of government(s) and/or ruling power(s). For example, China has now three different forms of provincial governments (i.e., $m=3$) including province (P), autonomous region (AR) and autonomous city (AC). Using the mathematical expression given above, we may obtain that China may at the most have 6 forms of 2-dimensional (i.e., $n=2$) border-regions: P–P, P–AR, P–AC, AR–AR, AR–AC[19], and AC–AC border-regions. Clearly, the P–P, AC–AC, and AR–AR border-regions are homogeneous, and the P–AR and AP–AC border-regions are heterogeneous.

Let us return back to the Tumen River area and spatially investigate its political composition. The delta area has been one of the most typical heterogeneous border-regions in the world. Among the three sovereign countries (China, Russia, and North Korea) under which three parts of the delta area are administered respectively, the socio-economic differences stemming from a transition from the centrally planned economies (CPEs)[20] can be clearly found in that the Russian Federation has adopted a radical strategy so as to quickly transform its socio-economy into a free-market system, while North Korea traditionally remains a virtually intact CPE system, China is nevertheless trying to reform its economy towards a socialist market one.

(3) *Spatial structure*. If adjacent political regions differing in number meet together, a border-region differing in spatial structure (or border dimension, i.e., the number of political authorities involved)[21] will be formed between them correspondingly. In terms of spatial structure, border-regions may be generally classified into $i$-dimensional border-regions (an $i$-dimensional border-region is one which is bordered by $i$ ($i=2$, 3, ..., $N$) political regions respectively). Given a set of border-regions with the same natural, geographic, social, and cultural conditions, as the degree of a

---

[19]Not geographically available.

[20]The centrally planned economy (CPE) is based upon the supposition that "society" (i.e., in practice the planning agencies, under the authority of the political leadership) knows or can discover what is needed, and can issue orders incorporating these needs, while allocating the required means of production so that the needs are economically met. (J. Eatwell, M. Milgate and P. Newman (eds.) (1987): *The New Palgrave: A Dictionary of Economics*, Vol. 4, p. 881, London: The Macmillan Press Limited, 1987.)

[21]In what follows, we will use the terms "spatial structure' and 'border dimension' interchangeably to characterize border-regions differing in number of political authorities involved.

border-region's spatial structure increases, so does the complexity of the cross-border economic relation.[22]

Border-regions with different spatial structures can be found in the world. Some examples are listed as below:

*2-d border-region.* The U.S.–Mexican border-region is a 2-d border-region which runs for 2,000 miles from East to West. The DMZ (Demilitarised Zone) divided by the 38th Parallel in Korean peninsula is also a 2-d border-region with 213 kilometers long from East to West and four kilometres wide extended to each side of North and South Korea. Under the separation between the former East and West Germany, Berlin used to be a 2-d border-city including the east and west parts between which a forbidden border wall (i.e., Berlin Wall) was established during the Cold War period. In 1922, a British High Commander, exasperated at the disputes involving Ibn Saud and the Amir of Kuwait, took a red pencil and himself fixed the boundaries between them. He also declined two "neutral zones" along Ibn Saudi's borders, one shared with Kuwait, the other, with Iraq, while both were two thousand or so square miles of barren desert – called "neutral" in both cases because the Bedouin would be able to pass back forth to graze their flocks and because each of them would have two landlords.[23]

*3-d border-region.* The Tumen River delta area (TRDA) is a 3-d border-region between China, Russia and North Korea; Nyas Lake area is jointly under three countries of Tanzania, Mozambique and Malawi in south-eastern Africa; Victoria Lake area is a 3-d border-region of Tanzania, Uganda and Kenya; Pickwick Lake area covers three states of Tennessee, Mississippi, and Alabama in U.S.A.

*4-d border-region.* Chad Lake area is a 4-d border-region of Chad, Cameroon, Nigeria and Niger; Huaihai Economic Zone (HEZ) (founded in 1986) is under the jurisdiction of four provinces (Jiangsu, Shandong, Henan, and Anhui) in East China. Michigan Lake area is also a 4-d border-region under the four states of Michigan, Wisconsin, Illinois, and Indiana in U.S.A.

---

[22]Consider a $m$-d border-region ($m \geq 2$) in which each sub-region has 2 cross-border channels (e.g., importation and exportation). If the reliability for each channel is a constant (i.e., $r_0$), the aggregate cross-border reliability for the $m$-d border-region is expressed as $r(m) = r_0^x$, where $x = m!/(m-2)!$. Obviously, given $r_0 < 1$, $r(m)$ is a decreasing function of $m$.

[23]For more details about the two "neutral zones", refer to D. Yergin (1992): *The Prize: the Epic Quest for Oil, Money and Power*, p. 281, New York: A Touchstone Book, Published by Simou & Schuster.

and Anhui) in East China. Michigan Lake area is also a 4-d border-region under the four states of Michigan, Wisconsin, Illinois, and Indiana in U.S.A.

*5-d border-region.* e.g., Caspian Sea area (between Kazakhstan, Turmenistan, Iran, Azerbijan, and Russia).

*6-d border-region.* e.g., Black Sea area (between Turkey, Bulgaria, Romania, Ukraine, Russia, and Georgia).

*7-d border-region.* e.g., Adriatic and Ionian Seas area (between Italy, Slovenia, Croatia, Bosnia and Herzegovinia, Yugoslavia, Albania, and Greece).

*8-d border-region.* e.g., Baltic Sea area (between Poland, Germany, Denmark, Sweden, Russia, Estonia, Latvia, and Lithuania); Persian Gulf area (between Oman, United Arab Emirates, Qatar, Bahrain, Saudi Arabia, Kuwait, Iraq, and Iran).

More broadly speaking, the Mediterranean Sea area can be known as an 18-d region which borders on 18 independent countries including France, Spain, Morocco, Algeria, Tunisia, Libya, Egypt, Israel, Lebanon, Syria, Turkey, Cyprus, Greece, Albania, Yugoslavia, Italy, Croatia, and Bosnia and Herzegovina, if some transfrontier issues (such as the water environmental protection, etc.) are raised.

CHAPTER 2
# BORDER-REGIONAL ECONOMICS

Regional economics, which is defined as a subject to explain the location of production and population within a national economy[1], experienced an exultant prosperity in both theory and practice along with the regional economic recoveries in the first decades of the post-World War II, while it recently seems to show a diminishing marginal development after those economies have come close to a maturity. Consequently, more and more regional scientists, economic geographers and policy makers have realized the importance of exploring the operational mechanisms and economic development laws of some special regions, among which the border-regions have been one of the most challenging topics due to their special geographical features and political structures.

## 2.1 Recent Literature

There have been many articles and monographs focusing squarely on a number of critical topics relative to border-regions. Mao Zedong (1929) argued about the special role of the inter-provincial border-regions in the existence of the Chinese Communist Party (CCP) during China's Warlord era in the 1920s.[2] A pioneer study in the geographical sphere of border-regions was conducted by R. Hartshorne (1933) who examined the economic disruptions arising from the division of the Upper Silesian Coalfield after World War I.[3] Further empirical works, particularly stemming from the spate of new frontier drawing in post-Versailles Europe, resulted in border-regions which were generally detected as economically

---

[1]R. J. Krumm and G. S. Tolley (1987): "Regional Economics", in J. Eatwell, M. Milgate and P. Newman (eds): *The New Palgrave: A Dictionary of Economics*, Vol. 4, p. 117, London: The Macmillan Press Limited, 1987.

[2]Mao Zedong (1929): "Why Has the Red Political Power Still Been Existing?", in *Mao's Selected Works*, pp. 47–84, Vol. 1, Beijing: Remin Press, 1977.

[3]See R. Hartshorne (1933): "Geographical and Political Boundaries in Upper Silesia", *Ann. Association of American Geography*, Vol. 23, pp. 195–228.

disadvantageous regions by regional scientists and economic geographers with an interest in locational theory and spatial economics.[4]

W. Christaller (1933) observed that towns and cities in border-regions could only develop partial hinterlands, which also pushed up the economic overhead cost of investment.[5] Using the Bureau of Economic Analysis Functional Economic Areas (FEAs) along the U.S.–Mexico border which include such cities as San Antonio, Texas, and Palm Spring, California, Niles Hansen (1981) studied the border-regional development in Southwest US.[6] The book entitled *The U.S.–Mexico: Borderland Development and the National Economies* edited by L. J. Gibson and A. C. Renteria (Boulder: Westview Press, 1985) looks at the structural characteristics of the border-region and the flow of goods, services, capital, and people crossing the border of the United States and Mexico. The contributors in this book addressed the cultural, economic, and demographic dimensions of the borderlands and focused on the critical problems relating to the region, such as environmental pollution, migration, and territorial issues with reference to the implications of border-zone industrial growth. In addition, there is a special journal devoted to the U.S.–Mexico border – one of the most interesting borders in the world, where economic and cultural factors are mixed in about equal proportions – which have published numerous studies of industrialization in border cities, and a growing environmental literature.[7]

From the viewpoint of D. Rumley and J. Minghi (1991), border-regions have the geographical disadvantages stemming from the peripherality in relation to their national cores, and the attendant *remoteness* from the

---

[4]Among those, A. Lösch (1954) analysed the disruptive impacts of tariff and the limited number of border crossing points on market areas and the disincentive of the constant threat of military incursions to investment distribution in border-regions. For more details, see A. Lösch (1954): *The Economics of Location*, New Haven: Yale University Press.

[5]W. Christaller (1933): *Die Zentrallen Orte in Suddeutschland* (The Central Locations in Southern Germany), Darmstadt: Wissenschaftliche Buchgesellschaft, reprinted in 1980; also cited in N. Hansen (1977): "Border Regions: A Critique of Spatial Theory and A European Case Study", *Ann. Regional Science*, Vol. 11, pp. 1–14.

[6]Niles Hansen (1981): *The Border Economy: Regional Development in the Southwest*, Austin: University of Texas Press.

[7]See, for example, L. A. Herzog (1990): *Where North Meets South: Cities, Space, and Politics on the U.S.–Mexico Border*, Austin, Tx: Center for Mexican American Studies, University of Texas.

centers of power and decision-making.[8] Using linear programming (LP) method, Guo Rongxing (1993a) analysed the agricultural production of a transprovincial border-region in China and revealed a more remarkable performance for the border-region given the removal of its internally border-related barriers.[9] Among the above researches, there is an absence of substantive case studies to draw upon the effects of the removal of political borders and the paper by Philip N. Jones and Trevor Wild (1994) may be considered as a pioneer venture in this field. Beginning with an introduction of the formulation of inner-German border during the Cold War period, this paper examines both the short- and the long-term socio-economic impacts of the removal of this impenetrable border after November 1989 on the North Bavarian section of the *Zonenrandgebiet* (*ZRG*) in former East Germany bordering on former West Germany and Czechoslovakia, which was characterized by its dispersed industrial base and lack of high-order urban centers.[10]

Border-related barriers exist when the intensity of interaction in space suddenly drops at places where a border is crossed. P. Rietveld (1993) distinguished various reasons for the existence of the barrier effects of international borders: (1) weak or expensive infrastructure services in transport and communication for international links; (2) preferences of consumers for domestic rather than foreign products and destinations; (3) government interventions of various types; and (4) lack of information on foreign countries. In his paper, P. Rietveld offered a quantitative measure of international barriers in European countries, expressed as a measure of service reduction between regions located in different countries as compared to regions located within the same country. He also measured the lack of accessibility due to border crossing by different modes of transportation and

---

[8]D. Rumley and J. Minghi (1991): *The Geography of Border Landscapes*, London/New York: Routledge. However, it should be noted that border-regions also have some additional advantages of economic development over their respective heartlands under some circumstances. For more theoretical and practical analyses, see Chapter 6.

[9]Guo Rongxing (1993a): "The Impacts of Spatial Organizational Structures on the Economic Development of the Provincial Border-Regions of China", *Scientia Geographica Sinica*, Vol. 13, pp. 196–204; also translated and published by *Chinese Geographical Science*, Vol. 4, pp. 204–10, 1994.

[10]See P. N. Jones and T. Wild (1994): "Opening the Frontier: Recent Spatial Impacts in the Former Inner-German Border Zone", *Regional Studies*, Vol. 28, pp. 259–73.

communications.[11] To analyse the impact of borders, N. Cattan and C. Grasland (1993) developed a framework in which two factors were distinguished to affect places in space: distance and borders. The impacts of distance and borders are specified for two types of variables: state variables relating to the situation in certain places; and flow variables relating to the interaction between different places. Two possible effects of borders were considered: (1) non-homogeneities between places at different sides of the border, and (2) discontinuities in flow between places at different sides of the border.[12] In addition, R. Ratti and S. Reichman (1993) formulated a theoretical hypothesis that emphases the overcoming of barriers through the construction of contact areas allowing inter-regional co-operation.[13] After some necessary specifications, R. Ratti (1990; 1993) also developed two different approaches to overcome the existing barriers and border effects: (1) a micro-economic approach which examines the frontier through the analysis of the economic actor's strategy behaviour, and is based on the theory of industrial organization; (2) a meso-economic approach which considers the role of "frontier" within a specific supporting space or milieu.[14]

In a broader sense, border-regions exist either economically or non-economically wherever borders are formed by adjacent political authorities. Suburbia, a fringe between rural and urban areas and one of the most dynamic regions, is also a border-region which has attracted many regional scientists and policy-makers. An urban place has necessarily a fringe, a zone that demarcates the outpace of what is considered as typically and predominantly 'urban'. Similarly, a rural fringe is a necessary outer zone of

---

[11]P. Rietveld (1993): "Transport and Communication Barriers in Europe", in Riccard Cappellin and Peter W. J. Batey (eds.): *Regional Networks, Border Regions and European Integration*, pp. 47–59, European Research in Regional Science serires, No. 3, London: Pion limited.

[12]N. Cattan and C. Grasland (1993): "Migratization of Population in Czechoslovakia: A Comparison of Political and Spatial Determinants of Migration and the Measurement of Barriers", *Trinity Papers in Geography*, forthcoming.

[13]R. Ratti and S. Reichman (eds.): *Theory and Strategy of Border Areas Development*, Bellinzona: IRE, 1993.

[14]See (1) R. Ratti (1990): "The Study of the Spatial Effects of the Borders: An Overview of Different Approaches", NETCOM, Vol. 4, pp. 37–50; (2) R. Ratti (1993): "How Can Existing Barriers and Border Effects Be Overcomed? A Theoretical Approach", in R. Cappellin and W. J. Batey (eds.), pp. 60–9, 1993.

what is considered as 'rural'. The concept of rural-urban border-region can thus be approached from two directions, and two perspectives: the first one reflects the urban view of the immediate countryside, whereby somewhere a zone of mixing exists, while the second one looks the other way round. Considering the tremendous increase in development at rural-urban fringe, three has been little empirical work to identify the characteristics of this landscape that matter to socio-economic activities. The nature of rurban fringes is described by van Den Berge (1984) in his monograph on the fringe of Lusaka, Zambia, as "... of uncertain and confusion".[15] In addition, H. Schenk (1993) developed in his paper a sufficient understanding for the fringe zone between Bangalore and its rural surrounding including the nature of the process that takes place there.[16]

## 2.2 Definition

Even though the concepts of both 'border' and 'border-region' have come into literature for a long history, border-regional economics exists only when and where the transborder economic interactions and inter-relations have been effectively established between adjacent political economies. How we should define border-regional economics is a multi-disciplinary question, and, to be sure, the arguments of which have to undergo a long period of time. This is obviously stemmed from the fact that our research object – border-region – varies from case to case and demonstrates large complexities and, sometimes, uncertainties in terms of nature, geography, social culture and political economy. From a general meaning, border-regional economics may be simply described as a subject that studies the spatial organization and economic development laws in border-regions. As border-regions are more complicated and special regions, border-regional economics should be specifically defined.

First of all, border-regional economics may be categorised as a branch of regional economics. Being geographically connected with each other, all adjacent sub-regions are usually similar in natural and geographic conditions

---

[15]L. M. van Den Berg (1984): *Anticipating Urban Growth in Africa, Land Use and Land Values in Rurban Fringe of Luska, Zambia*, Zambia Geographical Association, Occasional Study No. 13, Lusaka, Zambia.

[16]H. Schank (1993): "The Rurban Fringe: A Central Area Between Region and City: the Case of Bangalore, India", University of Amsterdam, The Netherlands.

and cultural customs. What is more, there usually exist cross-border socio-economic interaction and interdependence in border-regions. Therefore, border-regional economics cannot be studied independently on each side of a border-region but should be emphasised on the transborder region as a whole by taking into account the special regional economic problems such as regional structure changes, regional conditions and patterns of economic development as well as optimal approaches and models for regional co-operation and integration.

However, it should be noted that, unlike other regions, each border-region *per se* is decided by two or more independent political authorities and thus many cross-border heterogeneities in terms of political systems and economic policies exist in different locations. Furthermore, each side of the border-region has its own different economic interest and political expectation, some of which might not even be co-ordinated with those of the other side(s) across the border(s).[17] Therefore, traditional theories and methodologies in regional economics could not solve all the economic problems in border-regions perfectly.

Secondly, border-regional economics may be treated as a special kind of inter-regional economics. Inter-regional economics is defined here as an economics of interdependence, interaction and co-operation between two or more political regions (such as independent and dependent states, provinces, municipalities, counties, etc.).[18] According to this definition, border-regional economics may be methodologically treated as a branch of inter-regional economics (including inter-state economics, inter-provincial economics, inter-municipality economics, inter-county economics, etc.) in the border-regions. Therefore, border-regional economics should focus on the inter-regional and, particularly, cross-border interdependence and co-operation in border-regions, and examine the political and economic conditions which decide the inter-regional structure and spatial characteristics of cross-border economic activities, so as to explore both theoretically and practically the operational mechanisms and optimal patterns for the transborder economic development problems.

---

[17]For instance, the principles of comparative advantage in regional economics will never become convincing in those border-regions under totally antagonistic regimes.

[18]Inter-regional economic issues (but international economics is an exception) have been generally treated by regional economists. In this research, however, we give them a specific definition here so as to analytically support border-regional economics.

The economic performance in any border-region is influenced and/or decided at a large extent by two or more political authorities involved in the border-region. So there is no doubt that border-regional economics should be studied in inter-regional perspectives. Otherwise, the economic mechanisms of border-regions can't be effectively explored. However, it should be noted that it would be prejudiced that border-regional economics *simply* equals to inter-regional economics. As a matter of fact, the sub-regions belonging to different political authorities in a border-region share many common aspects – natural, geographical, social and cultural. They are more than usually treated as a naturally single society by the border citizens themselves who speak each other's tongue and may have more in common with each other than with the citified peoples of their respective heartlands. Therefore, the economic activities can be treated more inter-regionally between border-regions and their respective heartlands rather than between transborder sub-regions.

In conclusion, border-regional economics can be more generally defined as a special branch of regional and inter-regional economics, the research interests of which should include three aspects:

- Each independent economies in a border-region;
- Cross-border economic interactions and inter-relations;
- Cross-border economies as a whole.

## 2.3 Objectives

Border-regional economic research has broader contents in both theoretical and practical perspectives. As a first step to systematically investigate this new subject, we should clarify the research objectives that focus on the various economic aspects of the border-regions differing in natural, geographic, cultural, and political conditions. Generally, border-regional economists should at least pay attentions to the three aspects as below.

1. *To explore the spatial economic distributions in border-regions under the condition that production factors (such as capital, labour force, natural resource, technology, information, etc.) are heterogeneously distributed and cannot freely flow across borders. This suggests that border-regional economics should deal with (1) spatial divisions of*

*production factors in border-regions; (2) effectuations of cross-border trade and economic co-operation; and (3) economic relations between border-regions and their respective heartlands.*

Even though political regions positioned side by side and separated by a border are at sometimes very similar in natural geography, they display enormous differences in the economic performances of their own. The U.S.–Mexican border is a typical case in point. In Mexico in 1960, for example, border municipalities averaged $640(U.S.) in per capita income per year, approximately one-fifth the average income in the United States for the same year. Still, the Mexican figure represented more than twice the average per capita income of other cities in Mexico, suggesting that Mexican border cities are prosperous relative to the rest of the nation. Proximity to Mexico, however, appears to bring down the per capita income levels in many U.S. border cities. Wages levels in 1977 for border towns such as Calexico, Eagle Pass, Laredo, and Brownsville tended to represent only one half the average wage levels for the respective states. As one moves away from the border (El Centro, Yuma, or Tucson), or in cities that have a more diversified economy (San Diego), per capita incomes rise substantially.[19] One result of this disparity is that corporate capital is drown to the border region to take advantage of low wages, low tax rates, and lax public controls over labour standards, waste disposal, and such like. Mexican labour comes at 8 to 10 cents to the dollar compared to the United States. Under special provisions of legislation to encourage the location of assembly plant operations on the Mexican side, with production destined for American markets, U.S., Japanese, and Korean capitals have created nearly 500,000 jobs in Mexican border cities, from Tijuana to Brownsville in so-called *maquila* (in-bond) assembly plants. Some of them straddle the border in a unique arrangement of "twin" plants, with management and parts production located on the U.S. side and the labour-intensive assembly operations on the Mexican side.[20]

---

[19]L. A. Herzog (1990): *Where North Meets South: Cities, Spaces, and Politics on the US –Mexican Border*, p. 47, Austin,Texas: Center for Mexican American Studies, University of Texas.

[20]John Friedmann (1993): "Borders, Margins, and Frontiers: Notes Towards a Political Economy of Regions", unpublished draft, University of California at Los Angeles, U.S.A.

The Chinese transprovincial border-regions are another case in point. Including its newly established province in Hainan island, mainland China has been divided into 30 provincial regions (or provinces, autonomous regions, and autonomous cities) by 66 border lines. Along the 52,000 kilometer long inter-provincial borders, there are 849 counties and cities which account for 38.9 percent of the total number of the counties and cities of the nation. China's border-regions have plentiful resources. For instance, there have at least 40 per cent of the nation's 825 billion tons of coal reserves in the border-regions, among which are Inner Mongolia–Shanxi border-region (170 billion tons), Shanxi–Hebei–Shangdong–Henan border-region (8.25 billion tons), Shaanxi–Shanxi–Henan border-region (3.7 billion tons), Jiangsu–Shandong–Henan–Anhui border-region (2.82 billion tons), Yunnan–Guangxi Zhuang–Guizhou border-region (1.2 billion tons), etc.[21] Even though they are spontaneously endowed by the nature, most of the transprovincial border-regions still have less developed infrastructures than mainland China as a whole. The reason that lies behind this kind poverty vs. abundance is special but intuitively stems from the fact that, as most border-regions in China are far away from their respective provincial capitals which are usually the economic cores, the economic and technological exchanges between those border-regions and their respective political centers are much more costly. The more economical transborder co-operation in border-regions, however, lacked the effective supports from both provincial and local governments. For example, since the advent of the administrative decentralization in the early 1980s, China's national economy has become effectively "cellularized" into a plethora of semi-autarkic regional enclaves. To protect local market and revenue sources, provincial and local authorities erected a series of regulatory barriers against the importation (exportation) of various commodities, ranging from alcohol and tobacco to clothing, washing machines, TV sets, refrigerators, and even automobiles from (to) other provinces. These protectionist measures, which were often in violation of central directives, had been enforced through a patchwork system of roadblocks, cargo seizures, ad hoc taxes, commercial surcharges, and licensing fees, and in a number of well-publicised cases, outfight highway

---

[21]Guo Rongxing (1995a): "A Proposal on the Exploitation of Natural Resources in the Provincial Border-Regions of China", *Science and Technology Review*, No. 2, February, pp. 38–40.

robbery across the transprovincial borders. Moreover, this competition between provinces could be fierce in the "battlegrounds" of their border-regions, and there were numerous tales of "border commodity wars" between provinces. The central government's efforts to transprovincially open the internal economic borders were never enforced in depth.[22]

2.    *To reconstruct the spatial inter-relationship and regulate the policy instruments for border-regions in an attempt to promote the socio-economic development by the appropriate approaches of rational co-ordination and management of border-regions while not necessarily changing the political structures and social compositions. This implies that three aspects should be focused: (1) rational allocation of production factors and sustainable development; (2) possibilities and conditions of maximizing the economic outputs in border-regions; and (3) forms and organizations of cross-border co-operation and economic integration.*

Prior to the Second World War, international borders in the western Europe represented relatively rigid barriers between the independent countries, but in the post-war period the borders have become increasingly permeable to the mobility of persons, goods, services, technology, information, etc. Industrial and commercial expansion in border-regions has clearly generated economic benefits. However, it also has induced or intensified numerous problems that can not be solved by one side of the border alone.[23] Throughout the 1970s, it became increasingly evident that progress with respect to transborder co-operation in Europe would require a legal basis for guaranteeing accords reached by neighbouring regional and

---

[22]More details about the "border commodity wars" and their economic impacts on the inter-provincial border-regions may be found in Guo Rongxing (1993b): *Economic Analysis of Border-Regions: Theory and Practice of China*, Appendix A6 ("The Chinese Border Trade War"), pp. 201–5, Beijing: China Ocean Press.

[23]These problems include environmental pollution, transportation, public health, workers who commute across borders, legal and educational differences, and planning of land use. For more evidence, see N. Hansen (1985): "The Nature and Significance of Border Development Patterns", in L. J. Gibson and A. C. Renteria (eds.): *The U.S. and Mexico: Borderland Development and the National Economies*, p. 12–3, Boulder: Westview Press, 1985.

local authorities and for assuring central governments that national sovereignty would be respected in the process. Working through the Council of Europe, local and regional authorities from border-regions, and national ministers responsible for regional planning, developed a European Outline Convention on Transfrontier Co-operation. In 1979, this European Convention was endorsed by the Council of Europe's Parliamentary Assembly and it has since been signed by Austria, Belgium, Denmark, France, Ireland, Italy, Luxembourg, the Netherlands, Norway, Sweden, Switzerland, and West Germany. The nations that have signed the European Convention have agreed that they are resolved to promote transborder co-operation "as far as possible, and to contribute in this way to the economic and social progress of frontier regions and to the spirit of fellowship which unites the peoples of Europe".[24]

The appendix to the European Convention is particularly important because it sets forth an array of agreements, statutes, and contracts that could be used to formalize co-operative efforts in such areas as urban and regional development, transportation and communication, energy, environmental protection, education, health, tourism, disaster relief, culture, industrial development, and problems who commute across borders. The model co-operative mechanisms represent a graduated system ranging from simple consultation to the establishment of permanent organizations. Thus, transborder co-operation is implicitly treated as an evolving relationship that typically develops from a network of informal contracts to an increasingly number and complexity of concrete arrangements that could eventually result in planning harmonization across borders.[25]

Closed to the throbbing heart of Europe, Wallonia has common borders and links with many European regions – to the south, Nord–Pas-de-Calais, Picardie, Champagne–Ardennes, and Lorraines; to the east, the Grand Duchy of Luxembourg, the Rhineland–Palatinate, and the Rhineland of North Westphalia; to the north, the Netherlands and Flanders. The economic infrastructure in the Walloon economy remains dependant on traditional industries (steel-making, plant, etc.) with the emphasis on upstream

---

[24]See Council of Europe (1982): *European Outline Convention on Transfrontier Co-operation between Territorial Communities or Authorities*, p. 2, Strabourg, France: Council of Europe.
[25]N. Hansen (1985), p. 13.

production. There is consequently little opportunity for the creation of added value. In addition, the region is characterized by the insufficient services to enterprises with an imbalance between consumer, nonmerchantable, and production services: only 16.6 per cent of jobs for salaried employees are directly related to services rendered to companies as against an average ratio of 22.4 per cent for Belgium as a whole. In addition, within Belgium, Wallonia represents 55.2 per cent of the territory and 32.6 per cent of the population, and it contributes only 26 per cent to the gross national product (GNP).[26] The Walloon region has for many years been pursuing a voluntarist policy with regard to cross-border co-operation. In this respect, four particular cross-border programmes has been launched for this region: (1) the European Development Pole (EDP) for three countries (Belgium, Luxembourg, France) was an initiative launched in 1985; (2) the EUREGIO project (provinces of Liège and Limbourg and the regions of Aix-La-Chapelle and the Dutch Limbourg), in which the province of Liege has been participating since 1982; (3) the European Cross-border Co-operation Action Programme (province of Hainaut and the region of Nord–Pas-de-Calais) was implemented, in the initial stages, through a Joint Declaration signed by the region of Nord–Pas-de-Calais and by the Walloon region in 1986, and subsequently updated in 1989; and (4) the Champagne–Ardennes Programme was launched in 1989 through a feasibility study.[27]

In the course of the past decades, significant efforts have been made in Europe to strengthen co-operation on transboundary waters at bilateral, multilateral and pan-European levels. More than 100 conventions, treaties, and other arrangements have been concluded between European countries for that purpose. They bear witness to the concern and interest of European countries in striving together to prevent the deterioration of water quality in transboundary waters and to ensure reasonable and equitable use and joint conservation of transboundary waters.[28] An important function of the joint bodies established under several transboundary water agreements is to develop concerted action programmes to reduce pollution loads. For

---

[26]See M. Quévit and S. Bodson (1993): "Transborder Co-operation and European Integration: The Case of Wallonia", in R. Cappellin and P. W. J. Batey (eds.), p. 193, 1993.

[27]For more details about the European cross-border co-operation programmes, refer to Chapter 7.1.

[28]United Nations Economic Commission for Europe (1988): *Water Pollution Control and Flood Management in Transboundary Waters*, Geneva: ECE/ENVWA/7.

example, action programmes developed by the International Commission for the Protection of the Rhine against Pollution (1987), the International Commission for the Protection of the Moselle and Saar (1990), and the International Commission for the Protection of Elbe (1991), aim, *inter alia*, to (i) improve the riverine ecosystem in such a way that higher organisms which were once present can return; (ii) guarantee the production of drinking water; (iii) reduce the pollution of the water by hazardous substances to such a level that sediment can be used on land without causing harm; and (iv) protect the North Sea against the negative effects of the river waters.[29]

3.  *To propose strategies and policies for the border-regional developments from both overall and local perspectives. Without the overall point of view, border-regional economics would not be a science. But if border-regional economists do not care about the interest of each independent sub-region, this kind of border-regional economics would lose its foundation of existence and become barely a borderless economics. To implement this objective, three aspects should be appropriately co-ordinated between: (1) national preferences and border-regional characteristics; (2) border-regions and their respective sub-regions; and (3) sub-regions under the administrations of their respective political regions.*

Located in the southern and northern Wuling mountain range respectively and bordered by Mt. Qitian-ling in South China, Shaoguan municipality of Guangdong province and Chenzhou prefecture of Hunan province are similar in natural and geographic features and resource endowments but stepped on to different economic transitions. Before 1980, there had not been much difference between these two local economies. But since then, Shaoguan has possessed a relatively higher degree of "autonomy" in terms of public finance, credit and banking, material supply, trade, price, labour and wage system, personnel affairs, etc., while Chenzhou's transition from the centrally planned economy (CPE) to a market-oriented one has

---

[29]Secretariat of the United Nations Commission for Europe (1994): "Protection and Use of Transboundary Watercourses and International Lakes in Europe", *Natural Resources Forum*, Vol. 18(3), pp. 171–80.

unambiguously lagged behind that of Guangdong province. For example, when Guangdong provincial government began to implement a new fiscal policy entitled "*Dizheng Baogan*" (to fix the increased rate of the revenue turned over to the state), Hunan province continued to follow "*Zhong'e Fencheng*" (to proportionally share the total revenue between the state and local authorities) policy to Chenzhou prefecture. Apparently, the latter particularly lacks the incentives for the local government to accumulate its wealth. In addition, Shaoguan municipality had a more elastic tax system than Chenzhou prefecture. For example, the tin ore mining sector in Shaoguan was collected only 3 per cent product tax by the Guangdong provincial government, but as high as 20 per cent taxes and fees (including 10 per cent product tax, 3 per cent management fee, 5 per cent industrial and commercial tax, 1 per cent environmental protection fee and 1 per cent resource tax) for the same business in Chenzhou prefecture were charged by Hunan provincial government.[30]

The unequal policies have produced much large difference between the two sides of the border. In the 1950s, the two neighbours developed with almost an equal growth pace and same industrial structure. Both of them had 580 million yuan of gross value of industrial and agricultural output (GVIAO) coincidentally in 1958 and not much significant difference in the 1960s and the 1970s. Since the late 1970s, the two local economies have become more and more differentiated: Shaoguan municipality, for example, had 918 million yuan GVIAO higher than Chenzhou prefecture in 1980. But in 1987, however, the GVIAO difference between the two neighbours reached by 2,213 million yuan.[31]

Besides the uncertain political condition and less-developed economic infrastructure, environmental issue has also been a growing challenge to the sustainable development in border-regions. About 100 years ago, most of the Tumen River area was covered with a primitive forest and a sparse population. In the recent decades, the rapidly expanded population especially the unsustainable industrialization have generated water pollution and other environmental damages. According to a Chinese mission report of 1991, the

---

[30]Li Zhisheng (1988): "Influences, Disadvantages and Suggestions", in Zhang Ping (ed.): *Studies of the Economic Relations Between Hunan and Guangdong Provinces*, pp. 338–9, Changsha: Hunan Renmin Press, 1988.

[31]Source: *Yearbook of Provincial Statistics*, (Guangdong and Hunan), related issues.

Tumen River has been seriously polluted: the total suspended substances (TSS) averages at 1000 mg/l (sometimes, as high as 4590 mg/l) in the 350 kilometers long section from the Chongchuan River entrance in the upper reaches, and 200 mg/l (sometimes, as high as 870 mg/l) in the lower reaches.[32] The main pollution sources are (1) Maosan Iron Ore Plant of North Korea in the middle Tumen River, which excretes more than 150 million ton waste water (including 10 million ton sand tailings) annually; (2) Kaishantun Chemical and Fibre Plant of China in the middle River, which exudes about 300 million ton industrial waste water (including 18 thousand ton $BOD_5$ (biological oxygen demands) and 705.6 thousand ton COD (chemical oxygen demands) per year into the River; (3) Shijian Paper Making Plant of China in the middle Gaya River, which exudes 2.8 thousand ton waste water (including 13.9 thousand ton $BOD_5$ and 61.3 thousand ton COD) into the Tumen River every year; and (4) Awude Chemical Plant of North Korea in the lower Tumen River, which excretes more than 180 thousand ton waste water per year.[33]

The water pollution in Tumen River has negatively affected the delta area through many aspects – economic, social, and ecological. For example, Tumen River had been well known for its plentiful Walbaum, Dybuwski, and Dybowski, and other fishes. The fisheries in the River, however, have decreased drastically since the 1940s, particularly in the recent decades, due to the water pollution. The aquatic production in Hunchun municipality, for instance, decreased from 103.5 tonnes in 1948, with an increase to 180 tons in 1957, and sharply down to 13 tons in 1969, 9 tons in 1980, and 3.5 tons in 1983, respectively.[34] The citizens of Tumen city (located at the intersect in Tumen and Gaya Rivers) had mainly depended on the Tumen River water before it was seriously polluted. In 1976, the municipal government had to invest 11 million Chinese yuan to construct a new drinking water stream in

[32]Environment Monitoring Station (1991): "A Mission Report of the Environmental Quality in Yanbian Area (1986–1991)", Yanbian Korean autonomous prefecture, Jilin province, China.

[33] Zhu Chunme, Ren Huanying and Shen Hengzhe (1993): "The Environment Pollution in Tumen River and Its Impacts on the Tumen River Area", *Northeast Asia Forum*, pp. 64–7, No. 2.

[34]Source: The Aquatic Products Station: *Statistical Report*, each year, Hunchun municipality, Jilin province, China. Also Zhu Chunme et al. (1993, p. 66).

order to meet the demands. The environment damages in the Tumen River also affected the agricultural production.[35]

As the Tumen River area is bordering on China, North Korea, and Russia, the environmental protection needs a multi-national co-operation. The most crying task for the three nations is to work out an international standard and establish an international monitoring system. However, as is known that the transborder pollution control is not likely to be emphasized if the adjacent countries have markedly differing levels of developments as well as different attitudes and values with respect to environmental issues. For example, the adoption of common standards would imply that the relatively poor country would have to devote a higher proportion of its resources to pollution reduction than would the relatively rich country. Apart from abstract questions of justice, this circumstance would not lead itself to an agreement between the political regimes concerned.[36]

## 2.4 How to Study Border-Regional Economics?

Indeed, border-regions have posed a series of crucial issues and challenges to economists, geographers, and policy-makers. As a new branch of regional economics, border-regional economics should be treated as a cross-disciplinary subject between geography (especially economic geography) and economics. Although the basic theories and methodologies in economics are particularly important for the economic analysis of border-regions, they are, nonetheless, not enough to cope with the systematic interpretation of economic mechanisms of the border-regions with different physical environments as well as social and political structures. In order to handle the special problems, some multi-disciplinary approaches involving not only economics but also some other subjects such as geography, system

---

[35]The agricultural use of the polluted water of Tumen River has destroyed the soil structure at some extent and decreased 7–20 per cent rice production in Yanbaian area, the west side of the River. See Yanbian Agricultural Institute (1980): "The Impacts of Sand Tailings Pollution in Tumen River on the Farmland and Rice Production", Yanbian Korean prefecture, Jilin province, China.

[36]Notice that, an agreement on environmental issues including a framework for the sustainable economic and social development in the Tumen River area was signed by China, Russia, North and South Korea, and Mongolia in Beijing, May 30, 1995.

science, and history should be incorporated into the methodologies of border-regional economics.

## 2.41 Core-periphery theory

Regional scientists usually argue about the theoretical definition and geographic demarcation of 'core' and 'periphery', but few of them would doubt that a core is the most prosperous and densely populated area and concentralizes most of the social and economic activities of a political region, and that a periphery which is located at the margin of a political region is relatively far away from the region's center (core) and is usually the socio-economic scarcity. The central place theory suggests a theoretical definite ordering of communities with a region in terms of economic activities ranging from villages and towns, where only the lowest-order economic activity exists, all the way up to primary cities. The primary cities are the main suppliers of higher-order regions. A region with an economic core surrounded by a periphery may be understood as an extension of the central place concept. In a core-periphery framework, many peripheral regions specialize in the production of natural resource-based commodities in which they have a comparative advantage while the core regions usually provide higher-order goods and services. Based on the principle of comparative advantage, the trade flows between the core and peripheral regions, as David W. Hughes and David W. Holland (1994) suggested, influence economic activities in the periphery through positive spread effects and negative backwash effects. Spread effects include the diffusion of investment, innovation, and growth activities from core to peripheral regions, while backwash effects refer to the unfavourable effects of core economic growth on economic development in peripheral areas.[37]

There have been many papers on the socio-economic analyses of core and peripheral regions. For example, Brian W. Ilbery (1984) and David Keeble (1989) empirically examined the core-periphery contrasts and disparities in the European Community (EC).[38] Chiu-Ming Luk (1985)

---

[37]More evidence may be found in D. W. Hughes and D. W. Holland (1994): "Core-periphery Economic Linkage: A Measure of Spread and Possible Backwash Effects for the Washington Economy", *Land Economics*, Vol. 70, pp. 364–77.

[38]For more details, see (1) B. W. Ilbery (1984): "Core-periphery Contrasts in European Social Well-being", *Geography*, Vol. 69(4), pp. 289–302; (2) D. Keeble (1989): "Core-

demarcated the spatial distribution of core and periphery in China using the data of 1982.[39] D. R. Vining (1982) analysed the migration between core and peripheral regions,[40] while D. Plane (1989) used a net-constrained impact model to explore the demographic impacts of core-periphery net immigration on the individual regions, sub-regions, and states of the United States.[41] After analysing the Celts of the United Kingdom, M. Hechter (1975) suggested two different models (diffusion and internal colonialism) for the explanation of the economic relations between the core and peripheral areas. The diffusion model indicates that the social and economic structures of core regions will diffuse the peripheral regions gradually and finally narrow the economic differences between the two kinds of regions. The internal colonialism model means an opposite direction: like the imperialist countries treating their colonies, the model is essentially the political control and economic exploitation of peripheral regions by core regions. M. Hechter also concluded that the internal colonialism model is more suitable than diffusion model to explain the relationship between England and Celts.[42]

It seems that mainland China has 'colonially' treated its transprovincial border-regions in the past decades: a large portion of energy (including coal, petroleum, electricity, etc.), mineral and agricultural products, and primary processing products were purchased at the officially-fixed low prices from border-regions under mandatory plans so as to provide cheap raw materials that in effect amounted to subsidising the southern and coastal industrial (core) areas, while the latter produced consumer goods which were in turn distributed to the inland border-regions at market-based prices. From the central government's point of view, this kind transference did created the allocative efficiencies and increase the total wealth of the nation, as the

periphery Disparities, Recession and New Regional Dynamisms in European Community", *Geography*, Vol. 74(1), pp. 1–11.

[39]Chiu-Ming Luk (1985): "Core-periphery Contrasts in China's Development During the Early Eighties", *Socio-economic Planning Sciences*, Vol. 19(6), pp. 407–16.

[40]D. R. Vining (1982): "Migration Between Core and Periphery", *Scientific American*, Vol. 247, pp. 45–53 (December).

[41]D. Plane (1989): "The Interregional Impacts of U.S. Core-periphery Net Migration", in Gibson et al. (eds.): *Regional Structure Change and Prospects in Two Mature Economies*, Regional Science Research Institute, Peace Dale, Rhode Island, 1989.

[42]M. Hecter (1975): *Internal Colonialism: The Celtic Fringe in British National Development, 1576–1966*, pp. 6–11, London: Routledge and Kegan.

industrial (core) areas usually utilized these raw materials more efficiently than border-regions. However, the economic divergence between the resource-exploited and resource-consumed areas widened substantially. For instance, Huaihai Economic Zone (HEZ), a border-region between Jiangsu, Shandong, Henan, and Anhui provinces, is a key resources-rich area in East China. During 1988–92, HEZ produced about 6–9 per cent the country's raw coal and electric power per year, but about 40–50 per cent of which were purchased at lower costs by the state to fuel the south-eastern area's industrialization.[43] As a result of the 'internal colonialism' policy, the HEZ's economy demonstrated a relatively stagnation compared to China as a whole: per capita total financial revenue in HEZ increased annually by only 6.17 per cent from 1988 to 1992, much lower than that of China (10.50 per cent) during the same period.[44]

## 2.42 The economies of spatial scale

Microeconomists have suggested that relatively larger scales of economic units (such as farms, factories, etc.) may make higher efficient uses of fixed inputs (costs) and, therefore, produce larger economic outputs per unit of total cost. As a matter of fact, eliminating the economic borders among neighbouring countries (especially those countries with relatively smaller sizes in terms of both production and consumption) may also create extra returns from the economies of scale resulting from an improved productivity through the greater utilization of manufacturing resources, research and development, communication networking, transportation facilities and many other benefits.[45]

According to the Treaty of Rome signed in 1956, the European Community (EC) was formally established in January 1958. The EC included six countries of France, West Germany, Italy, the Netherlands,

---

[43]For example, Xuzhou, HEZ's largest city, produced about 20 million tonnes of raw coal and 10 billion kwh of electric power annually. However, it remained an average power shortage of 1.2 billion kwh which decreased industrial production by at least 10 per cent per year. (Source: Liaison Office of Huaihai Economic Zone, Xuzhou, China, 1988.)

[44]Sources: (1) *Zhongguo Tongji Nianjian*, (China Statistical Yearbook), related issues, Beijing: China Statistical Press; (2) *Huaihai Jingjiqu Tongji* (Statistics of Huaihai Economic Zone), related issues, Liaison Office of Huaihai Economic Zone, Xuzhou, China.

[45]More theoretical discussions may be found in Chapter 8.

Belgium, Luxembourg during the first years, followed by the participation of U.K., Denmark and Ireland in 1973, Greece in 1981, and Spain and Portugal in 1986 respectively. By the end of 1988, the EC had been composed of 12 member countries covering 2,253,300 square kilometres of land area with more than 312 million population. For a long time, many tariff and non-tariff barriers with tedious border control procedures and the diversification of production techniques, standards of product quality, as well as other border-related barriers, piled up a huge "economic wall" which hence impeded the exchanges and circulation of labour, commodity, and capital within the whole community. The Single European Act (SEA) was adopted by the governments of the EC in 1985, the aim of which was to create a true common market with free movement of goods, services, and factors of production within Europe by 1992. The 1992 programme (including about 300 directives identified by Lord Cockfield) as a whole was to design to remove all barriers to trade and to permit equal access in all European markets. The directives in the programme may be divided into three categories:[46] The first group aims to remove physical barriers to trade, such as frontier formalities and lack of mutual recognition of qualifications of labour. A second group focuses on the removal of technical barriers, such as differences in product standards and requirements, product law, and company law. Fiscal directives form a third group, the aim of which is to harmonize (but not equalize) rates of indirect taxation.

The open border implies a change from the concept of border economics to that of economics across borders (or borderless economics). The removal of the internal economic borders of all EC countries will produce greater benefits. P. Cecchini (1988) estimated in a study funded by the European Commission that the completion of the internal market will increase about 4.5 per cent GDP for EC countries. This includes: (1) 1.5 per cent from freer trade in financial services; (2) 0.5 per cent from the removal of frontier controls; and (3) 2 per cent from the improved competitiveness, economies of scale, and general supply side effects.[47] Many indirect economic and

---

[46]See Shelagh Heffernan and Peter Sinclair (1990): *Modern International Economics*, p. 149, Oxford/Cambridge: Basil Blackwell.

[47]More evidence may be found in P. Cecchini (1988): *The European Challenge 1992: The Benefit of a Single Market*, Hants: Wildwood House.

social benefits for a borderless Europe are also derived from the removal of the political borders substantially.

The geographical proximity and the political heterogeneity typically characterise border-regions and thus stimulate cross-border interdependence and flows of goods, services, capital, people, and information. In addition, as border-regions are always located at the geographic peripheries of their respective political regions, the interdependence between border-regions and their respective heartlands is not significant in many cases. All the above geographic and social features suggest that each border-region *per se* has a great potential to develop the transborder co-operation and integration so as to overcome the internal diseconomies of spatial sizes and benefit from the external economies of spatial sizes.

## 2.43 System science

The basic principle of system science tells us that the dynamic behaviour of a system is fundamentally dependent on the overall structure rather than some individual elements of the system.[48] Correspondingly, the economic analysis of border-regions as a special kind of spatial system should focus on each border-region as a whole rather than the individual sub-regions which partially constitute the border-region. Border-regions can get rid of the disadvantages resulting from cross-border separation only through the transborder economic co-operation and/or integration. If the cross-border economic interactions among all sub-regions in a border-region are artificially separated, the production factors in the border-region can only be boundly utilized within their respective sub-regions. As a result, the border-region will lose the comparative advantages and bear the diseconomies of spatial size. After being transformed and integrated into a borderless spatial system, however, the border-region will achieve a more harmonious behaviour than that under internal barriers. To systematically explore the operational mechanisms and dynamically illustrate the behaviours of a border-regional system, let's begin with the analysis of the border market mechanism using a modified Cobweb model.

Coined by N. Kaldor (1934), one strand of the Cobweb literature concentrates on how expectations are formed and the effect of the price

---

[48]Jay W. Forester (1965): *Principles of Systems*, p.10, Cambridge, MA: MIT Press.

expectation mechanism on the stability of equilibrium. The Cobweb theorem proves that the market behaviour will (not) converge to (long run) equilibrium price if the absolute value of the price elasticity of demand is larger (smaller) than the price elasticity of supply.[49] To mathematically illustrate the Cobweb theorem, economists usually construct a simple equilibrium model as below. Let $D_t$ denote the demand of a commodity at time $t$, $S_t$ denote the supply of the commodity at time $t$, $P_t$ denote the price of the commodity at time $t$. Assume that $\alpha$ and $\beta$ are used to express the marginal demand and marginal supply of the commodity respectively, and $D_0$ and $S_0$ are two constants. An equilibrium model becomes

$$D_t = D_0 - \alpha P_t \qquad (2\text{–}1)$$
$$S_t = S_0 + \beta P_{t-1} \qquad (2\text{–}2)$$

where, $\alpha > 0$ and $\beta > 0$. Using the market equilibrium condition (i.e., $D_t \equiv S_t$), a dynamic function of $P_t$ over time $t$ derives from Equations (2–1) and (2–2):

$$P_t = (P_0 - P_E)(\frac{\alpha}{\beta})^t + P_E, \text{ with } t \in (0, \infty). \qquad (2\text{–}3)$$

where, $P_0$=price level at time zero; $P_E = (D_0 - S_0)/(\alpha - \beta)$. Obviously, Equation (2–3) generates different dynamic patterns when parameters $\alpha$ and $\beta$ change in value. In particular, when $\alpha \geq \beta$, $P_t$ will not be estranged; when $\alpha < \beta$, $P_t$ will tend to a constant (i.e., $P_E$) when time $t \to \infty$.

However, trade barriers (such as tariff and non-tariff) usually exist in a border-region and hinder, under different conditions, the free circulation of commodities from one side to the other side(s) across the border(s). As a result of these border-related barriers, the market equilibrium condition ($D_t \equiv S_t$) does not exist in cross-border markets. In order to build a model being able to explain the economic mechanism and dynamic behaviours of a border market, we use $B_t$ to denote the remains between the demand and supply in the border market, i.e., $B_t = D_t - S_t$. $B_t$ may include two parts: i.e., $B_t = B_0 + rP_t$, where $B_0$=constant blockade of a commodity produced in the border market; $r$=marginal blockade of the commodity determined by the

---

[49]N. Kaldor (1934): "A Classificatory Note on the Determinateness of Equilibrium", *Review of Economic Studies*, Vol. 1, February, pp. 122–36.

market price. Being substituted by the expressions of $B_t$, $D_t$ and $S_t$, the border market condition (i.e., $B_t=D_t-S_t$) yields a dynamic equation as below:

$$P_t = (P_0 - P_E')(\frac{r+\beta}{r-\alpha})' + P_E', \text{ with } r\neq\alpha \text{ and } t\in(0, \infty). \qquad (2\text{–}4)$$

where, $P'_E=(D_0-S_0+B_0)/(\alpha-r)$, $P_0$=price level at time zero ($t$=0). It is very clear that, in Equation (2–4), the dynamic pattern of $P_t$ over time $t$ is determined by $\alpha$, $\beta$ and $r$. Consider that $\alpha$ and $\beta$ are fixed and $\alpha>\beta$, we may dynamically experiment Equation (2–4) by changing the parameter $r$. To summarize up, we may derive different patterns of $P_t$ over time $t$ as below:[50]

(1) When $r>0$, it implies the close border policy. Here are three circumstances: (1a) $0<r<(\alpha-\beta)/2$. This kind of border blockade policy cannot play any critical role in the restriction of cross-border circulation of the commodity, and the price can eventually reach an equilibrium level ($P'_E$) through a decreasing vibration (see Figure 2–1). The time that $P_t$ needs to reach $P'_E$ from $P_0$ depends on the value of $r$: the larger of the value of $r$, the longer time $P_t$ will need to reach $P'_E$. (1b) $(\alpha-\beta)/2<r<\alpha$. This kind of border blockade policy will serve as an accelerated vibrator for $P_t$ to change far away from $P'_E$ over time and destroy the market mechanism eventually (see Figure 2–2).[51] (1c) $r>\alpha$. This kind of border blockade policy will form a positive feed back mechanism and result in an infinite growth curve for $P_t$ as time $t$ increases (see Figure 2–3).[52]

(2) When $r<0$, it implies the open border policy. Here are two circumstances: (2a) $-\beta<r<0$. This kind of open border policy will mitigate the supply-demand contradiction in the border market and help $P_t$ to vibrate within a decreasing range over time and, finally, reach the equilibrium level (see Figure 2–4). (2b) $r<-\beta$. This kind of open border policy will form a negative feed back mechanism and stimulate $P_t$ to monotonously approach the equilibrium point ($P'_E$) without any vibration (see Figure 2–5).[53]

---

[50]As an example, let us assume that $P_0$=20, $P_E$=15, $\alpha$=10, $\beta$=5.
[51]$r=(\alpha-\beta)/2$ is the critical point between Policy (1a) and Policy (1b).
[52]$r=\alpha$ is the critical point between Policy (1b) and Policy (1c).
[53]$r=-\beta$ is the critical point between Policy (2a) and Policy (2b).

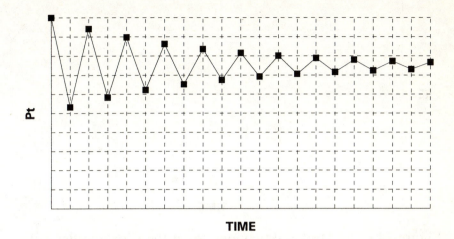

**TIME**

Figure 2–1 The Market Behaviour under the Close-border Policy
$(0 < r < (\alpha - \beta)/2)$

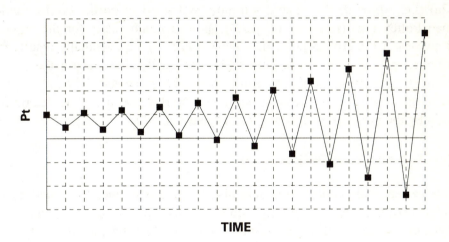

**TIME**

Figure 2–2 The Market Behaviour under the Close-border Policy
$((\alpha - \beta)/2 < r < \alpha)$

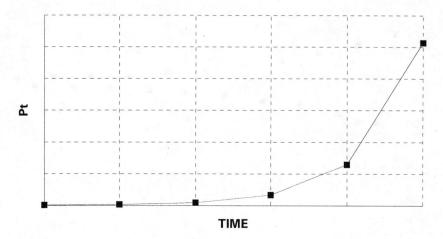

Figure 2–3 The Market Behaviour under the Close-border Policy
($r$>$\alpha$)

Notice that, even though there has a similar mechanism between Policy (1a) (shown in Figure 2–1) and Policy (2a) (shown in Figure 2–4), Policy (2a) (i.e., $-\beta<r<0$) demonstrates a more stable effect on the border market than Policy (1a) (i.e., $0<r<(\alpha-\beta)/2$), as it is much easier for the latter to draw nearer the critical point (i.e., $r=(\alpha-\beta)/2$)) which eventually results in a vibrated price curve, while Policy (2a) can easily draw nearer the critical point ($r=-\beta$) which eventually results in a stable price curve (i.e., $P_t=P'_E$). In addition, when $r=0$, it means a borderless market and that $P_t$ is determined only by the parameters of $\alpha$ and $\beta$ in Equation (2–3).

## 2.44 Historical geography

Border-regional economics should also be methodologically treated by the subjects of historical geography. Otherwise, the operational mechanisms and dynamic patterns of border-regions will not be understood easily. The evolution and developments of many international border-regions have been chronologically recorded either in the encyclopaedia or in the state documents. Let us look at two culturally distinctive border-regions which have been historically identified in geography.

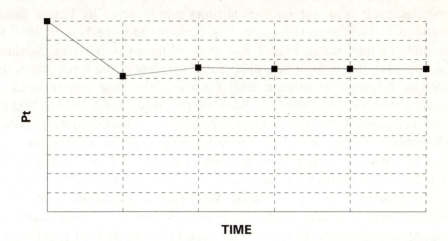

Figure 2–4 The Market Behaviour under the Open-border Policy
$(-\beta<r<0)$

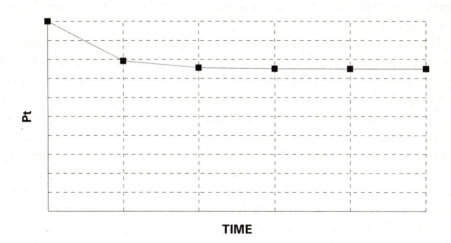

Figure 2–5 The Market Behaviour under the Open-border Policy
$(r<-\beta)$

The territory of the *Saar* came into existence in 1919, when the Treaty of Versailles made it an autonomous territory administered by France under League of Nations supervision, pending a plebiscite to be held in 1935 to determine its final status. France also received the right to exploit Sarrland coal field until that time. When more than 90 percent of the votes cast in the plebiscite favoured its reunion with Germany, the Saar was restored to Germany where it constituted the Saarland province. During World War II, Hitler incorporated it with Lorraine (annexed from France) into the province of Westmark. The scene of heavy fighting at the close of the war, the Saar was placed under French military occupation in 1945 and 1947 was given an autonomous government. In a referendum in 1947, the population voted for economic union with France. Strong West Germany's claims to the Saar, however, were a serious cause of friction in post-war France–Germany relations. An agreement between France and Germany in 1954 provided for an autonomous Saar under a neutral commissioner to be named by the West European Union; the economic union with France was to be maintained for 50 years. However, in a popular referendum, Saarland rejectected the agreement in October 1955 and, in accordance with subsequent French–German agreements, the Saar Territory became a state of the Federal Republic of Germany.

The autonomous Russian region of Karelia extends from the Finnish border in the west to the White Sea in the east, and from the Kola peninsula in the north to Lakes Lagoda and Onega, Europe's largest freshwater bodies, in the south. Russians now constitute a majority of its population of about three-quarter million, the rest consisting mainly of Karelians, Finns, and Lapps. Karelia was conquered in the 12th and 13th centuries by the Swedes who took the west, and by Novgorod who took the east. The eastern part was taken from Russia by the Sweden in 1617 but restored in 1721 by the Treaty of Nystad. The Russian empire was economically backward and was often a place of exile for political prisoners. In 1920 an autonomous oblast, known as the Karelian Workers' Commune, was set up in East Karelia; in 1923 it was made into the Karelian Autonomous SSR, which after the Soviet–Finnish War of 1939–40, incorporated most of the territory ceded by Finnish to the USSR. In March 1940, the region's status was raised to that of a constituent republic, called the Karela–Finnish SSA. During World War II, the Finns, who were allies of the Axis powers, occupied most of Karelia; but the region was returned to the USSR in 1944. Karelia returned to the status of an autonomous republic in 1956.[54]

---

[54]Adapted from *The New Columbia Encyclopaedia*, edited by W. H. Harris and T. S. Levey, New York/London: Columbia University Press, 1975. Also cited in J. Friedaman (1993).

# CHAPTER 3

# FROM CORE TO PERIPHERY

As the clearest symbol to territorial divisions, political borders physically and/or ideologically separate adjacent political regimes. In general, the economic mechanisms of border-regions intuitively stem from two facts: (1) border-regions are located in the geographical margins of their respective political regions (such as independent and dependent states, provinces, municipalities, counties, etc.) and usually far away from the cores; (2) each border-region is under the jurisdiction of two or more political authorities. Obviously, the former suggests that it is not a locationally better choice for border-regions to develop technological exchange and economic co-operation with their respective remote heartlands, while the latter implies that there always exist some geographical separations[1] and political and economic fragmentations within border-regions.

## 3.1 An Autarkic Economy

In his well-known monograph entitled *The Isolated State*, J. H. von Thünen (1826) locationally contributed to the theory of agricultural land use around a city. Indeed, more often than not, Thünen's model has been widely used in the past century's literature in which the land use within a city as a function of distance from the central business district to the urban fringe was extensively explained, even though it did not explain the demand for agricultural products emanating from the city and provide a complete theory of regions.[2] The economic difference between core and peripheral areas within an independent state has been now generally recognised by economic geographers and regional scientists, the phenomenal uncertainty and economic complexity, however, still exist in different regional environments. Therefore, before wandering throughout an economy to basically discover the different scenarios between its core and peripheral areas, we should make a number of regional assumptions as below:

---

[1]As analysed in Chapter 1, the geographical separations in border-regions are usually identified by natural and artificial barriers between adjacent political regions.

[2]For more evidence, see J. H. von Thünen (1826): *The Isolated State*, Translated by C. M. Wartenburg, London: Pergamon Press, 1966.

1. The target political region is an isolated country or at least one which is economically operated with infinitely high level tariff and non-tariff barriers for the importation (exportation) from (to) its outside world;
2. All necessary production factors (such as labour force, capital, technology, natural resources, etc.) are uniformly distributed throughout the country's territory;
3. An isotropic communication and transport network exists in the country;
4. All regional preferences and price discriminations are absolutely ignored by the economic players (both supply and demand sides); and
5. The economic activities (both buying and selling) are solely motivated by the principle of profit-maximization within the country.

Based on the above assumptions, we may construct a core-peripheral model for the autarkic economy. For simplicity of exposition, we use one dimensional case: consider that $A$ and $B$ (with the coordinates of $0$ and $L$ respectively) in Figure 3–1 symbolize the borders of the country, $O$ (with the coordinate of $L/2$) is the geographic center of the country. Let $r$ and $l$ denote the trade benefit and distance between point $x$ ($x \in (0, L)$) and any other point $x'$ (again, $x' \in (0, L)$) in the one-dimensional country respectively. The relationship between $r$ and $l$ may be expressed by a decreasing function as $r=r(l)$, $dr/dl=r'(l)<0$. Characterized by Assumptions (2)–(5), function $r(l)$ has two extremes: (1) when $l=0$, $r(0)=r_0=$ max, (2) when $l=\infty$, $r(\infty)=0=$min. In addition, when $0<l<\infty$, $0<r(l)<r_0$. For the sake of computational ease, the function $r=r(l)$ may be approximately expressed by $r=r_0/(1+l)$. Finally, we derive the total trade benefit of point $x$ with all parts of the country (i.e., from $A$ to $B$) by the integral calculus

$$R(x)=\int_0^x \frac{r_0}{1+l}dl + \int_0^{L-x} \frac{r_0}{1+l}dl =r_0(\ln(1+x)+r_0\ln(1+L-x), \text{ with } x\in (0, L). \quad (3\text{–}1)$$

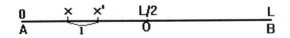

Figure 3–1 An One-dimensional Region

Equation (3–1) has three kinds of marginal properties for $R(x)$ with respect to $x$: (1) when $0 \leq x < L/2$, $dR/dx > 0$, i.e., $R$ is an increasing function of $x$, (2) when $x = L/2$, $dR/dx = 0$; and (3) when $L/2 < x \leq L$, $dR/dx < 0$, i.e., $R$ is a decreasing function of $x$. In particular, $R(x)$ is maximized in the geographic center (i.e., $x = L/2$) and is minimized in the peripheral lines (i.e., $x = 0$ and $x = L$) of the autarkic country, i.e.,

$$\text{when } x = 0, \ R(0) = r_0 \ln(1+L) = \min \tag{3–2}$$
$$\text{when } x = L, \ R(L) = r_0 \ln(1+L) = \min \tag{3–3}$$
$$\text{when } x = L/2, \ R(L/2) = 2r_0 \ln(1+L/2) = \max \tag{3–4}$$

The domestic trade benefit expressed by Equation (3–1) yields an inverted–U shape curve (as shown in Figure 3–2), from which we can conclude that the local trade benefit in the autarkic country always decreases from its center (i.e., $O$ in Figure 3–1) to its peripheral areas (i.e., $A$ and $B$ in Figure 3–1). With this simple core-peripheral model, we can also easily understand the regional economic differences within any isolated country.[3]

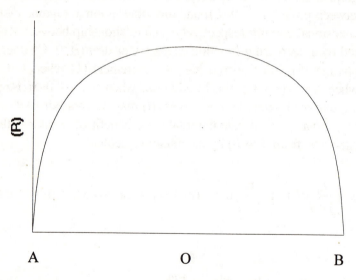

Figure 3–2 An Inverted–U Shape Trade Curve for an Autarkic Economy

---

[3]Similarly, if an economy is freer to importation (exportation) from (to) the outside world, the domestic and foreign trade benefit as a whole still follows an inverted–U shape curve, while the convex degree of which increases with respect to the border-related barriers.

## 3.2 How to Calculate the Border Effects?

The economic developments of any adjacent territories separated by a border are not solely determined by one of the territories but by both together. Political borders have been the power limits beyond which the governments and/or ruling powers can not extend the economic decisions of their own. As a result of the locational disadvantages, border-regions, in contrast with their respective core regions, have been rarely paid attention by the governments and/or ruling powers involved. In addition, border-regions have always been known as the disadvantageous localities by investors because each of the border markets being available for both the producers and the consumers has been separated into two or more parts and only one part can be treated domestically, while the rest can only be partially utilized under the border-related barriers.

To intuitively illustrate the spatial mechanisms of cross-border separation and their economic effects, let's look at a simple case. Consider a firm that is located at point "$O$" and makes profits by selling its products within a circular area (horizontally demonstrated as $ADBFA$ in Figure 3–3). Assume that the firm's profit per unit of product is maximised as $r_0$ at point "$O$" in which the transport is almost costless and is minimised as zero at the peripheral line of $ADBFA$ area where the gross profit is counteracted by the increased cost of transportation. The distance between $O$ and each point in the peripheral line is $L/2$. Based on Assumptions (2)–(5) in Section 3.1, we use a decreasing linear function[4] to express the profit ($r$) with respect to $l$ ($0 \le l \le L/2$), i.e., $r = r_0(L-2l)/L$. Finally, the firm's total profit ($R_c$) in an one-dimensional case[5] is aggregated by deriving the integral calculus function of $r$ from $-L/2$ to $L/2$, i.e.,

$$R_c = r_0 \int_{-L/2}^{L/2} \frac{L-2l}{L} dl = 2r_0 \int_{0}^{L/2} \frac{L-2l}{L} dl = \frac{r_0 L}{2} \qquad (3-5)$$

---

[4]The use of any other forms of decreasing functions (both linear and non-linear) may also be easily done. However, the result generated by different decreasing functions are only different in quantity but not in quality.

[5]This is only for the sake of computational ease. A two-dimensional case may also be done using the same methodology.

We now consider a political border (*AB* in Figure 3–3) which separates the market that the firm may potentially use into approximately two equal parts:

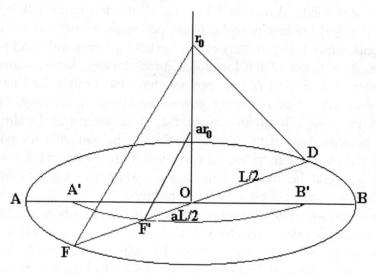

Figure 3–3 A Market Separated by a Border (*AB*)

(1) Domestic market (horizontally demonstrated as *ADBA* area in Figure 3–3): The firm's total profit within this part is half of $R_c$, i.e.,

$$R_{DP} = R_C / 2 = r_0 \int_0^{L/2} \frac{L - 2l}{L} dl = \frac{r_0 L}{4}$$

(2) Foreign market (horizontally demonstrated as *AFBA* area in Figure 3–3): Suppose that the border (*AB*) enables the firm to make a profit in each point of the foreign market by a constant portion $\alpha$ ($0 \leq \alpha \leq 1$)[6] of that in its domestic market under the same distance of transportation. Then, the firm's net profit in the foreign market will be only maximized to $\alpha r_0$ at point "*O*" and be minimized to zero at the peripheral line (*A'F'B'*). Notice that, the distance between *O* and each point in the peripheral line (*A'F'B'*), now,

---

[6]The parameter $\alpha$ decreasingly reflects the level of tariff and non-tariff barriers across the border (*AB*).

decreases from $L/2$ to $\alpha L/2$ correspondingly. The firm's total profit within the foreign part of the market is

$$R_{FP} = \alpha r_0 \int_0^{\alpha L/2} \frac{L-2l}{L} dl = \frac{(2-\alpha)\alpha^2 r_0 L}{4}$$

Finally, the total net profit of the firm in the border market becomes

$$R_p = R_{DP} + R_{FP} = \frac{(1+(2-\alpha)\alpha^2)r_0 L}{4} \tag{3-6}$$

When $0<\alpha<1$, $R_p$ in Equation (3–6) is always less than $r_0 L/2$ and larger than $r_0 L/4$, i.e., $R_{DP}<R_p<R_C$. In particular, when $\alpha=1$, $R_p=R_C=r_0 L/2$; when $\alpha=0$, $R_p=r_0 L/4=R_C/2$. Figure 3–4 illustrates an increasing tendency of $R_p$ with respect to $\alpha$ (assume $r_0=1$, $L=100$). Clearly, the total loss of the firm in the 2-d border market (i.e., $R_p-R_C$) is positive and decreases when $\alpha$ changes from 0 to 1.

$$R_C - R_p = \frac{(1-(2-\alpha)\alpha^2)r_0 L}{4} \tag{3-7}$$

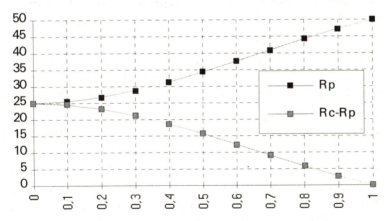

Figure 3–4 The Economic Effects of a Border with Respect to $\alpha$
($r_0=1$, $L=100$)

## 3.3 Cross-border Separation

A traditional approach sees the border as a dividing line, the source of a long series of discriminating effects. According to the locational principle of separation, the higher priority of socio-economic developments should never be given by the governments to their peripheral areas. There have been many locational scenarios stemming from the cross-border separations in terms of geography, economy, and politics. Below are five typical cases in the special landscape of the earth, from which we may obtain more evidences in detail.

[Case I] The Korean peninsula has rarely been the "calm land" since her last dynasty, Chosen (the land of morning calm), was forcedly replaced by the Japanese colonialism at the end of the 19th century. The peninsula was separated into two antagonistic economies as soon as it was liberated from the Japanese control by the two superpowers (former USSR and USA) at the end of the World War II. The DMZ (Demilitarised Zone) – an area of 213 kilometers in length along the 38th Parallel and four kilometers wide extending into both North and South Korea's territories – was selected by the Korean War participants to moderate the confrontation between the North and South regimes in the peninsula at the end of the Korean War (1950–53). Since then, the DMZ has been really a natural protection zone where many wild animals which were confirmed to be extinct in the rest of the peninsula have been living together peacefully, while it has been still a forbidden zone for the mankind.[7] The division of the country by external forces extends through all phases of Korean life – political, economic, and social. The artificial division at the 38th Parallel destroyed national unity, led to tragedy of fratricidal war and produced many other human and national agonies, as noted by Bong-youn Choy (1984): "The division broke the mutual complementarities between the northern and southern parts of the economy. For example, before the division of the country, northern Korea had almost 70 to 80 per cent of the heavy industry including most sources of hydroelectric power supply, while southern Korea dominated most of the light industry as well as rice production. The consumer-goods industry of the south depended upon northern supply of both electrical power and raw

---

[7]See *Information Times*, p. 2, August 2, 1992.

and semi-finished materials. The south depended on the chemical fertilizer produced in the north, while the north needed the rice from the south."[8]

The spatial distribution of socio-economic activities in South Korea's capital, Seoul, has been also greatly affected by its proximity to the border between the North and South in the peninsula. Seoul used to economically concentrate on Chung-gu (central district), northern Han-gang River. Since the Korean War (1950–53), the city's urbanization has expanded into the far southern Han-gang River through 18 bridges rather than into the northern fringe, simply due to the latter's much closer proximity to the forbidden 38th Parallel (i.e., the North–South border). The unevenly distributed economic activities were particularly obvious in Seoul Special municipality. For example, the business of the real estate in southern Han-gang River area increased hundreds of times in price level in the early 1990s compared with that of two decades before. Gangnam-gu (south Han-gang River district) has been one of the most prosperous districts in Seoul with many economic, trade, educational and research centers, and modern buildings (e.g., the 1988 Olympic Complex, KOEX Exhibition Center, etc.). However, few South Korean people have been willing to set up their business offices and dwell in the northern urban fringe because of its geographically closer to the North Korean regime.[9]

[Case II] The territorial division of Germany after the World War II by the Allies born an 1,380 kilometer length of border line from Lubek to Hof. The inner-German border-region was characterized by a sinuous disregard for the realities of local topography, and daily patterns of social life and economic activity. Initially, during the short period of the inter-Allied co-operation and unrestricted cross-border movement, this was not considered to be so significant. However, with the progressive intensification of the Cold War, the creation of separate currencies in 1948, and the foundation of the two German states in 1949, the boundary became a forbidden division between the two starkly different political and economic entities. In 1952, what then had become known as the *innerdeutsche Grenze* was sealed by the

---

[8]Bong-youn Choy (1984): *A History of the Korean Unification Movement: Its Issues and Prospects*, p. 14, Ill: Bradley University; also cited in Eui-Gak Hwang (1993): *The Korean Economies: A Comparison of North and South*, p. 1, Oxford: Clarendon Press.

[9]Notice that, in the spring of 1994, the North Korean threatened to make Seoul into a sea of fires in case of another Korean War, when I was visiting Korea University in Sungbuk-gu, the district of northern Seoul, South Korea.

German Democratic Republic (GDR) against all but carefully supervised and controlled movement. It was at the same time consolidated on the eastern side by the first rudimentary border fortifications, together with the creation of a 500m–wide ploughed 'guarded' strip. Bus and rail travel cross this border was curtailed, and the GDR began the process of tearing up road and railway crossings, eventually involving the disconnection of thirty-two railways, three autobahns, thirty-one main roads, 140 secondary roads, and innumerable minor roads and tracks.[10] The former inner-German separation which caused to the transportation network was severe, besides other ideological isolations. From the Shell Generalkarte 1: 200,000 Sheet 14 (Geographischer Verlag), one may clearly discovers the former frontier area which exacerbated its psychological impact and lengthened the reorientation of external communication links to new sources of supply and markets located elsewhere in West Germany or in foreign countries. K.-H. Braun and J. Maier (1983) also estimate that the extra distance created by the latter amounted to a penalty of between 150–200 kilometers for industries in the Coburg-Hof salient of the northern Bavaria area.[11] The very limited number of crossing points along the frontier, coupled with the marked contrasts in the density of the road network, were also evident.

[Case III] Despite the emphasis on economic integration, the planning and operation of infrastructures in most of the West European countries have still been predominantly done by the individual countries using a narrow national perspective. The existing transport network in West Europe clearly demonstrates a national orientation, even though the international dimension has recently grown in importance, as can be seen from initiatives such as the Channel Tunnel, a bridge between Sweden and Denmark, and a high-speed railway connection between France, Belgium, Germany, and the Netherlands. Below is an example in which P. Rietveld (1993) used a density indicator to investigate the role of borders in infrastructure networks. In Table 3–1, the numbers are calculated relative to the density in the border-region. For example, the number of 0.25 for the Germany–Belgian

---

[10]G. Bayerische (1981): *Bayerns Landesgrenze Zur DDR*, Bayerisches Staatsregierung, Munich.

[11]K.-H. Braun and J. Maier (1983): *Industrie im Peripheren Raum unter dem Einfluss der Grenze Zur DDR und CSSR*, Institut für Geowissenschaften, Bayreuth. Also cited N. P. Jones and T. Wild (1994): "Opening the Frontier: Recent Spatial Impacts in the Former Inner-German Border Zone", *Regional Studies*, Vol. 28, p. 264.

border means that the railway density (measured as the length (in km) of the railway network divided by the area (in km$^2$)) on this border is only 25 per cent of the density in the German and Belgian border-regions. Table 3–1 shows very clearly that substantial barrier effects exist for the international borders. In all cases, the border-crossing densities are much lower than the average densities in border-regions and the West Europe as a whole.[12]

Table 3–1 Network Densities for Rail and Road on Borderlines of Europe, 1989

| Border between countries | Network density on borderline relative to border area | |
| --- | --- | --- |
| | Railway | Highway |
| Belgium–the Netherlands | 0.10 | 0.21 |
| Belgium–France | 0.20 | 0.29 |
| Germany–the Netherlands | 0.12 | 0.31 |
| Germany–Belgium | 0.25 | 0.36 |
| Germany–France | 0.18 | 0.22 |
| Switzerland–Austria | 0.20 | 0.00 |
| Switzerland–France | 0.23 | 0.31 |
| Italy–France | 0.12 | 0.16 |
| Italy–Switzerland | 0.16 | 0.11 |

Source: P. Rietveld (1993): "Transport and Communication Barriers in Europe", p. 53, Table 1, in R. Cappelline and P. W. J. Batey (eds.): *Regional Networks, Border Regions and European Integration*, European Research in Regional Science Series No. 3, London: Pion Limited, 1993.

[Case IV] Being both culturally homogeneous and economically interdependent on each other, the United States and Canada have been known as a model of friendly neighbours. But when the two countries decided to build the 28 railways on the two sides along their about 700 mile common border before the 1980s, only 8 railways (less than 30 per cent of the total number) were extended up to the border so as to connect the two

---

[12]For a more detailed account of the empirical results, refer to the work of F. Bruinsma and P. Rietveld (1992): "De Structurerende Werking van Insfrastructuur", Economische Faculteit, Vrije Universiteit, Amsterdam.

nations' communication networks. Moreover, the United States and the Canadian governments each independently built a railway line along the border in its own territory. The two national railways are both very close and in parallel to each other. One may simply image that there would have not been such a communication network had the two sides of the border belonged to one single sovereign country.

[Case V] Even inside a political region, some internal cross-border separations have also stemmed from sub-political borders. According to China's provincial maps which were published in 1983, among the ten provincial regions (provinces, autonomous regions and autonomous cities), there were 453 highways in the provincial border-regions, of which only 269 (about 60 per cent) highways were transprovincially connected and 184 (about 40 per cent), however, were cut off near the borders.[13] As stated in Chapter 1, borders between political regions are usually expressed by natural barriers (such as rivers, mountains, lakes, oceans, etc.) or artificial barriers. The geographic and political separations in border-regions have shown in space many negative influences on the industrial allocation and socio-economic developments.

For example, separated by Wuyi mountain range with an average height of more than 1,000 meters from the sea level, the border-region of Zhejiang, Fujian, and Jiangxi provinces in Southeast China is covered by about 80 per cent mountainous and hilly lands. The highway network in the border-region is basically characterized by WMPs (winding-mountain-paths). A research project conducted by Zhu Wuxiang (1990) demonstrated that the border-region's highway transport flows of goods ranged between 500 and 1,000 trucks per day and were decreasingly related to the proximity to the border.[14] The inferior physical conditions have socio-economically affected the border-region. In Lishui prefecture of Zhejiang province, for example, 20 per cent of the rural area did not install post offices and more than two-

---

[13]Calculations by the author based on *Zhongguo Ditu Ce* (China Atlas), Beijing: China Map Publishing House, 1983. The ten provincial regions include Beijing, Shanghai, Tianjin autonomous cities, Hebei, Shanxi, Liaoning, Gansu, Qinghai provinces and Inner Mongolia, Ningxia Hui autonomous regions.

[14]Zhu Wuxiang (1990): "A Preliminary Study of the Economic Development in the Border-Region of Zhjiang, Fujian, and Jiangxi Provinces", unpublished MBA thesis, School of Economics and Management, Qinghua University, Beijing.

third villagers could not read newspapers in 1989.[15] From the statistical data, the border-region's sub-economies each experienced a relative stagnation compared with its respective provincial level. In 1987, Lishui prefecture's gross value of industrial output (GVIO) made up only 1.30 per cent that of the province, while this proportion remained 1.70 per cent in 1980. Nanping prefecture accounted for 12.69 per cent gross value of industrial and agricultural output (GVIAO) of Fujian province in 1978, and decreased to 12.40 per cent in 1980, 11.68 per cent in 1984, and 9.79 per cent in 1987 respectively. Again in 1987, Shangrao prefecture ranked number ten in the eleven prefectures and municipalities in Jiangxi province in terms of per capita GVIAO, while the number eleven was Ganzhou prefecture which borders on Guangdong province in the south-west.[16]

## 3.4 Evidence from 117 Counties[17]

Fundamentally stemmed from the physical disparity as well as the institutional diversification, political economies have usually developed different regional economic mechanisms and policy instruments from each other and generated economic heterogeneity in their cross-border regions. In this section, we select a study area in Central China and try to economically differentiate border-regions using the cross-section data.

With an area of 167 thousand square kilometers and a population of more than 80 millions, Henan is one of the largest provinces in China.[18] It has a great diversity in terms of natural geography and topography. For example, three mountainous areas of Qinba-shan in Southwest, Dabie-shan in Southeast, and Taihang-shan in Northwest cover a total number of 298

---

[15]Source: The Prefectural Bureau for Statistics of Lishui, Zhejiang province, China.

[16]Data source: *Yearbook of Provincial Statistics*, various issues of Zhejiang, Fujian, and Jiangxi provinces.

[17]This research was done in partial collaboration with Research Institute of Economics, Henan Provincial Planning Commission in 1990 and resulted in a chapter of my Ph. D. thesis (1991) and a paper entitled "The Economic Comparison of Border-Regions: The Case of Central China" (Guo Rongxing, 1994), in Lou Zhaomei et al. (eds): *Advances in Management Science*, pp. 417–22, Beijing: International Academic Publishers, 1994.

[18]As noted by Guo Wenxuan et al., Henan province can basically characterize mainland China in terms of nature, geography, socio-culture and political economy more than other provinces of the country. For more discussions, see Guo Wenxuan (ed.) (1989): *An Introduction to Henan's Economy*, in Chinese, Zhengzhou: Henan Renmin Press.

towns and villages of 40 counties in Henan province. Henan is one of China's provinces with plentiful natural resources. Coal reserves abound in the eastern, north-eastern, and central areas, petroleum and natural gas in the southern and north-eastern areas, gold in the western area, bauxite in the north-western and southern areas, molybdenum in the western area, natural soda in the southern area and blue asbestos in the south-western area.[19] In order to make a comparative analysis of sub-economies differing in nature, geography, resource, and spatial organization, we classify Henan's 117 sub-regions (counties or cities) into 12 different groups by composition of: (i) geographic location (GL) by which core (C) and periphery (P) regions are identified; (ii) natural topography (NT) by which plain (P) and mountain (M) regions are identified; (iii) natural resource (NR) by which agricultural (A) and mineral (M) regions are identified; and (iv) border dimension (BD) by which two and three dimensional border-regions are identified.

Henan province has approximately a 3,130 kilometer long border across which 42 counties are directly exposed to six neighbouring provinces (i.e., Hebei in the north, Shanxi in the north-west, Shaanxi in the west, Hubei in the south, Anhui in the south-east, and Shandong in the north-east). Among the 42 border counties, seven counties are adjacent to two outside provinces (we define them as 3-dimensional border-regions) and 35 counties are adjacent to one outside province (we define them as 2-dimensional border-regions). Furthermore, we use the number of a border-county's towns and/or villages bordering on the outside province(s) to approximately express the marginal degree (MD) of the border county. Summarizing up, the variables used here and data source are listed below:

(1) NIPC (national income per capita, measured in yuan[20]), for 117 counties. Source: *Henan Yearbook of Economic Statistics (1989)*, Henan Provincial Bureau for Statistics, Zhengzhou, Henan province, China.

(2) GL (geographic location), for 117 counties. Source: calculation by the author based on the map of Henan province.

(3) NT (natural topography), for 117 counties. Source: calculation by the author based on the map of Henan province.

---

[19]Date source: Guo Wenxuan (ed.) (1989), pp. 50–3, ibid.

[20]The official exchange rate of Chinese yuan (or RMB) to US dollar was around 3.2: 1 in the mid-1980s. Nonetheless, the more rational exchange rate of yuan to US dollar should be larger than the officially fixed one if the purchasing power parities (PPP) methodology suggested by the World Bank is introduced.

(4) NR (natural resource), for 117 counties. Source: *An Introduction to Henan's Economy*, by Guo Wenxuan (ed.) (1989), Henan Renmin Press.

(5) BD (border dimension), for 42 border counties (i.e., for GL= periphery). Source: calculation by the author based on the map of Henan province.

(6) MD (marginal degree, i.e., the number of villages and/or towns bordering on the outside province(s)), for 42 border counties (i.e., for GL= periphery). Source: Joint Investigation Team sponsored by the Provincial Planning Economic Commission, Zhengzhou, Henan province, 1988.

Table 3–2 gives the data of Henan's 42 border counties.[21]

Table 3–2 Geographic and Economic Conditions of 42 Border Counties, China

| County | NO | NIPC | BD | NT | NR | MD |
|--------|-----|---------|----|----|----|----|
| Lankao | 11 | 569.40 | 2 | P | A | 5 |
| Xin'an | 14 | 597.08 | 2 | M | A | 1 |
| Linxian | 27 | 467.69 | 3 | M | M | 5 |
| Anyang | 28 | 590.93 | 2 | M | M | 10 |
| Neihuang | 31 | 520.32 | 2 | P | A | 3 |
| Huixian | 34 | 1084.84 | 2 | P | M | 6 |
| Changyuan | 41 | 492.07 | 2 | P | A | 6 |
| Xiuwu | 42 | 1092.19 | 2 | M | M | 3 |
| Buo'ai | 43 | 1138.35 | 2 | M | A | 3 |
| Miyang | 44 | 1206.26 | 2 | M | A | 1 |
| Jiyuan | 46 | 1350.49 | 2 | M | A | 4 |
| Qingfeng | 49 | 574.90 | 2 | P | A | 5 |

*to be continued*

---

[21]For the data of the 75 counties, see Guo Rongxing (1991): "A Preliminary Study of Border-Regional Economics: Theory and Practice of Economic Development in the Provincial Border-Regions of China", Table 15, Ph.D. thesis, School of Economics and Trade, CUMT, Xuzhou, China.

Table 3–2 (*continued*)

| | | | | | | |
|---|---|---|---|---|---|---|
| Taiqian | 50 | 517.49 | 3 | P | A | 9 |
| Fanxian | 51 | 559.87 | 2 | P | A | 7 |
| Nan'le | 52 | 353.48 | 2 | P | A | 7 |
| Mianchi | 62 | 698.52 | 2 | M | M | 4 |
| Shaanxian | 63 | 918.66 | 2 | P | M | 2 |
| Lingbao | 64 | 884.74 | 3 | P | M | 6 |
| Lishi | 65 | 520.06 | 2 | M | M | 5 |
| Yucheng | 67 | 483.59 | 2 | P | A | 8 |
| Shangqiu | 68 | 516.28 | 2 | P | A | 5 |
| Minquan | 69 | 525.84 | 2 | P | A | 4 |
| Xiayi | 72 | 466.80 | 3 | P | A | 5 |
| Yongcheng | 74 | 422.78 | 2 | P | M | 13 |
| Luyi | 80 | 514.49 | 2 | P | A | 6 |
| Danxian | 81 | 516.43 | 2 | P | A | 6 |
| Shenqiu | 83 | 494.89 | 2 | P | A | 7 |
| Tuocheng | 84 | 525.89 | 2 | P | A | 2 |
| Xincai | 92 | 357.75 | 2 | P | A | 2 |
| Pingyu | 93 | 346.87 | 2 | P | A | 7 |
| Xichuan | 96 | 504.53 | 2 | P | A | 4 |
| Xixia | 99 | 472.64 | 2 | M | M | 3 |
| Xinyie | 103 | 412.98 | 3 | M | M | 7 |
| Dengzhou | 105 | 353.03 | 2 | P | A | 5 |
| Tanghe | 106 | 602.32 | 2 | P | A | 3 |
| Tongbai | 107 | 725.92 | 2 | M | M | 6 |
| Neixiang | 110 | 286.61 | 2 | P | A | 6 |
| Xinyang | 111 | 508.81 | 2 | M | A | 5 |
| Huaibin | 114 | 299.66 | 2 | M | A | 13 |
| Gushi | 115 | 357.19 | 3 | M | A | 6 |
| Shangcheng | 116 | 394.31 | 2 | M | A | 3 |
| Xinxian | 117 | 346.58 | 3 | M | A | 9 |

Notes: NO (ordinal number of observation)$\in (1, 117)$; NIPC (national income per capita) is measured in Chinese yuan; BD (border dimension)=2 or 3; NT (natural topography)= P(lain) or M(ountain); NR (natural resource)=A(griculture) or M(ineral); MD (marginal degree)=number of villages and/or towns bordering on the outside province(s).

Table 3–3 Average NIPCs of 12 Kind Regions, 117 Counties, China

| Type of topography and resource | Core | Periphery | | Total |
|---|---|---|---|---|
| | | 2-d | 3-d | |
| **Plain and** | | | | |
| mineral resource | 552.8 (4)(181.98) | 673.43 (6)(214.83) | 470.17 (2)(2.48) | 599.36 |
| agricultural resource | 651.73 (10)(265.24) | 784.99 (7)(400.33) | 351.89 (2)(5.31) | 669.26 |
| **Mountain and** | | | | |
| mineral resource | 937.07 (11)(359.24) | 808.76 (3)(281.23) | 884.74 (1)(0) | 907.92 |
| agricultural resource | 738.42 (50)(343.81) | 489.40 (19)(85.45) | 492.15 (2)(25.35) | 664.84 |
| TOTAL | 746.10 | 607.44 | 501.88 | 690.00 |

Notes: Figures in parentheses below each average NIPC estimation are the number of observations and standard error respectively.
Source: Calculations based on (1) Table 3–2 and (2) Guo Rongxing (1991, Table 15).

From the estimated average NIPCs and their respective standard errors (shown in Table 3–3), we may draw some economic differences between the 12 kinds of sub-regions (counties). Generally, Henan's core regions, with an average NIPC of 746.10 yuan, have a favourable location compared to peripheral regions, as the 2-d and 3-d border-regions of the latter have only the average NIPCs of 607.44 yuan and 501.88 yuan respectively. As the average NIPC of all 2-d border-regions is 105.56 yuan higher than that of all 3-d border-regions, we can conclude that the economic development in peripheral regions is negatively related to the border dimension. Furthermore, Table 3–3 also shows that the average NIPC of the agricultural resource-based counties (669.26 yuan) is higher than that of the mineral resource-based counties (599.36 yuan) in plain regions and that the average

NIPC of the mineral resource-based counties (907.92 yuan) is higher than that of the agricultural resource-based counties (664.84 yuan) in mountain regions. Indeed, more often than not, this causality stems from the fact that the plain regions in China have an advantage for agricultural production while the mountain regions usually possess more high value-added mineral and forest resources for industrial production.

It should be noted, however, that some average NIPCs in Table 3–3 demonstrate relatively much larger standard errors in border-regions, such as the 2-d border-region of plain with agricultural resource (with a standard error of 400.33 yuan), the core region of mountain with mineral resource (with a standard error of 359.24 yuan), etc. Furthermore, Table 3–3 also shows some facts that do not explicitly fit the above results: for example, regarding the mountain with mineral resource-based regions, the 2-d border-region has even a lower average NIPC (808.76 yuan) than the 3-d border-region (884.76 yuan). The main reason that lies behind the above results might be either the dearth of the sample (for example, only one county, i.e., Xiuwu labelled as No. 42 in Table 3–2, is available for the estimation of the average NIPC for the 3-d mountain border-region with mineral resource) or the fact that Henan's peripheral economy had been more or less promoted by the sources of the outside provinces.[22]

We may go further to quantitatively analyse the correlation between the NIPC and the marginal degree (MD). Using the data given in Table 3–2, we may estimate two linear equations for the 42 border counties:

$$NIPC_{2\text{-}d} = 651.09 - 15.40\,MD_{2\text{-}d} \qquad (3\text{–}8)$$
$$(9.82)\ (-1.24)$$
$$(N=35,\ R^2=0.03,\ F=1.54)$$

$$NIPC_{3\text{-}d} = 603.87 - 16.79\,MD_{3\text{-}d} \qquad (3\text{–}9)$$
$$(13.97)\ (-1.10)$$
$$(N=7,\ R^2=0.02,\ F=1.20)$$

---

[22]Notice that, the substantial measures for the development of some peripheral areas may overcome the locational disadvantages of border-related separation. For more evidence, see Chapters 6.

where NIPC$_{2-d}$ and NIPC$_{3-d}$ are national incomes per capital for 2-d and 3-d border-regions respectively; MD$_{2-d}$ and MD$_{3-d}$ are marginal degrees for 2-d and 3-d border-regions respectively. Even though both are not generated by significant statistical values in Equations (3–8) and (3–9), the estimated NIPCs of the 2-d and 3-d border-regions each demonstrates a decreased tendency with respect to the marginal degree (MD) (see Figure 3–5). Furthermore, the coefficients in Equations (3–8) and (3–9) may also help us to find the economic difference between the 2-d and 3-d border-regions: apart from a net increased average NIPC of 47.22 yuan compared to 3-d border-region, 2-d border-region's marginal decrease of NIPC stemmed from the marginal degree is estimated at 15.40, i.e., the average NIPC will be decreased by 15.40 yuan after one unit of marginal degree (expressed by the number of villages and/or towns bordering on the outside province(s)) increases. But the marginal decreased effect on 3-d border-region's NIPC is estimated at 16.79 which is 1.39 yuan higher than that on 2-d border-region. This difference implies that the marginal degree (MD) impedes the economic development of 3-d border-region more than 2-d border-region.

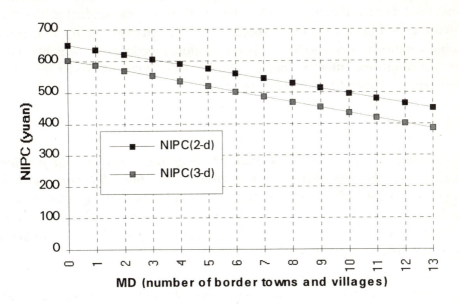

Figure 3–5 The MD-related NIPCs of 2- and 3-d Border Counties

# CHAPTER 4

# IN SEARCH FOR ECONOMICS

The concept 'interdependence' can be traced back to the 19th century, while it did not come into the literature of the economic analysis of interactions and inter-relations among countries and regions until the Second World War.[1] In the 1970s and the 1980s, a large number of papers, books and reports had been conducted on the topics of the categories, structures, and measures for interdependence and the macro-economic policy and co-ordination between the increasingly interdependent industrial economies.[2] The general phenomena of interdependence, fostered by international and inter-regional events and developments, of course, have produced and are still producing tremendous increases in terms of flows of information, technology, capital, people, and cultural influences across political borders, which, therefore, witnesses the most evident in the economic performances of border-regions. In addition to three basic propositions which are focused on the spatial aspects of economic interdependence with respect to distance, size, and border dimension (i.e., the number of independent authorities involved in a border-region) respectively in this chapter, we try to explore some empirical evidences for border-regional economics which, under certain conditions, may be transformed from the status of border-separated economics to that of borderless economics.

## 4.1 Proposition 1

Proposition 1. *Given the same natural, geographic, social, and political conditions, the interdependence between any two different political regions is negatively related to the distance between them.* In other words, assuming that $L$ and $R_1$ are used to express the distance and the degree of interdependence between the two political regions respectively, we obtain a negative differential of $R_1$ with respect to $L$, i.e.,

---

[1]For more discussions, see Zhang Yunling (1989): *The Interdependence in the World's Economies*, p. 2, Beijing: The Economic Science Press.

[2]See, for example, H. R. Alker (1974): "Analysing Global Interdependence", Center for International Studies, Massachusetts Institute of Technology; G. Oudis and J. Sachs (1984): "Macroeconomic Co-ordination among the Industrial Economies", *Brookings Paper*, No. 1.

$$dR_1/dL<0 \qquad\qquad (4\text{--}1)$$

This proposition axiomatically implies that the adjacent political regions will usually have more opportunities to develop economic and technological exchanges and social interactions, while the political regions which are far away from each other will have only relatively lower efficient inter-relations. To intuitively demonstrate this point, the geographical composition of the international trade in the last decades, for instance, has shown that trade between neighbouring countries has grown with exceptional rapidity: bilateral trade flows across the U.S.–Canadian border, between France, Italy, UK, Germany, and the Netherlands in West Europe, and between Japan and the countries once known as her 'co-prosperity' sphere in East Asia have risen a great deal more quickly than between those remote and isolated countries.

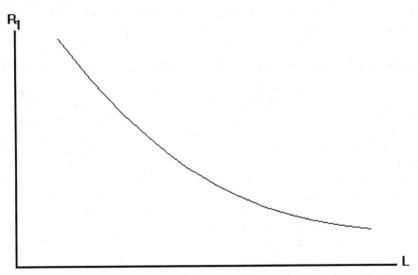

Figure 4–1 The Relationship between Interdependence and Distance

The evidences provided by J. Frankel, S.-J. Wei and E. Stein (1994) and B. Eichengreen and D. A. Irwin (1995) can help us to understand the correlation between the distance and the interdependence between sovereign countries,[3] even though their results need to be further clarified as Frankel and Stein used data of the 1980s and obtained slightly larger coefficients (around 0.5 to 0.6) on distance compared with the interwar estimates (around 0.3 to 0.6) based on the data of the 1930s derived by Eichengreen and Irwin, which clearly provides no evidence that declining transportation cost should have an increasingly important influence on pattern of trade.[4]

In order to provide more evidences for Proposition 1 and apply it to locationally characterize the economic activities in border-regions, we investigated 187 peasants of eight towns and villages (Fengxian, Huankou, Huashan, Liangzhou, Lizhai, Shonglou, Shunhe, and Zhaozhuang) which differ in distance to the border (i.e., 15.0 km, 6.0 km, 20.0 km, 4.5 km, 1.5 km, 5.5 km, 7.5 km, and 5.5 km respectively) between Jiangsu, Shandong and Anhui provinces in East China.[5] For simplicity of analysis, the peasants' socio-economic activities in this investigation were roughly classified into three groups: (1) visiting-activity (VA) which includes visiting relatives, friends and attending social and religious activities; (2) selling-activity (SA) which includes selling what are produced by the peasants themselves; and (3) buying-activity (BA) which includes buying what are needed in the peasants' production and daily lives. Furthermore, we use "homeland"

---

[3]Both Eichengreen et al. and Frankel et al. used a similar log-form specification as $\ln(1+TRADE_{ij})= \beta_0+ \beta_1\ln(GNP_i \cdot GNP_j)+ \beta_2\ln([GNP_i/POP_i]\cdot [GNP_j/POP_j])+ \beta_3 DIST_{ij} +\beta_4 CONT +u_{ij}$ where $TRADE_{ij}$ is the nominal value of bilateral trade between countries $i$ and $j$, $GNP_i \cdot GNP_j$ is the product of the two countries' nominal national incomes, $[GNP_i/POP_i]\cdot [GNP_j/POP_j]$ is the product of the two countries' per capita national incomes (also in nominal terms), $DIST_{ij}$ is the distance between the economic centers of gravity of the two countries (measured in miles or kilometers), and $CONT$ is a dummy variable for whether the two countries are contiguous. More details may be found in J. Frankel, S.-J. Wei and E. Stein (1994): "APEC and Regional Economic Agreements in the Pacific", unpublished manuscript, University of California at Berkeley, USA; B. Eichengreen and D. A. Irwin (1995); "Trade Blocs, Currency Blocs and the Reorientation of World Trade in the 1930s", *Journal of International Economics*, Vol. 38, pp. 1–24.

[4]This phenomenon may be plausibly explained by the increasing tendency of regional integration among the neighbouring countries (such as EC, NAFTA, ASEAN, etc.) in the recent decades.

[5]This household investigation was made in collaboration with the Research Office of the Magistrate, Fengxian county. I also benefited from the students of Class–788-SM of CUMT School of Economics and Trade for the data collection in 1990.

Table 4–1 Number of Socio-economic Activities Per Peasant, Fengxian County, China

| Town/village | DTB (km) | N | Homeland activities | | | | Cross-border activities | | | |
|---|---|---|---|---|---|---|---|---|---|---|
| | | | HLVA | HLSA | HLBA | HLTA | CBVA | CBSA | CBBA | CBTA |
| Fengxian | 15.0 | 28 | (0.2)3.2 | (1.8)7.4 | (1.2)4.9 | 15.5 | (0.05)0.2 | (0.5)1.3 | (0.4)1.0 | 2.5 |
| Huankou | 6.0 | 20 | (0.4)3.1 | (1.6)6.8 | (1.0)4.4 | 14.3 | (0.2)0.4 | (0.6)1.8 | (0.5)1.3 | 3.5 |
| Huashan | 20.0 | 28 | (0.1)3.5 | (1.9)7.8 | (1.3)5.2 | 16.5 | (0.02)0.1 | (0.4)1.1 | (0.2)0.8 | 2.0 |
| Liangzhai | 4.5 | 22 | (0.3)2.3 | (1.2)6.1 | (0.9)4.1 | 12.5 | (0.4)1.0 | (0.5)2.1 | (0.4)1.4 | 4.5 |
| Lizhai | 1.5 | 18 | (0.5)1.7 | (1.3)5.0 | (1.0)3.4 | 10.1 | (0.4)1.5 | (0.9)2.8 | (0.8)1.9 | 6.2 |
| Shonglou | 5.5 | 25 | (0.3)2.6 | (1.1)6.5 | (0.8)4.3 | 13.4 | (0.2)0.8 | (0.7)1.9 | (0.6)1.3 | 4.0 |
| Shunhe | 7.5 | 22 | (0.4)3.2 | (1.5)7.0 | (0.9)4.7 | 14.9 | (0.1)0.3 | (0.7)1.6 | (0.4)1.1 | 3.0 |
| Zhaozhuang | 5.5 | 24 | (0.2)2.6 | (1.2)6.5 | (0.7)4.3 | 13.4 | (0.3)0.8 | (0.9)1.8 | (0.7)1.2 | 3.8 |

Note: (1) DTB=distance to the border; N=number of observations; HLTA=homeland total activity; HLVA=homeland visiting activity; HLSA=homeland selling activity; HLBA=homeland buying activity; CBTA=cross-border total activity; CBVA= cross-border visiting activity; CBSA=cross-border selling activity; CBBA=cross-border buying activity; (2) The figures in parentheses are standard erorrs of what follow respectively.
Source: provided by Li Yan, Lian Xiaotong, Zheng Chaokun, Guo Xiuling, Liang Zhuyong, Qu Gushi, Liu Qinghua, Tian Gang, Ma Haiying. Calculations by the author.

(HL) and "cross-border" (CB) terms to identify the socio-economic activities by two parts: (1) the activities that happen in the homeland; (2) the activities that happen in other province(s) across the border(s). Using the compiled data in Table 4–1, we estimate the relationships between the socio-economic activities and the distance to the border (DTB) by means of the OLS regression (see Table 4–2 and Figures 4–2).

Table 4–2 Estimated Number of Socio-economic Activities by DTB

| Equation | $R^2$ | F |
|---|---|---|
| HLVA=2.14+0.77 DTB<br>(9.16) (3.30) | 0.64 | 10.82 |
| HLSA=5.64+0.12 DTB<br>(20.33) (4.37) | 0.76 | 19.05 |
| HLBA=3.75+0.77 DTB<br>(23.07) (4.87) | 0.80 | 23.76 |
| HLTA=11.55+0.28 DTB<br>(17.40) (4.19) | 0.74 | 17.52 |
| CBVA=1.15–0.06 DTB<br>(6.23) (–3.40) | 0.66 | 11.53 |
| CBSA=2.41–0.07 DTB<br>(14.70) (–4.53) | 0.77 | 20.56 |
| CBBA=1.62–0.04 DTB<br>(14.37) (–4.00) | 0.73 | 16.06 |
| CBTA=5.18–0.18 DTB<br>(11.72) (–4.12) | 0.74 | 17.00 |

Note: (1) The figures in parentheses are t-statistical values of the estimated coefficients respectively; (2) Variables are defined in Table 4–1.

From the above results, we may find that the socio-economic performances of the border-region depend critically on the geographical proximity to the border through two reverse directions: all the homeland activities (HLAs) are positively related to the distance to the border (DTB) while all the cross-border activities (CBAs) are negatively related to the DTB. In addition, it should be noted that, among the three HLAs and CBAs, the DTB-related HLVA and CBVA are most insignificantly estimated with the lowest R², F, and t-statistical values while the DTB-related HLBA and CBSA are most significantly estimated with the largest R², F, and t-statistical values respectively. This simply implies that DTB is more important in explaining the spatial distribution of the local economic activities (i.e., HLBA and CBSA) rather than that of the local social activities (i.e., HLVA and CBVA).

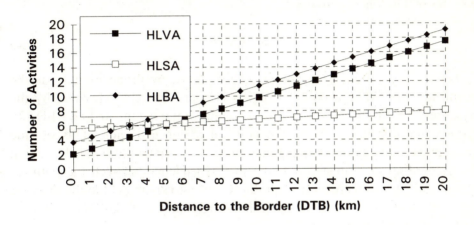

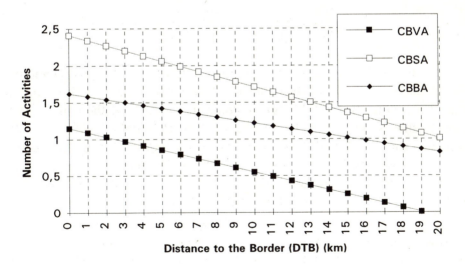

Figure 4–2 The Socio-economic Impacts of the Distance to the Border (DTB)

## 4.2 Proposition 2

Proposition 2. ***Given the same natural, geographic, social, and political conditions, the dependence of a political region on its outside world is negatively related to the territorial size of the region.*** In other words, if $S$ and $R_2$ are used to express the territorial area and the degree of dependence of a political region on its outside world respectively, the differential of $R_2$ with respect to $S$ is negative, i.e.,

$$dR_2/dS < 0 \qquad\qquad (4\text{--}2)$$

*Proof.* Proposition 2 may be plausibly proved by Proposition 1. As the territorial area ($S$) of a political region is approximately expressed by the equation $S = \pi r^2$ (where $r$ is the average radius of the region, and $\pi \approx 3.14159$), the average distance between the political region and each of its outside economies ($L$) is an increasing function of the average radius of the region ($r$). According to Proposition 1, the interdependence between the political region and each of its outside economies is negatively related to the distance between them, i.e., $dR_2/dL < 0$. Correspondingly, $dR_2/dr < 0$. Differentiating $R_2$ with respect to $S$, we obtain

$$\frac{dR_2}{dS} = \frac{dR_2}{dr} \cdot \frac{dr}{dS} = \frac{dR_2}{dr} \cdot \frac{1}{2\pi r} < 0$$

Proposition 2 may also be empirically illustrated by the economic performances of the existing countries differing in size. Let S=territorial area of a country (km²); GDP=gross domestic products of the country (US dollar); and IP=import value of the country (US dollar). We take the generated variable IR (=IP/GDP) to reflect a country's economic dependence on the outside world, i.e., when a country's IR increases, so does the country's dependence on the outside world. Using the statistical data of 27 countries, we obtain a relationship between IR and S:[6]

---

[6]Data source: *The World Yearbook of Economic Statistics*, 1983–84. The 27 countries include USA, Japan, Germany (W), France, UK, the Netherlands, Switzerland, Sweden, Norway, Spain, Canada, Australia, Austria, India, Indonesia, Saudi Arabia, South Korea, Philippines, Singapore, Thailand, Egypt, Libya, Argentina, Brazil, Chile, Mexico, and Peru.

$$IR=0.1957+1230.76/S \qquad (4-3)$$
$$(10.73)\ (21.01)$$
$$(N=27,\ R^2=0.95,\ F=441.52)$$

Equation (4–3) unambiguously demonstrates the fact that a country's economic dependence on the outside world (IR) increases (decreases) when its territorial areas (S) decreases (increases). The causes for the decreasing effect of size on a country's economic dependence may also be illustrated by the relationship between the supply and the demand of basic resources for those countries which differ in size. To make a further clarification, let's select 15 major metals (i.e., copper, lead, tin, zinc, iron ore, manganese, nickel, chromium, cobalt, molybdenum, tungsten, vanadium, bauxite, titanium, lithium) of 93 countries from *World Resources 1992–93* and calculate the number of major metals (NMM) for different countries.[7] The relationships between the number of major metals and the territorial sizes for the 93 countries are dotted by Figure 4–3 and approximately expressed by a linear estimation as below:[8]

---

[7]Notice that the calculation of NMM for each country is subject to the following criteria: if the reserves of a metal equal to zero, are less than 0.5 million metric tons of content, or even not available in a country, the metal will then be excluded from the total number of the major metals (i.e., 15) of the country.

[8]Data source: *World Resources 1992–93*, pp. 262–3 and pp. 322–3, Oxford: Oxford University Press, 1992. The 93 countries include (1) AFRICA: Algeria, Angola, Botswana, Burkina Faso, Cameroon, Congo, Egypt, Ethiopia, Gabon, Ghana, Guinea, Kenya, Liberia, Libya, Madagascar, Mauritania, Mozambique, Namibia, Niger, Nigeria, Sierra Leone, South Africa, Tanzania, Tunisia, Uganda, Zaire, Zimbabwe; (2) NORTH & CENTRAL AMERICA: Canada, Costa Rica, Cuba, Dominican Rep., Haiti, Honduras, Jamaica, Mexico, Panama, USA; (3) SOUTH AMERICA: Argentina, Bolivia, Brazil, Chile, Colombia, Ecuador, Guyana, Peru, Surinname; (4) ASIA: China, Cyprus, India, Indonesia, Iran, Iraq, Japan, North Korea, South Korea, Laos, Malaysia, Mongolia, Myanmar, Oman, Pakistan, Philippines, Saudi Arabia, Sri Lanka, Thailand, Turkey, Vietnam, Yemen; (5) EUROPE: Albania, Austria, Bulgaria, Czechoslovakia, Finland, France, Germany, Greece, Hungary, Ireland, Italy, Norway, Poland, Portugal, Romania, Spain, Sweden, UK, Yugoslavia; (6) FORMER USSR; and (7) OCEANIA: Australia, New Zealand, Papua New Guinea, Solomon Islands.

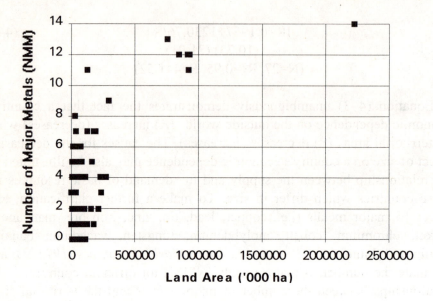

Figure 4–3 The 93 Countries' NMMs and Land Areas

$$NMM=2.63807+0.754375\times10^{-5}LA \qquad (4\text{--}4)$$
$$(9.84) \qquad (9.00)$$
$$(N=93, R^2=0.47, F=81.06)$$

where NMM (number of the major metals) ranges between 0 and 15; LA (land area) is measured in thousand ha; the t-statistical values which are given in parentheses and $R^2$ and F values are all significant.

From Equation (4–4), we find that NMM is positively related to the land area (LA), or more precisely, that a new metal will increase for each increment of $1/0.754375\times10^5$ (i.e., about 132,560) thousand ha land area in a country. This conclusion implies that those geographically small countries will be potentially possessed of a great import dependence on their outside world, because, compared with geographically large countries, they have only relatively limited variety of resources and have to import those basic resources which don't exist in their territories, in an attempt to meet their diversified needs of production and consumption. As either a cause or a result, the increased imports will eventually stimulate the exportation in order to macro-economically manage a balance of the economy.[9]

## 4.3 Proposition 3

Proposition 3. *In a set of i-dimensional border-regions (an i-d border-region is defined as one which includes i (i=2, 3, ..., N) independent political regions) with same natural, geographic, social, and political conditions, the cross-border interdependence in the i-d border-region is positively related to the number of political regions (i) involved in the border-region.* In other words, if $R_3=f_3(i)$ is used to express the degree of cross-border interdependence in an *i*-dimensional border-region ($i$=2, 3, ..., N), we obtain

$$f_3(i) > f_3(i-1) \tag{4-5}$$

*Proof.* Assume that the total territorial area of a border-region (expressed by $S$) is equally divided by $i$ ($2 \leq i \leq N$) independent sub-regions, the average area of each sub-region is $S/i$. It is very easy to understand that the average territorial area for each of the $i$ sub-regions (i.e., $S/i$) in the $i$-d border-region is a decreasing function of $i$, i.e., $S/2 > S/3 > ... > S/N$. According to Proposition 2, the degree of cross-border interdependence for each sub-region in the $i$-d border-region follows an increasing tendency when $i$ changes from 2 to $N$, i.e., $f_2(S/N) > f_2(S/(N-1)) > ... > f_2(S/i) > ... > f_2(S/2)$. Obviously, this expression is plausibly equivalent to $f_3(N) > f_3(N-1) > ... > f_3(i) > ... > f_3(2)$. That is to say, *ceteris paribus*, the degree of cross-border interdependence in a $N$-d border-region will always exceed that in a $N$–1-d border-region, *par analogie*. While the 2-d border-region has the lowest degree of cross-border interdependence in all border-regions.

Proposition 3 intuitively illustrates the disparities of cross-border interdependence of border-regions which differ in border dimension ($N$). In actual practice, peoples on both sides of a political border have usually developed common ties that are some ways stronger than those with their respective heartlands. Furthermore, the opening of political borders results

---

[9]According to the principle of macro-economics, the import (M) and export (X) in an open economy ought to follow an equilibrium equation: W+S+T+X=C+I+G+M (where, W=wage, C=consumption, S=save, T=tax, I=investment, G=government expenditure).

in new and different forms of cross-border interaction from that across the previously closed borders. Increased and sustained cross-border interaction of this nature can, itself, generate greater political trust and economic benefit between different adjacent territories.

Besides exclusionary, borders are also continuative. Along the border, folks speak each other's tongue and may have more in common with each other than with the citified people of their respective heartlands. Moreover, the borders can be seen as a contact factor. In this sense, a border is no longer a separate line, but a functional space as an intermediate element between different societies. In conclusion, the above three propositions in fact imply something more for border-regional economics:

- There are many similarities and homogeneities in terms of natural and geographic conditions and cultural and linguistic systems in border-regions where the borderers are closely related to each other.[10] Notwithstanding their political convictions, the independent economies are also operating in an interdependent way across border(s) – one side decides and depends on the other side(s), and *vice versa*.
- The uneven distribution of natural resources and the heterogeneity of socio-economic developments among different political regions also generate different comparative advantages for each political region over the other(s). After the border-related barriers are overcomed, cross-border exchange and co-operation can be more effectively established in various fields and dynamically promote the socio-economic developments in the adjacent border areas.
- Located at the margins of political regions, border-regions could only sustain relatively low efficient exchanges and flows of goods, capital, and technology with their respective remote heartlands. As indicated by a Chinese saying, "*Yuanqin Buru Jinlin*" (the remote kinsfloks are not as helpful as the nearby neighbours), better economic outcomes could be generated between border-regions and their "*Jinlin*" (nearby neighbours) than between border-regions and their "*Yuanqin*" (remote heartlands).

---

[10]For example, in a semi-farming and semi-herding area, Fuchun, Inner Mongolia, China, more than two-thirds of the Han-Chinese and Mongolian have established relations through marriages. (See Pan Naigu and Ma Rong (eds.): *Papers on the Frontier Areas Development*, pp. 110–20, Beijing: Peking University Press, 1993.)

## 4.4 More Evidences

The economics of border-regions varies in cases and relatively depends on the condition of either conflict or peace which exists between a political regime and its neighbours. The ultimate definition of a region as constituting a "political border" is often dependent on the nature of the border separating the territories of adjacent regimes. Under conditions of conflict, border-regions often undergo intensive fortification and/or are the focus of local development. Under conditions of peace, border-regions may transform into the geographical focus on the cross-border co-operation and development in terms of peoples, capital, technology, information, etc. which provide the substantial evidence for the formulation of border-regional economics. Let us look at some examples.

4.41 Israeli–Palestinian co-operation

> *"Recognizing the mutual benefit of co-operation in promoting the development of the West Bank, the Gaza and Israel, upon the entry into force of this Declaration of Principles, an Israel–Palestinian Economic Co-operation Committee will be established in order to develop and implement in a co-operation manner the programs..."* (Quoted from Israel–PLO (1993): "Declaration of Principles on Inter Self-Government Arrangements", signed in Washington, D. C., USA, September 13.)

As a conflictual territory between the Israeli and Arab societies, the West Bank of Jordan River has been a typical binational area which is populated mainly by the Arabians while dotted by many Jewish-based settlements since 1967. This area has been jointly operated by the State of Israel and the Palestinian Liberation Organization (PLO) in accordance with the Declaration of Principles on Inter Self-Government Agreement signed by the two parties in Washington D. C. on September 13, 1993 with the witness of the U.S. president. Two years later, the Israeli prime minister and PLO leader signed another historic agreement concerning the establishment of the Palestinian self-rule in most of the West Bank on September 28, 1995. According to the 1995 Israeli–Palestinian Agreement, the Israeli army should "redeploy" from the seven largest Palestinian towns on the West

Bank, including a partial withdrawal from Hebron; and, tentatively, from 450 smaller towns and villages. Together, these two areas contain the great bulk of the West Bank Palestinians – but less than 30 per cent of the territory. The rest of the West Bank, which includes the Israeli settlements and so-called state land, is to stay under Israeli army control.[11]

The Israelis and Palestinians have eventually make history with a handshake. The problems are, however, still existing. The main difficulty was how Israel could withdraw its troops from the West Bank towns while continuing to protect physically every single Israeli settler dotted throughout the region. The compromise, as argued by *The Economists* (1995), is an intricate jigsaw that fits together, though not easily. The Israelis fear that the cities, where (with the crucial exception of Hebron) the Palestinians will have full responsibility, could become safe havens for terrorists. The Palestinians fear that the small towns and village, where the Palestinians will be responsible for public order but the Israelis retain overall control, could be isolated, cut off by Israeli checkpoints from markets and farms. A clash between the Palestinian police and Israeli settlers is foreshadowed in the threats from a handful of outraged settlers.[12] Furthermore, the successful transformation of the West Bank from a bi-ethnic conflict to economic co-operation is a matter of not two-dimensional but multi-dimensional coalition between different political groups. In the Israeli side, the peace agreement is still facing fierce opposition from extremist Jewish settlers, especially those living in or near the West Bank towns of Hebron, and from the right-wing opposition Likud party. In the Palestinian side, the PLO also faces challenges from its internal rivals, including the Hamas Islamic opposition group, while continuing to bargain with the Israelis.

Even though the peace process still needs time and patience of the both sides before all the territorial and cultural conflicts are peacefully solved by the Israeli and Palestinian authorities, it increasingly demonstrates that, along with the end of the Cold War, the West Bank would eventually become a calm land for the Israelis and Palestinians, both of whom have

---

[11]Israel–PLO (1995): "Agreement on Establishing the Palestinian Self-Rule in Most of the West Bank", signed in Washington D. C., USA, September 28.

[12]*The Economists*, p. 17, September 30, 1995.

been the losers in the non-cooperative game of territorial conflict and expect a long and stable co-operation for their common interest.[13]

## 4.42 The Southwest US border economic growth

The U.S.–Mexican border runs 2,000 miles from East to West and makes 23 counties of four states of the United States be completely exposed to Mexico. The Seven Standard Metropolitan Statistical Areas (SMSAs) shown in Table 4–3 account for over 90 per cent of the total population in U.S. border counties. All these SMSAs grew more rapidly during the 1970s than the 1960s. El Paso, which had the lowest 1970–80 border SMSAs population growth rate, still grew at over three times the corresponding national rate of 11 per cent, and by well over the respective rates for the relatively rapidly growing South and West. McAllen's demographic growth (at the rate of 56 per cent) was five times that of the United States as a whole, and Tucson (at the rate of 51 per cent) and Brownsville (at the rate of 49 per cent) grew almost as rapidly as the former.

Moreover, the economic growth in the Southwest US border-region also experienced a great leap forward during the same period. The data from the U.S. Bureau of the Census (1983) which reflect the distribution of income in the 25 counties along the U.S. side of the U.S.–Mexico border demonstrate dramatic changes in terms of income per capita in most of the 25 border counties from 1969 to 1979.[14] Among the factors contributing to the phenomenal growth of SMSAs border-region has been manufacturing decentralization favouring the West and the South, climate and environmental amenities (as well as air conditioning to ameliorate the harsher aspects of the southern climate), migration of retired persons to the Southwest, and the diffusion of transportation, communications, education, and other social and economic infrastructures that have made it more

---

[13]According to *Financial Times* (p. 4, September 29, 1995), 51 per cent of Israelis backed the 1995 Agreement and throughout the West Bank and Gaza Strip support for Mr Yasser Arafat, the PLO leader, personally increased to 54 per cent after the agreement was signed, up from 49 per cent in July, 1995.

[14]More detailed analyses may be found in J. T. Peach (1985): "Income Distribution in the U.S.–Mexico Borderlands", in L. J. Gibson and A. C. Renteria (eds.): *The U.S. and Mexico: Borderland Development and the National Economies*, p. 57–80, Boulder: Westview Press, 1985.

feasible for people to live in once-remote areas.[15] According to the data presented in Table 4–4, per capita income in three of four border states (California being the only exception) was lower in both 1979 and 1969 than in the United States as a whole. In both 1969 and 1979, New Mexico had the lowest per capita income of the four border states, while California had the highest level. In Arizona, per capita income increased from 94.2 per cent of the nation's average in 1969 to 96.5 per cent of the national level in 1979. Per capita income in New Mexico in 1969 was only 78.1 per cent of the national figure, but had reached 83.9 per cent of the national figure by 1979. Texas' per capita income increased from 89.5 per cent of national average in 1969 to 98.7 per cent of the national figure by the year of 1979.

Table 4–3 Population Change in U.S. SMSAs Bordering Mexico, 1970-80

| Area | 1970 ('000) | 1980 ('000) | Change 1970–80 (%) |
|---|---|---|---|
| San Diego | 1,357 | 1,861 | 37 |
| Tucson | 352 | 531 | 51 |
| Las Cruces | 70 | 96 | 38 |
| El Paso | 359 | 480 | 34 |
| Laredo | 73 | 99 | 36 |
| McAllen | 182 | 283 | 56 |
| Brownsville | 140 | 210 | 49 |
| South | 63,000 | 75,000 | 19 |
| West | 35,000 | 43,000 | 23 |
| U.S. | 203,000 | 227,000 | 11 |

Source: U.S. Department of Commerce, Bureau of Census, Statistical Abstract of the United States, the U.S. Government Printing Office, Washington DC, 1981.

---

[15]N. Hansen (1985): "The Nature and Significance of Border Development Patterns", in L. J. Gibson and A. C. Renteria (eds.), ibid.

Table 4–4 Per Capita Income Change in the 25 Border Counties, USA, 1969–79

| State County | Per capita income 1969 | | Per capita income 1979 | | Change 1969–79 (%) |
|---|---|---|---|---|---|
| | US$ | % of U.S. | US$ | % of U.S. | |
| California | 3,614 | 115.9 | 8,303 | 113.8 | 229.7 |
| San Diego | 3,392 | 108.8 | 7,969 | 109.2 | 234.9 |
| Imperial | 2,459 | 78.8 | 5,809 | 79.6 | 236.2 |
| Arizona | 2,937 | 94.2 | 7,043 | 96.5 | 239.8 |
| Cochise | 1,709 | 54.8 | 5,738 | 78.6 | 335.8 |
| Santa Cruz | 1,782 | 57.1 | 5,447 | 74.6 | 305.7 |
| Pima | 1,892 | 60.7 | 7,149 | 98.0 | 377.9 |
| Yuma | 1,761 | 56.5 | 5,681 | 77.8 | 322.6 |
| New Mexico | 2,437 | 78.1 | 6,120 | 83.9 | 251.1 |
| Hidalgo | 1,369 | 43.9 | 5,242 | 71.8 | 382.9 |
| Luna | 1,256 | 40.3 | 4,790 | 65.6 | 381.4 |
| Dona Ana | 1,487 | 47.7 | 5,284 | 72.4 | 355.3 |
| Texas | 2,792 | 89.5 | 7,206 | 98.7 | 258.1 |
| El Paso | 1,594 | 51.1 | 5,306 | 72.7 | 332.9 |
| Hudspeth | 1,046 | 33.5 | 4,480 | 61.4 | 428.3 |
| Culberson | 1,174 | 37.6 | 4,290 | 58.8 | 365.4 |
| Jeff Davis | 1,425 | 45.7 | 5,675 | 77.8 | 398.2 |
| Presidio | 1,071 | 34.3 | 3,751 | 51.4 | 350.2 |
| Bresidio | 1,181 | 37.9 | 4,837 | 66.3 | 409.6 |
| Terrell | 1,281 | 41.1 | 7,069 | 96.9 | 551.8 |
| Val Verde | 1,250 | 40.1 | 4,542 | 62.2 | 363.4 |
| Kinney | 799 | 25.6 | 4,146 | 56.8 | 518.9 |
| Maverick | 1,038 | 33.2 | 3,100 | 42.5 | 298.9 |
| Dimmit | 871 | 27.9 | 3,922 | 53.7 | 450.3 |
| Webb | 1,352 | 43.3 | 3,980 | 54.5 | 294.4 |
| Zapata | 1,121 | 35.9 | 4,395 | 60.2 | 392.1 |
| Starr | 1,102 | 35.3 | 2,668 | 36.6 | 242.1 |
| Hidalgo | 1,006 | 32.3 | 4,040 | 55.4 | 401.6 |
| Cameron | 1,091 | 35.0 | 4,336 | 59.4 | 397.4 |
| United States | 3,119 | 100.0 | 7,298 | 100.0 | 234.0 |

Source: U.S. Bureau of the Census (1983): *Summary Characteristrics for Governmental Units and Standard Metropolitan Statistical Areas* (*PHC 80–3–33*), Appendix B, Washington, D. C., USA.

The changes stemmed from the proximity to the U.S.–Mexico border appear more significant when per capita income in the 25 border counties are examined in 1969 and 1979 respectively. Although in both 1969 and 1979, San Diego county, California, was the only one of the 25 border counties with per capita income exceeding the nation's average figure, the remaining 24 border counties along the border all exhibited an increase in per capita income as a percentage of the national level.

### 4.43 The economic recovery in the inner-German border

From the locational point of view, the economic and political integration of the adjacent nations can be seen as the integration of different factor endowments that are at different levels of development. More specifically, economic interdependence between the former rival economies can be interpreted as adding qualified labour force, land, capital stock, and technology to each side of the newly unified economy across the border that was previously closed. Eventually, the national wealth per capita in the enlarged territory will be equalized.

On November 9, 1989, the fifty-first anniversary of Hitler's Crystal Night rampage against the synagogues, a most tricking event which symbolized the end of the Cold War era occurred in the Berlin Wall, as was described latter by Elizabeth Pond (1990):

"At 7:00 p.m., Politburo member Gunter Schabowski told stunned reporters that East Germans could henceforth cross the border into West Germany.

...

With minutes of the announcement, there was a popular "explosion", as one East German official described it. East Berliners, hearing the news, rushed to the exits to West Berlin that had been barred to them for twenty-eight years, and found them still barred. The crowds and the tension mounted over the next three hours. "The choice was either to let them through or shout", explained an anxious Allied officer responsible for West Berlin Security.

By 10:30 p.m., the East German border guards at four crossing points in the center of the city, still lacking instructions, did the unthinkable. These servants of the most rigidly prison code of obedience in the entire Soviet bloc took authority into their own hands and opened the gates.

By 11:00 p.m., East Germany Interior Minister Frederick Dicker confirmed the desperate decision of the local commanders with an official order. The dike had been breached. It was no long possible to turn back the flood."[16]

Besides the political and national unification, the removal of the impenetrable border after November 1989 has created a dynamic socio-economic situation.[17] Within the enlarged space-economy of the unified Germany, the former inner-German border-region has to compete with far more powerful concentrations of population and economic activity. Below briefly illustrates two geographical zones which were dreadfully identified in the former inner-German border and are now experiencing the drastic changes in the unified German economy.

The Bavarian section of the former inner-German border-region has demonstrated a vigorous economic growth since the removal of the border. This area connected three countries of West and East Germany and Czechoslovakia during the Cold War era. The employment trends indicate the strong upsurge of economic activity in the border zone following the frontier opening. This growth has largely occurred through the expansion of the existing firms, which have seen their businesses prospects transformed by the addition of new markets at local, regional, and national levels within the former GDR, ultimately involving the addition of population of 18,564,000. In addition, more than 80 per cent of over 700 enterprises in the areas within the entire ZRG (i.e., *Zonenrandgebiet*, which included the Baltic coastland in east Schleswig–Holstein and the elongated strip of territory bordering on Czechoslovakia and was first designed in 1953 as a 30–60 kilometer wide zone, running along the eastern border of the four Federal states of Schleswig–Holstein, Lower Saxong, Hesse, and Bavaria) had expanded their business as a result of frontier opening.[18]

---

[16]E. Pond (1990): *After the Wall: American Policy Toward Germany*, A 20th Century Fund Paper, New York: Priority Press Publication.

[17]A brief history of East-West German unification is as below: (1) November 9, 1989, the crossing points from East to West Germany were opened without restriction; (2) July 1990, the two German economies were unified with the introduction of the single DM currency; (3) October 3, 1990, political unification was confirmed when GDR (German Democratic Republic) officially acceded to the Federal Republic of Germany in accordance with Article 23 of the Basic Law.

[18]For more details about this zone, see T. Wild and P. N. Jones (1993): "From Periphery to New Centrality? The Transformation of Germany's Zonenrandgebiet",

Berlin had a peculiar constitutional status during the Cold War era. Its eastern side was the apex of the centrally planned economy, while its western side followed the market capitalism and was heavily subsidized by the Federal government. The disappearance of this special status arose the process of modernisation for the two spatial economies. After the World War II, the public sectors which had been under the control of the Berlin government before 1945, gradually split up following the establishment of the two independent states (i.e., the German Democrat Republic and the Federal Republic of Germany). Separate entities in both east and west Berlin were formed, with the governments of both cities exercising full ownership over them. To speed up the process of industrialisation and urbanisation of the unified Berlin, the Federal Republic's financial support for both sides of the city increased a great deal. Furthermore, water, electricity, gas, telecommunication and transport companies are busy marrying the two halves of the city through an investment programme aimed at modernising the entire infrastructure. By the end of the 20th century, more than DM26 billions (about US$18 billions) will have been spent on this project. At the same time, Berliner Wasserbetriebe, which looks after the city's water and sewerage system, accounts for DM5 billions of the total investment, to be spent on replacing old pipelines modernising the drainage system and building new filtering plants. Bewag and Gasag, the electricity and gas companies, will each invest nearly DM2 billions. Deutsche Telekom, the state-owned telecommunications network, will have invested more than DM13 billions by 2000, and BVG, the city's transport authorities, will spend DM4 billions on laying new tracks and power lines.[19]

*Geography*, Vol. 78, pp. 281–94. P. N. Jones and T. Wild (1994): "Opening the Frontier: Recent Spatial Impacts in the Former Inner-German Border Zone", *Regional Studies*, Vol. 28, pp. 259–73.

[19]J. Dempsy (1995): "Berliners Pay Prices for Wall around Utilities", *Financial Times*, p. 3, September 6.

# CHAPTER 5
# CAN BORDER-REGIONS BE ECONOMICALLY OPTIMIZED?

What are the functional differences between a region which is administered by a single political authority and one which is under the jurisdiction of more political authorities? How can border-regions differing in number of political authorities (i.e., spatial structure, or namely, border dimension) be economically differentiated? Theoretically, border-regions with different spatial structures will yield different spatial mechanisms and, furthermore, different economic performances. To quantitatively explore these spatial economic problems, we build a $N$-dimensional static model of spatial economies in this chapter and apply it to economically compare border-regions with different spatial structures. Using this model, we find that, *ceteris paribus*, the largest output of an $i$-dimensional border-region ($F_i^*$) ($i$=1, 2, ..., $N$) follows a decreasing tendency with respect to $i$, i.e., $F_1^* \geq F_2^* \geq ... F_i^* \geq ... \geq F_{N-1}^* \geq F_N^*$. In addition, we also present an application of the $N$-d model in the agricultural production, which shows a substantially increased potential of benefit from the cross-border co-operation after the border-related barriers are removed.

## 5.1 Necessary Assumptions

Before starting our discussions, let us first look at some literature which is helpful to analytically addressing the cross-border issues.

In his paper entitled "International Environmental Agreements as Games", S. Barrett (1992) demonstrates a phenomenon in which the inter-governmental behaviours are effectively described by an interesting fishermen dilemma: "If a fishery is subject to open access, every fisherman will harvest too many fish because each has little to gain from conservation. If the current rate of harvest is reduced, growth in the total stock of the fishery is likely to be greater and hence the stock should support a greater rate of harvest in the future. But if one fisherman reduces his harvest, and this fisherman is only one among many, he could only hope to recover (at best) only a small portion of the extra future harvest, most (if not all) of it will be garbled by the other fishermen. Every other fisherman faces exactly the same incentive. Although every fisherman could be better off if use of the resource were reduced by all, each has a private incentive to overexploit the fish population."[1]

Obviously, under the shadowy influence of the incentives, the most possible consequence would be that all the fishermen will match to overexploit the scarce fishery resource until it is exhausted. The fishery example illustrates a phenomenon that is common to many social and economic problems in which the private incentives of independent agents (like the slippery fishermen as above) prevent the agents from reaching an outcome which makes all the agents better off. If the resource is under the jurisdiction of a single government, the exploitation of it can be easily co-ordinated by the government itself. But if the resource is located at the border-regions and subject to open access to more than one regimes, the problem cannot be solved so easily by one side of the border alone but need consistent cross-border co-operation between all parties concerned.

It is often asserted that international agreement become less effective with respect to the increase of the number of countries involved. S. Barrett (1992), for example, shows that as the number of countries increases, so do the differences between them. Agreement on the basis of simple rules like uniform abatement levels without side payments will then become very difficult to reach; and yet this is often the basis upon which treaties are negotiated. Even if agreement can be reached, it may not be sustainable. As the number of countries increases, the incentive for signatories to punish non-signatories falls, and free riding becomes more irresistible.[2]

Another analytical framework which can be extended to cope with the cross-border issues has been developed by C. Carraro and D. Siniscalco (1993). With a consideration of $N$ countries ($N \geq 2$) that interact in a common environment, they analyse the profitability and stability of international agreements to protect the environment in the presence of transfrontier or global pollution[3] by assuming that each country may decide whether or not to co-ordinate its strategy with other countries. They conclude that a coalition is formed when conditions of profitability and stability (free-riding) are satisfied. It is also shown that such coalitions exist; that they tend

---

[1]S. Barrett (1992): "International Environmental Agreements as Games", p. 11, in R. Pethig (ed.): *Conflicts and Co-operation in Managing Environmental Resources*, Berlin: Springer-Verlag, 1992.

[2]For more evidence, see S. Barrett (1992), pp. 11–36, ibid.

[3]Of course, they can also be extended to other international and cross-border issues.

to involve a fraction of negotiation countries; and that the number of signatory countries can be increased by means of self-financed transfers.[4] Their analytical framework is highly simplified, but the results show a promising route for research and policy analysis between sovereign countries, especially in their common border-region. Furthermore, the environment and technological co-operation between sovereign nations are also analysed by Carraro and Siniscalco (1995) as two separate negotiations in which the environmental protection is proved to be profitable but unstable while technological co-operation is proved to be profitable and stable. The joint negotiation, however, is more profitable and more stable than the two separate negotiations as it uses the gains from technological co-operation to offset the environmental free-riding incentives and to reach full co-operation both on technology and on the environment.[5]

As discussed in Chapter 1, border-regions can be classified in terms of the number of independent sub-regions. A $N$-dimensional border-region ($N$=2, 3, ...) is one which is directly under the jurisdiction of $N$ independent authorities. Apparently, given the same natural, geographic, social, and political conditions, a border-region directly under more independent authorities (or policy-makers) will bear relatively larger diseconomies of spatial scale, and become more difficult to reach a stable coalition of cross-border co-operation among the authorities than that under fewer independent authorities. In order to quantitatively estimate the differences of economic performances between border-regions which differ in spatial structure (i.e., the number of political authorities involved), we need to construct a generalised mathematical model.

Frankly speaking, it is really not an easy task to construct such a complex model as to involve border-regions with all kinds of conditions – natural, geographic, technical, social, cultural, and political. The only feasible way we can do is to make some simplifications and assumptions. To this end, we have to stipulate that our research area is divided by $N$ autarkic sub-regions ($N$=1, 2, 3, ...) which can be effectively administered by $N$ independent

[4]C. Carraro and D. Siniscalco (1993): "Strategies for the International Protection of the Environment", *Journal of Public Economics*, Vol. 52, pp. 309–28.

[5]For more discussions, see C. Carraro and D. Siniscalco (1995): "Policy Co-ordination for Sustainability: Commitments, Transfers and Linked Negotiations", in I. Goldin and Winter L. Alan (eds.): *The Economics of Sustainable Development*, Cambridge: Cambridge University Press, 1995.

policy-maker(s) respectively. In addition, in order to build a $N$-dimensional static model of spatial economies ($N$=1, 2, 3, ...) from which the optimal solutions of $N$-d border-regions can be quantitatively derived, five necessary assumptions should be organized as below:

1. All necessary production factors (such as labour force, capital, technology, natural resource, information, etc.) are both scarcely and unevenly distributed within the research area.
2. The production factors cannot freely flow between the $N$ autarkic sub-regions across the border(s) when $N\geq2$;
3. Each of the $N$ autarkic sub-regions has at least one comparatively advantageous (or disadvantageous) production sector over any other sub-region(s) in the research area when $N\geq2$;
4. The cost of transport and communication in the $i$th sub-region in the research area ($i$=1, 2, 3 ... $N$) is too little to influence the $i$th policy-maker's locational preference within the $i$th sub-region;
5. The objective(s) of the policy-maker(s) in this research area is (are) to purely maximize its (their) profit(s) within its (their) own territory(ies).

In fact, the first two assumptions are not ad hoc. They are basically charcterized by almost all border-regions where the border-related barriers exist. Assumption (3) is a necessary condition for the independent sub-regions to develop cross-border co-operation in the research area after the border-related barriers are removed. Assumption (4) allows that the internal economic operation becomes consistently efficient within each of the $N$ independent sub-regions of the research area when $N$ decreases to 1. Finally, Assumption (5) serves as a sufficient condition under which the optimal solutions of the $N$ sub-regions in the research area can be derived.

## 5.2 A N-dimensional Static Model

Based on the above assumptions, we may build a generalized static model of $N$-dimensional spatial economies under 1, 2, ..., and $N$ independent policy-maker(s) respectively, from which the economic differences between border-regions differing in border dimension can be unambiguously discovered.

## 5.21 The 1-d regional system

Consider a regional system which is economically administered by a single policy-maker. For the sake of expositional ease, $m$ policy variables are used here to denote the production factors like labour force, capital, technology, natural resource, information, etc. in the regional space $(S)$, i.e., $X^1=(X_{111}, X_{112}, ..., X_{11m})$. In addition, the production constraints[6] for the $m$ policy variables in the regional system are noted as $g_1(X^1) \in g_1$, and the objective of the regional system is defined as a function of the policy variable set $(X^1)$, i.e., $f_1(X^1)$. According to Assumption (5), the economic output for this political region should be maximized, i.e., $\max \{f_1(X^1)\}$. Till now, we can organize a simplified mathematical programming model for the 1-d regional economy:[7]

$$\min d_1 \qquad\qquad (5\text{-}1)$$

$$\text{subject to} \begin{cases} f_1(X^1) + d_1 = M_1 \\ g_1(X^1) \in g_1 \\ X^1 \in (0, \infty) \\ d_1 \geq 0 \\ M_1 \to \infty \end{cases}$$

in which the gap $(d)$ between the economic output $(f_1(X^1))$ and the policy-maker's goal $(M_1)$ is minimized by the policy-maker. According to Assumptions (1)–(5) in Section 5.1, the optimal solution for the policy

---

[6] They are also noted as *technical constraints* by operations researchers.

[7] Of course, this kind of mathematical programming problems can also be built as a shorter form, i.e.,

$$\max f_1(X^1)$$

$$\text{subject to} \begin{cases} g_1(X^1) \in g_1 \\ X^1 \in (0, \infty) \end{cases}$$

but the form in Model (5–1) can be more easily extended to $N$-d border-regions.

variable set ($X^1$) in the 1-d regional system can be feasibly obtained from Model (5–1), i.e., $F_1^* = f_1(X^{1*})$, where $X^{1*} = (X_{111}^*, X_{112}^*, ..., X_{11m}^*)$.

## 5.22 The 2-d border-regional system

Assume that the regional space ($S$) defined in Section 5.21 is now divided into two autarkic sub-regions (i.e., $S = S_1 + S_2$), the policy variables of which are defined as $S_1$: $X^{21} = (X_{211}, X_{212}, ..., X_{21m})$ and $S_2$: $X^{22} = (X_{221}, X_{222}, ..., X_{22m})$ respectively. The economic implications of $X^{21}$ and $X^{22}$ are as same as that of $X^1$. The production constraints for the two independent sub-regional systems are noted as $g_{21}(X^{21})$ and $g_{22}(X^{22})$ respectively. As the two sub-regions are now economically separated from their formerly united community, $g_{21}(X^{21})$ and $g_{22}(X^{22})$ are subject to $g_{21}(X^{21}) \subset g_1$, $g_{22}(X^{22}) \subset g_1$ and $g_{21}(X^{21}) \cup g_{22}(X^{22}) = g_1$. Similarly, $f_{21}(X^{21})$ and $f_{22}(X^{22})$ are defined as two independent objective functions for the sub-regions $S_1$ and $S_2$ respectively. According to Assumption (5), the economic outputs for the two sub-regions in the 2-d border-region are independently maximized by the two policy-makers respectively, i.e., max $\{f_{21}(X^{21}), f_{22}(X^{22})\}$. Finally, we obtain a two-objective programming model for the 2-d border-region

$$\min d_{21} + d_{22} \tag{5-2}$$

$$\text{subject to} \begin{cases} f_{21}(X^{21}) + d_{21} = M_{21} \\ f_{22}(X^{22}) + d_{22} = M_{22} \\ g_{21}(X^{21}) \in g_{21} \\ g_{22}(X^{22}) \in g_{22} \\ X^{21} \in (0, \infty), \; X^{22} \in (0, \infty) \\ d_{21} \geq 0, \; d_{22} \geq 0 \\ M_{21} \to \infty, \; M_{22} \to \infty \end{cases}$$

in which the gaps ($d_{21}$ and $d_{22}$) between the economic outputs $\{f_{21}(X^{21}), f_{22}(X^{22})\}$ and their respective goals ($M_{21}$ and $M_{22}$) are both minimized. According to Assumptions (1)–(5), the optimal solutions for the two sub-regions ($S_1$ and $S_2$) in the 2-d border-regional system can be feasibly obtained from Model (5–2) as below: $F_{21}^* = f_{21}(X^{21*})$, where $X^{21*} = (X_{211}^*,$

$X_{212}{}^*$, ..., $X_{21m}{}^*$); $F_{22}{}^*=f_{22}(X^{22*})$, where $X^{22*}=(X_{221}{}^*, X_{222}{}^*, ..., X_{22m}{}^*)$. The total value of the two objective functions in the 2-d border-regional system are $F_2{}^*=F_{21}{}^*+F_{22}{}^*=f_{21}(X_{21}{}^*)+f_{22}(X_{22}{}^*)$. Based on Assumptions (1)–(5) in Section 5.1, Guo Rongxing (1995b) has proved that the maximized output of the 2-d border-regional system ($S$) expressed by Model (5–2) will not in any case exceed that of the 1-d regional system expressed by Model (5–1), i.e.,

$$F_2{}^* \le F_1{}^{*8}$$

## 5.23 The $N$-d border-regional system

Assume that the regional space ($S$) is now composed of $N$ autarkic sub-regions (i.e., $S= S_1+ S_2+ ...+ S_N$). The policy variable set of the $i$th sub-region ($S_i$) is defined as $X^{ni}=(X_{ni1}, X_{ni2},..., X_{nim})$ ($i=1, 2, ..., N$). The definition of $X^{ni}$ (where $i=1, 2, 3, ..., N$) is as same as that of $X^l$. The production constraints for the $i$th independent sub-regional systems are noted as $g_{ni}(X^{ni})$ (where $i=1, 2, ..., N$). In addition, as all sub-regions in the research area are now economically separated each other, the $N$-d production constraints may be expressed as $g_{ni}(X^{ni}) \subset g_1$ ($i=1, 2, 3, ..., N$), and $g_{n1}(X^{n1}) \cup g_{n2}(X^{n2}) \cup ... \cup g_{nN}(X^{nN})=g_1$. $f_{ni}(X^{ni})$ ($i=1, 2, ..., N$) stands for the objective function of the $i$th independent sub-region. As defined in Assumption (5), the economic outputs of the $N$ sub-regions in the $N$-d border-region are independently maximized by the $N$ policy-makers respectively, i.e., max $\{f_{n1}(X^{n1}), f_{n2}(X^{n2}), ..., f_{nN}(X^{nN})\}$. Finally, a $N$-objective programming model for the border-region may be written as

$$\min \sum_{i=1}^{N} d_{ni} \tag{5-3}$$

---

[8]More details on the mathematical proof may be found in Guo Rongxing (1995b): "The Impacts of Provincial Borders on the Economic Development of China: The $N$-dimensional Model of Spatial Economies", *Xitong Gongcheng Lilun Yu Shijian* (Journal of China System Engineering Society), Vol. 15, No. 4, pp. 38–43.

$$\text{subject to} \begin{cases} f_{ni}(X^{ni}) + d_{ni} = M_{ni} \\ g_{ni}(X^{ni}) \in g_{ni} \\ X^{ni} \in (0, \infty) \\ d_{ni} \geq 0 \\ M_{ni} \to \infty \\ (i = 1, 2, ..., N) \end{cases}$$

in which the $i$th sub-region's gap ($d_{ni}$) between its economic output $f_{ni}(X^{ni})$ and goal ($M_{ni}$) is minimized. Similarly, Model (5–3) yields an optimal solution for the $i$th independent sub-region ($S_i$), i.e., $F_{ni}{}^* = f_{ni}(X^{ni*})$, where $X^{ni*} = (X_{ni1}{}^*, X_{ni2}{}^*, ..., X_{nim}{}^*)$ ($i = 1, 2, ..., N$). The total value of the $N$ independent objective functions in the $N$-d border-regional system is $F_N{}^* = F_{n1}{}^* + F_{n2}{}^* + ... + F_{nN}{}^*$. Applying the same approach as that used by Guo Rongxing (1995b), we may prove that, under Assumptions (1)–(5) in Section 5.1, the largest output of an $i$-d border-regional system ($F_i$) (where $i = 1, 2, ..., N$) will follow a decreasing tendency with respect to $i$, i.e.,

$$F_N{}^* \leq F_{N-1}{}^* \leq ... F_i{}^* \leq ... \leq F_2{}^* \leq F_1{}^* \tag{5–4}$$

It should be noted here that Formula (5–4) does not contradict with Proposition 3 (which yields an increasing tendency of cross-border interdependence with respect to border dimension) in Chapter 4. As a matter of fact, both of the two analytical results coincidentally illustrate the same economic mechanism for an $i$-d border-region in which the cross-border interdependence is increasingly related to, while at the meantime, the economic output is decreasingly related to border dimension ($i$).[9] Based on Formula (5–4), the economic impact of cross-border separation on the $i$-d border-region may be written as

$$\frac{F_1{}^* - F_N{}^*}{F_1{}^*} \geq 0$$

---

[9] We may thus conclude that, in a border-region, the less maximized economic output stemming from border-related barriers plausibly implies a greater potential for cross-border co-operation (interdependence), and *vice versa*.

and the marginal economic impact of cross-border separation on the $N$-d border-region may also be written as

$$\frac{F_{N-1}^* - F_N^*}{F_{N-1}^*} \geq 0$$

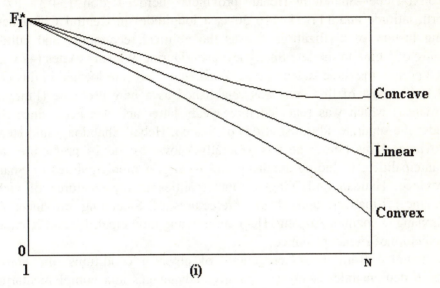

Figure 5–1 The Maximized Outputs ($F_i^*$) with Respect to Border Dimension ($i$)

The property of the maximized output function ($F_i^*$) varies in different border conditions[10] and generally results in three different patterns with respect to border dimension ($i$) (where $i$=1, 2, 3, ..., $N$) in the research area (see Figure 5–1): (1) linearity, (2) concavity, and (3) convexity. More specifically, the linear property constantly demonstrates a negative effect of border dimension ($i$) on the maximised output ($F_i^*$) of a border-region; the concave property decreasingly demonstrates a negative effect of border dimension ($i$) on the maximised output ($F_i^*$) of the border-region, i.e., the maximized output curve with respect to border dimension is above pattern (1); the convex property increasingly demonstrates a negative effect of

---

[10]These border conditions include political forms, economic institutions, tariff and non-tariff barriers, etc.

border dimension ($i$) on the maximized output ($F_i^*$) of the border-region, i.e., the maximized output curve with respect to the border dimension is below pattern (1).

## 5.3 The Case Study[11]

Shanxi–Hebei–Shandong–Henan provincial border-region (34°31'–37°41' north latitude and 111°51'–116°30' east longitude) in Central China has a long history of civilization. It was the political, economic, and cultural centre of China in the late Shang Dynasty. During Warring States (475–229 BC) period, the three states of Han, Zhao, and Wei were located in this area. In 1949, most of this area was established as a new province (Pingyuan province) which was repealed three years latter and has been since then under the separate administrations of Shanxi, Hebei, Shandong, and Henan provinces. This border area is generally known as the 14 prefectures and municipalities, including Jincheng and Changzhi municipalities of Shanxi province, Handan and Xingtai municipalities and prefectures of Hebei province, Liucheng and Hezhe prefectures of Shandong province, and Xinxiang, Jiaozhuo, Anyang, Hebi and Puyang municipalities and Xinxiang prefecture of Henan province.

Stemmed from the heterogeneity of physical conditions, the border-region demonstrates many comparative advantages and complementarities between different sides of the 4-d border. The agricultural production of the border-region is taken here as an example. Table 5–1 gives the outputs per ha for four agricultural products (grain, cotton, vegetable, and fruit) for the 11 border prefectures and municipalities of the four provinces in this area, from which we may clearly derive the regional differences in agricultural production. For example, Liucheng prefecture of Shandong province produces 7204.9 kg of grain per ha, while Jiaozhuo municipality of Henan province produces only 1818.8 kg per ha; the cotton productivity in Xinxiang of Henan province is 947.9 kg per ha which is more than four times that of Jincheng municipality of Shanxi province. The output of vegetable per ha in Jincheng municipality reaches 16279.1 kg, which is less than 1/4 that in Shandong province as a whole. The production of fruit in

---

[11]This section is based on a paper by Guo Rongxing (1993a): "The Impact of Spatial Organizational Structures on the Economic Development of the Provincial Border-Regions of China", *Scientia Geographica Sinica*, Vol. 13, pp. 196–204.

Hezhe prefecture of Shandong province is 5906.6 kg per ha which is more than 10 times that in Puyang municipality of Henan province.

Table 5–1 Agricultual Productivities of Shanxi–Hebei–Shandong–Henan Border-Region (Unit: kg per ha)

| Sub-region | No. | (1) Grain | (2) Cotton | (3) Vegetable | (4) Fruit |
|---|---|---|---|---|---|
| Shanxi | (1) | | | | |
| Changzi | (1.1) | 3274.2 | 387.0 | 20400.6 | 4182.6 |
| Jincheng | (1.2) | 2236.2 | 221.0 | 16279.1 | 3521.1 |
| Hebei | (2) | | | | |
| Xingtai | (2.1) | 2646.0 | 789.5 | 20828.7 | 3447.9 |
| Handan | (2.2) | 4973.4 | 654.9 | 36145.8 | 2906.3 |
| Shandong | (3) | | | | |
| Liucheng | (3.1) | 7204.9 | 884.5 | 67367.8 | 2115.5 |
| Hezhe | (3.2) | 6358.4 | 789.5 | 67387.8 | 5906.3 |
| Henan | (4) | | | | |
| Anyang | (4.1) | 3113.6 | 469.9 | 29225.6 | 4154.8 |
| Xinxiang | (4.2) | 3646.5 | 947.9 | 40076.0 | 4135.7 |
| Jiaozhuo | (4.3) | 1818.8 | 755.1 | 50740.2 | 4145.7 |
| Hebi | (4.4) | 2286.2 | 343.7 | 40209.5 | 4540.4 |
| Puyang | (4.5) | 3013.7 | 682.5 | 17150.6 | 587.1 |

Note: Xingtai includes Xingtai prefecture and municipality; Handan includes Handan prefecture and municipality; Xinxiang includes Xinxiang prefecture and municipality.
Source: The Liaison Office of Zhongyuan Association for Economic and Technological Co-ordination (ZYAETC), Handan, China, 1986.

Obviously, according to the principles of comparative advantage and mutual complementarity, the cross-border co-operation could be greatly benefited by all participants in the area. However, the administrative borders had seriously cut off the cross-border economic relations and rigidly formed a self-reliant agricultural system for each side before an association for economic and technological co-ordination was established by the 14 municipalities and prefectures of the border-region in 1985.[12] For the sake of computational ease, we consider only one production constraint,

---

[12]For an introduction of this Association, see Chapter 7.3.

cultivable land[13] and apply the methodology developed in Section 5.2 to analyse the agricultural production for the area under different border conditions, from which the economic effects of the border-related barriers on the agricultural production can be quantitatively derived.

### 5.31 The case under 4-d border condition

Let policy variable $X_{ijk}$ stand for the cultivable land input of the $k$th agricultural production in the $j$th sub-region (prefecture or municipality) of the $i$th province (see Table 5–2). The 4-d linear programming model for the border-region is built as below.

Table 5–2 Specification of Policy Variables ($X_{ijk}$) (Unit: thousand ha)

| Sub-region | No. | (1) Grain | (2) Cotton | (3) Vegetable | (4) Fruit | Total |
|---|---|---|---|---|---|---|
| Shanxi | (1) | | | | | |
| Changzi | (1.1) | $X_{111}$ | $X_{112}$ | $X_{113}$ | $X_{114}$ | 299,400 |
| Jincheng | (1.2) | $X_{121}$ | $X_{122}$ | $X_{123}$ | $X_{124}$ | 221,900 |
| Hebei | (2) | | | | | |
| Xingtai | (2.1) | $X_{211}$ | $X_{212}$ | $X_{213}$ | $X_{214}$ | 901,400 |
| Handan | (2.2) | $X_{221}$ | $X_{222}$ | $X_{223}$ | $X_{224}$ | 1,029,800 |
| Shandong | (3) | | | | | |
| Liucheng | (3.1) | $X_{311}$ | $X_{312}$ | $X_{313}$ | $X_{314}$ | 533,500 |
| Hezhe | (3.2) | $X_{321}$ | $X_{322}$ | $X_{323}$ | $X_{324}$ | 734,700 |
| Henan | (4) | | | | | |
| Anyang | (4.1) | $X_{411}$ | $X_{412}$ | $X_{413}$ | $X_{414}$ | 450,000 |
| Xinxiang | (4.2) | $X_{421}$ | $X_{422}$ | $X_{423}$ | $X_{424}$ | 416,100 |
| Jiaozhuo | (4.3) | $X_{431}$ | $X_{432}$ | $X_{433}$ | $X_{434}$ | 384,700 |
| Hebi | (4.4) | $X_{441}$ | $X_{442}$ | $X_{443}$ | $X_{444}$ | 60,400 |
| Puyang | (4.5) | $X_{451}$ | $X_{452}$ | $X_{453}$ | $X_{454}$ | 763,300 |

[13]Other factors, such as labour force, fertilizer, conditions of irrigation and cultivation, etc., are also very important in agricultural production. But their influences on the optimal solutions will be insignificant if they are not the critical constraints.

(1) The cultivable land use for the agricultural production in the *j*th sub-region of the *i*th province should not in any case exceed the total cultivable land area, i.e.,

$$\sum_{k=1}^{4} X_{ijk} \leq CLA_{ij} \qquad (5\text{--}5)$$

where $CLA_{ij}$ is the total cultivable land area of the *j*th sub-region $(j \in 5)$[14] of the *i*th province $(i=1, 2, 3, 4)$, the data of which are given in the last column of Table 5–2. Formula (5–5) generates 11 cultivable land constraints.

(2) In the 4-d spatial system, we suppose that each independent side (province) in this area expects a larger agricultural production so as to sustain its increasing demand. So the output constraint for the *k*th agricultural production of the *i*th province is constructed as

$$\sum_{j} C_{ijk} X_{ijk} \geq PYO_{ik} \qquad (5\text{--}6)$$

where $C_{ijk}$ (for the computational ease, let's fix it as a constant) is the output per ha of the *k*th agricultural product $(k=1, 2, 3, 4)$ of the *j*th sub-region $(j \in 5)$ in the *i*th province $(i=1, 2, 3, 4)$ (given in Table 5-1); $PYO_{ik}$ is the previous year's output of the *k*th agricultural product $(k=1, 2, 3, 4)$ of the *i*th province $(i=1, 2, 3, 4)$ which is given in Table 5–3. Based on the above definitions, we derive 16 linear constraints for the four provinces from Formula (5–6).

(3) The objective function of each province is to maximise its agricultural output, i.e.,

$$\max F_{4i} = f_{4i}(X^{4i}) = \sum_{j} \sum_{k=1}^{4} P_{k} C_{ijk} X_{ijk}$$

---

[14]Obviously, when $i=1, j=1, 2$; when $i=2, j=1, 2$; when $i=3, j=1, 2$; when $i=4, j=1, 2, 3, 4, 5$.

where $C_{ijk}$ is given in Table 5–1, $P_k$ is the price of the $k$th product ($k$=1, 2, 3, 4). For simplicity of computation, the price of the $k$th product in the border-region is supposed to be a constant at all circumstances in the case study:[15] $P_1$=0.488 yuan per kg, $P_2$=2.442 yuan per kg, $P_3$=0.068 yuan per kg, and $P_4$=0.058 yuan per kg.[16]

Table 5–3 Outputs for the Border-Region, 1985 (unit: million kg)

| Sub-region | No. | (1) Grain | (2) Cotton | (3) Vegetable | (4) Fruit |
|---|---|---|---|---|---|
| Shanxi | (1) | 1334.3 | 1.1 | 433.2 | 92.5 |
| Changzi | (1.1) | 889.3 | 0.1 | 294.2 | 42.5 |
| Jincheng | (1.2) | 445.0 | 1.0 | 140.0 | 50.0 |
| Hebei | (2) | 2937.2 | 219.1 | 1590.5 | 219.9 |
| Xingtai | (2.1) | 799.4 | 57.7 | 613.5 | 127.3 |
| Handan | (2.2) | 2137.8 | 161.4 | 978.0 | 92.6 |
| Shandong | (3) | 4849.4 | 383.8 | 1226.4 | 129.5 |
| Liucheng | (3.1) | 1877.1 | 201.4 | 987.5 | 55.0 |
| Hezhe | (3.2) | 2972.5 | 182.4 | 238.9 | 74.5 |
| Henan | (4) | 5622.0 | 137.6 | 1295.0 | 86.3 |
| Anyang | (4.1) | 1177.2 | 22.9 | 407.0 | 38.5 |
| Xinxiang | (4.2) | 2242.3 | 107.4 | 325.7 | 39.8 |
| Jiaozhuo | (4.3) | 314.6 | 6.8 | 145.5 | 0.3 |
| Hebi | (4.4) | 40.9 | 0.2 | 64.3 | 1.2 |
| Puyang | (4.5) | 1847.0 | 0.3 | 352.5 | 6.5 |
| TOTAL | | 15742.9 | 741.6 | 4545.1 | 528.2 |

Note: Xingtai includes Xingtai prefecture and municipality; Handan includes Handan prefecture and municipality; Xinxiang includes Xinxiang prefecture and municipality.
Source: The Liaison Office of the ZYAETC, Handan, China.

---

[15]In market-based economies, the price of a product is never a constant but determined by both supply and demand factors. But the simplification seems to be reasonable here, as most of the agricultural products were purchased and re-distributed at the officially-fixed prices under mandatory plans in mainland China before the 1990s.

[16]Source: *Zhongguo Tongji Nianjian* (China Statistical Yearbook), 1988.

Then, we can establish a minimized multi-objective function for the 4-d border-regional system: $Z_4=d_1+d_2+d_3+d_4$, where $d_1=M_{41}-F_{41}$, $d_2=M_{42}-F_{42}$, $d_3=M_{43}-F_{43}$, $d_4=M_{44}-F_{44}$; $M_{4i}$ ($i$=1, 2, 3, 4) is a considerably large figure.

The linear programming model includes 44 policy variables and 31 production constraints. The optimal solution of the model is: $X_{111}$=296500, $X_{121}$=162500, $X_{112}$=2800, $X_{123}$=26600, $X_{124}$=32900, $X_{212}$=241000, $X_{221}$=792700, $X_{222}$=44000, $X_{223}$=191400, $X_{214}$=660400, $X_{331}$=391600, $X_{312}$=140800, $X_{332}$=328500, $X_{323}$=391600, $X_{324}$=14600, $X_{411}$=450100, $X_{421}$=416100, $X_{431}$=144600, $X_{432}$=182200, $X_{433}$=25500, $X_{434}$=31200, $X_{441}$=61100, $X_{451}$=763300, other variables are all zero. The largest output values for the four provincial sides of the border-region become $F_{41}$=751130000, $F_{42}$=4268640000, $F_{43}$=4170720000, $F_{44}$=3242530000. The total output value of the border-region is $F_4=F_{41}+F_{42}+F_{43}+F_{44}$=12433.02 million yuan.

## 5.32 The case under 1-d (borderless) condition

To make a comparison, let us analyse the optimal solution for the border-region's agricultural production under the borderless condition or that the 4-d border-region has been merged as a new province. In actual practice, the elimination of the 4-d economic border means that the cross-border trade has been unboundly promoted and that the potentials of comparative advantages have been fully utilized in the agricultural production between the four formerly separate sub-economies. Therefore, under the borderless condition, Formula (5–6) becomes

$$\sum_{i=1}^{4} \sum_{j} C_{ijk} X_{ijk} \geq PYTO_k \qquad (5–7)$$

where $PYTO_k$ is the previous year's total output of the $k$th agricultural product ($i$=1, 2, 3, 4) of the border-region (given in the last row of Table 5–3). Therefore, compared to Formula (5–6) under 4-d border condition, Formula (5–7) generates now only four production constraints for the grain, cotton, vegetable and fruit.

Other production constraints and objective functions are as same as that of the case under the 4-d border condition. The new linear programming model includes 44 policy variables and 19 production constraints, which produces an optimal solution as $X_{114}=299400$, $X_{124}=215300$, $X_{212}=901400$, $X_{221}=1029800$, $X_{311}=533500$, $X_{321}=241600$, $X_{323}=493200$, $X_{411}=450100$, $X_{421}=384700$, $X_{422}=31600$, $X_{434}=383600$, $X_{441}=61100$, $X_{451}=763300$, other variables are all zero. The largest output values for the four sides are $F_{11}=1191690000$, $F_{12}=4236610000$, $F_{13}=4884830000$, $F_{14}=3562900000$. The total output value of the whole region, now, becomes $F_1=F_{11}+F_{12}+F_{13}+F_{14}=13876.02$ million yuan.

We now are able to compare the two spatial systems using their optimal solutions. The difference between the two systems' total output values may be treated as the economic loss of the 4-d border, i.e., $\Delta=F_1-F_4=1442.99$ (million yuan). This means that, after the removal of the 4-d provincial border, the border-region may increase its annual agricultural production by 1442.99 million yuan (about 10.4 per cent of that in the 4-d border case). This also simply means that agricultural production in the border-region has been decreased by the same amount per year due to the existing 4-d border-related barriers.

## 5.33 The case under 11-d border condition

Using the above methodology, we may go further: assume that the border-region is now administered by not 4 but 11 independent policy-makers (i.e., $N=11$), we obtain an optimal solution for each side of the 11-d border-region by the model developed in Section 5.2 (the results are given in Table 5–4). The largest output values of the 11 sub-divisions are given in Table 5–5. The total output value of the whole region ($F_{11}$), now, is only maximized to $F_{11}=F_{111}+F_{112}+\ldots+F_{1111}=9951.95$ (million yuan).

## 5.34 Conclusion

Based on the above results (compiled in Table 5–5), we find that the maximized agricultural output in the border-region under the 11-d condition is 3924.07 million yuan (about 28.28 per cent) and 2481.07 million (about 19.96 per cent) lower than that under the 1-d and 4-d conditions respectively. After comparing the three maximized outputs, we may also examine the relationship between the maximized output of the regional system ($F_i$) and the number of the independent sub-regions involved in the

Table 5–4 Optimal Solutions for Three Regional Systems ($X_{ijk}$), (Unit: 1000 ha)

| (i.j) | (1) Grains | | | (2) Cotton | | | (3) Vegetables | | | (4) Fruits | | |
|---|---|---|---|---|---|---|---|---|---|---|---|---|
| | 4-p | 1-p | 11-p | 4-p | 1-p | 11-p | 4-p | 1-p | 11-p | 4-p | 1-p | 11-p |
| 1.1 | 296.5 | 0.0 | 274.7 | 2.8 | 0.0 | 0.2 | 0.0 | 0.0 | 14.4 | 0.0 | 299.4 | 10.2 |
| 1.2 | 162.5 | 0.0 | 194.5 | 0.0 | 0.0 | 4.6 | 26.6 | 0.0 | 8.6 | 32.9 | 215.3 | 14.2 |
| 2.1 | 0.0 | 0.0 | 680.0 | 241.0 | 901.4 | 155.0 | 0.0 | 0.0 | 29.4 | 660.4 | 0.0 | 36.9 |
| 2.2 | 791.6 | 1029.8 | 429.8 | 44.0 | 0.0 | 246.5 | 194.1 | 0.0 | 270.5 | 0.0 | 0.0 | 31.9 |
| 3.1 | 392.7 | 533.5 | 260.4 | 140.8 | 0.0 | 227.7 | 0.0 | 0.0 | 14.7 | 0.0 | 0.0 | 26.0 |
| 3.2 | 0.0 | 241.6 | 467.4 | 328.5 | 0.0 | 231.1 | 391.6 | 493.2 | 3.5 | 14.6 | 0.0 | 12.6 |
| 4.1 | 450.1 | 450.1 | 327.8 | 0.0 | 0.0 | 4.9 | 0.0 | 0.0 | 13.9 | 0.0 | 0.0 | 9.3 |
| 4.2 | 461.1 | 384.7 | 78.7 | 0.0 | 31.6 | 70.0 | 0.0 | 0.0 | 8.8 | 0.0 | 0.0 | 9.6 |
| 4.3 | 144.6 | 0.0 | 78.7 | 182.2 | 0.0 | 8.9 | 25.5 | 0.0 | 2.9 | 31.2 | 383.6 | 29.3 |
| 4.4 | 61.1 | 61.1 | 17.9 | 0.0 | 0.0 | 0.4 | 0.0 | 0.0 | 1.6 | 0.0 | 0.0 | 0.3 |
| 4.5 | 763.3 | 763.3 | 327.8 | 0.0 | 0.0 | 0.4 | 0.0 | 0.0 | 20.6 | 0.0 | 0.0 | 22.3 |

Note: (1) 4-p=the solution of the regional system under four provinces; 1-p=the solution of the regional system as an economically united one; 11-p=the solution of the regional system under 11 provinces. (2) The errors resulted from the computation are possibly done by computer.

*i*-d regional system (*i*=1, 4, and 11): as $(F_1-F_4)/(4-1)=(13876.02-12433.02)/3=481.00$ is larger than $(F_4-F_{11})/(11-4)=(12433.02-9951.95)/7=354.43$, the maximized output $(F_i)$ with respect to the border dimension *i* $(1 \leq i \leq 11)$ in the border-region is approximately characterized by the concave curve in Figure 5–1, i.e., the border dimension (*i*) shows a decreasingly marginal effect on the maximized output of the border-region.

Table 5–5 Maximized Outputs for the Three Different Regional Systems (Unit: million yuan)

| Sub-region | (No) | (1) 4-p | (2) 1-p | (3) 11-p | (4)=(1)–(2) | (5)=(3)–(2) | (6)=(3)–(1) |
|---|---|---|---|---|---|---|---|
| Shanxi | 1 | 751.13 | 1191.69 | 737.56 | –440.56 | –454.13 | –13.57 |
| Changzhi | 1.1 | | 483.95 | | | | |
| Jincheng | 1.2 | | 253.61 | | | | |
| Hebei | 2 | 4268.64 | 4236.61 | 3467.88 | 32.03 | –768.73 | –800.76 |
| Xingtai | 2.1 | | 1293.17 | | | | |
| Handan | 2.2 | | 2174.71 | | | | |
| Shandong | 3 | 4170.72 | 4884.83 | 3461.70 | –714.11 | –1423.13 | –709.02 |
| Liucheng | 3.1 | | 1506.50 | | | | |
| Hexhe | 3.2 | | 1955.20 | | | | |
| Henan | 4 | 3242.53 | 3562.90 | 2284.91 | –320.37 | –1277.99 | –957.62 |
| Anyang | 4.1 | | 553.68 | | | | |
| Xingtai | 4.2 | | 327.54 | | | | |
| Jiaozhuo | 4.3 | | 786.20 | | | | |
| Hebi | 4.4 | | 103.61 | | | | |
| Puyang | 4.5 | | 513.88 | | | | |
| TOTAL | | 12433.02 | 13876.02 | 9951.95 | –1443.0 | –3924.07 | –2481.07 |

Note: 4-p=the solution of the regional system under four provinces; 1-p=the solution of the regional system as an economically united one; 11-p=the solution of the regional system under 11 provinces.

From Table 5–5, we may also find that each provincial side obtains a different return from the cross-border co-operation in our case study. For example, after co-operation, Shanxi's agricultural production will increase by 440.55 million yuan (about 58.65 per cent of that in the 4-d border case). In Hebei's side, however, there will be a loss of 32.03 million yuan (about 0.75 per cent of that in the 4-d border case). The net benefit from cross-border co-operation is also different between Shandong (714.16 million yuan or about 17.12 per cent of its previous output) and Henan (320.36 million yuan or about 9.88 per cent of its previous output) respectively.

Summarizing up, due to the cross-border separation, the border-region cannot be economically optimized. In this section, we have estimated the economic impacts of the "sub-political borders" and apply it to analyse the border-region of Shanxi, Hebei, Shandong, and Henan provinces in Central China. The result shows that the economic potentials in the border-region have not been fully utilized and that the annual agricultural production has been decreased by about 10.4 per cent due to the cross-border separations between the four provinces.

If the area falls under the jurisdiction of a single political authority, the economic relationship between its internal locations and sectors may be easily regulated by the single authority by means of unified economic policies, and the inefficiencies of allocation of production factors can be therefore eliminated. But the resources in the border-region have been administered by four provincial authorities, the problem cannot be solved easily.

## CHAPTER 6
# BORDER-REGIONAL DEVELOPMENT

Strategically, a successful border-regional development plan is a dynamic function of economic growth. Such growth can be achieved in border-regions by various approaches such as the direct investment by central government and the substantial cross-border co-operation, all of which, obviously, are the most fundamental tasks to border-regional economists. In this chapter, two basic approaches (i.e., core-peripheral approach and cross-border approach) for the border-regional development are proposed with an extensive interpretation of the spatial mechanisms and conditions of applications of the two approaches. In addition, three cases are briefly introduced, which are: (i) Mexico's border industrialization programme (BIP); (ii) China's frontier development programmes; and (iii) Shenzhen Special Economic Zone (SEZ).

## 6.1 The Basic Approaches

Besides the natural and artificial separations across borders and the low efficient exchanges and flows of goods, capital, and people with their respective heartlands, border-regions also possess the characteristics of pioneer areas and laboratory to test the modifications that might eventually affect the central areas. With the regional life cycle, border-regions, which are thought to be marginal, fragile, and vulnerable, are in fact outposts for the shifts which might economically reach the central levels of their respective national territories. Instead of being marginal or abandoned areas, the border-regions, being far away from the centres, can also achieve a fundamental transition from the culturally avant-garde peripheries to the national cores under some appropriate approaches.

6.11 Core-peripheral approach (CPA)

This approach may also be intuitively called 'development strategy from core to periphery'. That is to say, the economic developments of the border-regions are 'domestically' fuelled by their respective core areas.

By core we generally mean the most prosperous, stable, and powerful region, while from which to the periphery, a decrease in population density and human well-being exists in many cases. Theoretically, the development of a region implies an importation of advanced technologies and behaviours, and different people, from that were previously there. A source region for these import exists, typically a core, where is wealthy enough to contemplate the spread of its prosperity to its peripheral areas. In order to illustrate the basic mechanism of border-regional development guided by the core-peripheral approach, let us construct a simple model. Assume that *PE* and *CE* stand for the economic levels in peripheral and core areas respectively; *L* denotes the distance between the core and peripheral areas; *k* is the regional conductivity[1]. We obtain a simple equation

$$PE=f[CE/(L/k)] \tag{6--1}$$

In Equation (6–1), *k* is positively related to the density of communication and transport networks of the region. For the simplicity, the regional conductivity (*k*) may sometimes be assumed to be an isotropic variable or even a constant in all directions within the region. *PE* is positively related to both *CE* and *k*, while it is negatively related to *L*.

Notice that the applications of the core-peripheral approach are subject to two conditions: (1) the core areas have comparatively economic and technological advantages over the peripheral areas, i.e., *CE* is a large figure; (2) the peripheral areas are close proximity to the core areas and/or have a high regional conductivity, i.e., *L/k* is a small figure. However, border-regions, being usually far away from their respective political and economic cores, have been neither efficiently nor incentively fuelled by the economic and technological sources of the cores particularly when the peripheral and core areas are poorly connected with transport and communication networks. The applications of the CPA may be efficient in those peripheral economies with relatively well-developed cores and that the economic inter-relationships between core and peripheral areas are efficiently supported by advanced transport and communication networks. For instance, the border developments in the North America and many of the West European nations are the successful cases.

---

[1]The term, regional conductivity (*k*) is specifically defined here to express the quality and efficiency of circulation in terms of capital, labour force, technology, etc. within a region.

## 6.12 Cross-border approach (CBA)

In case of unavailability of either one or both of the above two conditions, the application of the core-peripheral approach (CPA) will inevitably become inefficient. Fortunately, another measure – cross-border approach (CBA) – may be possibly applied by the governments to economically develop their peripheral areas.

Undoubtedly, the uneven distribution of production factors as well as the heterogeneity of socio-economic developments among adjacent political regions usually generate different comparative advantages from each other. Border-regions are located at the margins of political regions and usually maintain relatively low efficient exchanges and flows of goods, capital, and people with their respective cores. Under such conditions as the border-related barriers are removed, cross-border co-operation, however, may become an efficient way to promote the border-regional development than the co-operation between border-regions and their respective core areas. In order to illustrate the basic mechanism of the border-regional development guided by the cross-border approach, let us construct another simple model. Consider that $BE$ and $BE'$ stand for the economic and technological levels of the target side and the other side of a border respectively. $\lambda$ denotes the cross-border condition. The growth potential for the border economy (noted as $\Delta BE$) may be approximately expressed as

$$\Delta BE = f[\lambda(BE' - BE)] \qquad (6\text{–}2)$$

The cross-border condition ($\lambda$) is defined in Equation (6–2) as an index of extent to which border openness in the border-region is valued. Usually, $\lambda$ ranges between 0 and 1. In particular, $\lambda = 1$ implies the complete removal of all border-related barriers and that the cross-border co-operation and trade can be unboundedly established between the neighbouring economies; while $\lambda = 0$ implies a totally autarkic policy. $\Delta BE$ is positively related to both $\lambda$ and the gap between $BE'$ and $BE$. It should be noted that, when $\lambda = 0$, $\Delta BE$ will always become zero no matter how different the $BE$ and $BE'$ are.

The application of the cross-border approach in a border-region is subject to two conditions: (1) the outside world has comparative economic and technological advantages over the target side of the border-region, i.e.,

*BE'–BE* is positive[2]; (2) the border-related barriers (both physical and ideological) between the target side and its outside world may be easily removed, i.e., $\lambda$ is able to increase to 1 from zero. However, as demonstrated in Chapter 3, border-regions are usually separated by cross-border barriers in terms of physical environment, political structure, and economic policy. Therefore, the value of $\lambda$ is usually less than 1 or sometimes even equals to zero given the condition that the border-related barriers exist. The applications of CBA may be successful in those peripheral economies with relatively wealthy and friendly neighbours. Typical cases have been, among others, Mexico's border industrialisation programme (BIP) which was promoted by its close proximity to the world's largest economy, USA and China's special economic zones (SEZs) in the south-eastern coastal areas *vis-à-vis* the newly industrialized "small dragons" of Hong Kong, Taiwan and other NIEs in East Asia.

## 6.13 A mixed CPA–CBA model

In different cases of the border-regional development, there have obstacles for both the core-peripheral approach and the cross-border approach due to the special physical and political conditions in border-regions. The most efficient way, therefore, is to combine the two approaches together. To illustrate the operational mechanism for the border-regional development jointly promoted by the above two approaches, let us construct a potential model for a capital-based economy.[3] Assume that $NIPC(x, y)$ stands for national income per capita at point $(x, y)$ in a given political region $(\Omega)$ with a boundary $(l)$. A basic knowledge in economics tells us that capital flow is usually generated from a place with a higher level of income per capita to a place with a lower level of income per capita. Mathematically, the capital

---

[2]Notice that, when *BE'–BE* is not positive, the cross-border approach is still effective in at least the following aspects (1) application of low-cost labour force and other resources; (2) extension of consumers' market; and (3) regional economic integration for an increased return from the economies of spatial sizes. Nevertheless, the condition that *BE'–BE* is positive is very important for border development.

[3]The model is highly simplified and has indeed some shortcoming, because an economy is usually fuelled by, besides capital, many other production factors (such as technology, labour force, etc.). But it will not matter here. Our aim is only to sketch the basic mechanism of CPA and CBA on regional development, nothing more.

circulation within a tiny area d$A$ can be expressed by a simple differential function:

$$q_n = k\frac{\partial NIPC}{\partial n}dA \qquad (6\text{--}3)$$

where $q_n$=amount of capital inflow through the area d$A$; $k$=regional conductivity in the area (d$A$); $n$=direction at which the income gradient is the largest. The amount of capital inflow ($q_n$) through the area (d$A$) in Equation (6–3) is positively related to both the gradient of *NIPC* (i.e., $\partial NIPC/\partial n$) and the regional conductivity ($k$) in the area (d$A$). In addition, $q_n$ can be divided into two parts from the directions of $x$ and $y$ in the area (d$A$) respectively, i.e., $q_n=q_x+q_y$. Finally, the capital circulation may be expressed by a static balance (inflow–outflow) equation in the sub-region d$A$=d$x$d$y$ if the capital loss is ignored:

$$q_x+q_y+I(x, y)=q_{x+dx}+q_{y+dy} \qquad (6\text{--}4)$$

In Equation (6–4), $q_x$ and $q_y$ are the capital inflow rates in the sub-region d$A$ at the sub-region's border lines $x$ and $y$ respectively; $q_{x+dx}$ and $q_{y+dy}$ are the capital outflow rates in the sub-region d$A$ at the sub-region's border lines $x+dx$ and $y+dy$ respectively. As an exogenous variable, $I$ is the investment per period of time by the government in the area of d$A$ at point ($x, y$). If $\partial NIPC/\partial x$ and $\partial NIPC/\partial y$ are the *NIPC* gradients at point ($x, y$) in the area (d$A$), $k_x$ and $k_y$ are defined as the regional conductivities in the area (d$A$) in the directions $x$ and $y$ respectively. Replacing $q_x$, $q_y$, $q_{x+dx}$ and $q_{y+dy}$ in Equation (6–4) by their respective differential functions[4], we obtain a second order potential equation:

---

[4]According to Equation (6–3), we obtain $q_x = k_x\dfrac{\partial NIPC}{\partial x}dy$; $q_y = k_y\dfrac{\partial NIPC}{\partial y}dx$;

$q_{x+dx} \approx q_x + \dfrac{\partial q_x}{\partial x}dx = k_x\dfrac{\partial NIPC}{\partial x}dy + \partial(k_x\dfrac{\partial NIPC}{\partial x}dy)/\partial x dx = k_x\dfrac{\partial NIPC}{\partial x}dy +$

$k_x\dfrac{\partial^2 NIPC}{\partial x^2}dxdy$; $q_{y+dy} \approx k_y\dfrac{\partial NIPC}{\partial y}dx + k_y\dfrac{\partial^2 NIPC}{\partial y^2}dxdy$

$$k_x \frac{\partial^2 NIPC}{\partial x^2} + k_y \frac{\partial^2 NIPC}{\partial y^2} - I = 0, \text{ with } (x, y) \in \Omega \qquad (6\text{–}5)$$

For the sake of computational ease we may simply assume that the regional conductivity is isotropic or $k_x=k_y=$constant in Equation (6–5). According to Equation (6–2), as to an autarkic economy (i.e., $\lambda=0$), the *NIPC* gradients with respect to the directions $x$ and $y$ in the border line ($l$) are zero; as to an open economy (i.e., $\lambda>0$), the *NIPC* gradients with respect to the directions $x$ and $y$ in the border line ($l$) are positively related to the degree of border openness ($\lambda$), the length of the border line in the directions $y$ and $x$ (i.e., $l_y$ and $l_x$) and the comparative cross-border advantage of the outside's *NIPC* (labelled as $NIPC^\infty$) over the target side's *NIPC* (i.e., $NIPC^\infty$ –*NIPC*). Finally, the border conditions are approximately expressed as

$$\left. \frac{\partial NIPC}{\partial x} \right|_l = \lambda \left[ NIPC^\infty - NIPC \right] l_y \qquad (6\text{–}6)$$

$$\left. \frac{\partial NIPC}{\partial y} \right|_l = \lambda \left[ NIPC^\infty - NIPC \right] l_x \qquad (6\text{–}7)$$

In Equations (6–5)–(6–7), the *NIPC* field in the region ($\Omega$) is dependent on the variables of $I$, $k$ (or $k_x$ and $k_y$), $NIPC^\infty$, $\lambda$ and $l$. By solving the regional economic model, one may simulate the regional capital circulation and economic growth by changing the values of $I$, $k$, $NIPC^\infty$, $\lambda$, and $l$.

## 6.2 Mexico's Border Industrialization Program (BIP)

*"Mexican government has been willing to take advantage of the proximity and wealth of the United States in order to solve part of its own national unemployment problem and, at the same time, find the income necessary to maintain its political 'stability'. Since the Second World War, the privileges enjoyed by the border states have given not so much to promote development and help solve local problems but rather to satisfy the political and economic interests of the country's*

*power structure located in Mexico City."* (Quoted from Antonio Ugalde (1978): "Regional Political Process and Mexican Politics on the Border", in Stanley R. Ross (ed.): *Views Across the Border: The United States and Mexico*, pp. 108–9, Albuquerque: University of New Mexico Press, 1978.)

During the Second World War, Mexico and the United States signed an agreement that allowed Mexican labourers, principally agricultural workers, to cross into the United States to work. This program was conceived as a temporary measure to ease the manpower shortage created in the United States by the need to expand the number of men under arms during the war. After the war, Mexico came to depend on the program as a source of foreign exchange earnings and as an outlet for its "excess" supply of labour. The program continued until 1964 when it was unilaterally  terminated by the United States, largely in response to pressure exerted  by organized labour in the United States. The abrogation of the program led to a substantial increase in unemployment in the border-regions of Mexico, and partly as a measure to alleviate this problem, the new Mexican president, Diaz Ordaz, announced in 1965 a new program that would permit  United States' firms to import into Mexico capital equipment and materials for re-export.[5] The Johnson Administration agreed to this proposal, whereby use would be made of items 806.30 and 807.00 of the United States tariff schedules which permit reimport of finished or partially finished goods with duty to be paid only on that value added to the product while outside of the United States. In Mexico, the plants set up under the Border Industrialization Program (BIP) are called *"maquiladoras"* and the industry is called the *"maquila"* industry. *Maquila* means "measure" in Spanish in the sense that a miller of grain kept a measure or plant of the grain in payment for this services. The parallel here is that the Mexican plants provide only labour services, never owning the products. The plants are also called "in-bond" plants, since the

---

[5]A history of the border industrialization program (BIP) can be found in M. van Waas (1981): "The Multinationals' Strategy for Labour: Foreign Assembly Plants in Mexico's Border Industrialization Program", unpublished Ph. D. thesis, Standford University (University Microfilms International), pp. 143–191.

products they assemble never legally leave the parent company, although they may be out of the home country.[6]

It should not be surprising that Mexico and the United States have most interdependent assembly activities. As a developing country, Mexico shares a nearly 2,000 mile border with one of the world's largest producer. The border is fairly accessible and transportation from almost any point in the United States to the border is cheap when compared to overseas trade. Not only geographically but also culturally, the distance between the two countries are not very great. Since the United States has a relatively high real-wage economy in comparison to that of Mexico, its firms have amply incentive to move segmental production processes that are labour intensive to lower real labour cost areas. Real labour cost as a whole is lower in Mexico because labour productivity in general is lower, and because Mexico has abundant supplies of unskilled labour. Furthermore, more than three quarters of the labour force in Mexican assembly industries are women, most of whom are very young (about two thirds of the women are less than 25 years of age) and were previously not in the labour force.[7] The country has been one of the most frequently chosen locations for labour intensive production processes, mainly assembly. The industries represented in the *maquila* sector include those of television receivers and parts, semi-conductors, toys, textiles, office machines, scientific instruments, electric motors lumber and paper products, electrical equipment, motor vehicle parts, ceramic parts and luggage, among others.[8] Since 1965, when the Border Industrialization Program got under way, a significant number of assembly plants have been established almost every year. Table 6–1 gives the number of plants, employment and value added in the assemble plants.

---

[6]H. C. Goddard (1985): "Evaluating the Benefits and Costs of Mexico's Border Industrialization Program", in L. J. Gibson and A. C. Renteria (eds.): *The U.S. and Mexico: Borderland Development and the National Economies*, p. 141, Boulder: Westview Press, 1985.

[7]For more evidence, see J. Grunwald (1985) "Internationlization of Industry: U.S.–Mexican Linkages", in L. J. Gibson and A. C. Renteria (eds.): *The U.S. and Mexico: Borderland Development and the National Economies*, p. 110–1, Boulder: Westview Press, 1985.

[8]See H. C. Goddard (1985), p. 141.

Table 6–1 Geographic Locations of Mexico's Assemble Plants, 1973–81

| YEAR | Number of plants | | | Employment (all workers) | | | Value added (million US$) | | |
|---|---|---|---|---|---|---|---|---|---|
| | Border | Interior | Total | Border | Interior | Total | Border | Interior | Total |
| 1973 | 247 | 10 | 257 | 60,100 | 4,200 | 64,300 | 177.5 | 19.5 | 197.0 |
| 1974 | 429 | 26 | 455 | 71,125 | 4,852 | 75,977 | 289.2 | 26.5 | 315.6 |
| 1975 | 418 | 36 | 454 | 62,144 | 5,069 | 67,213 | 290.0 | 31.1 | 321.2 |
| 1976 | 406 | 42 | 448 | 67,532 | 6,964 | 74,496 | 314.4 | 37.7 | 352.2 |
| 1977 | 398 | 45 | 443 | 70,681 | 7,752 | 78,433 | 276.3 | 38.1 | 314.9 |
| 1978 | 480 | 37 | 457 | 82,387 | 8,317 | 90,704 | 386.5 | 52.0 | 438.6 |
| 1979 | 480 | 60 | 540 | 100,537 | 10,970 | 111,365 | 539.7 | 98.2 | 637.9 |
| 1980 | 551 | 69 | 620 | 106,576 | 12,970 | 119,546 | 539.7 | 109.6 | 770.8 |
| 1981 | 533 | 72 | 605 | 116,450 | 14,523 | 130,973 | 661.2 | n.a | n.a |

Sources: (1) J. Grunwald (1985): "Industrialization of Industry: U.S.–Mexican Linkage", pp. 114–5, Table 2; (2) H. C. Goddard (1985): "Evaluating the Benefit and Cost of Mexico's Border Industrialization Program", p. 143, Table 1. All in L. J. Gibson and A. C. Renteria (eds.): *Borderland Development and the National Economies*, Boulder: Westview Press, 1985.

Most of the Mexico's assembly activities are located along the border with the United States, concentrating on six towns from Tijuana, just south of San Diego, California, on the Pacific Ocean, to Matamores opposite Brownsville, Texas, near the Gulf of Mexico, while the proportion of the assembly plants in the interior of the country has been increasing steadily even though being still very small. (see Table 6–1) The development in Mexico's northern border area has been strongly influenced by the proximity to the United States, and it has been both a cause and an effect of migration from Mexico's heartland. As shown in Table 6–2, during 1970–80, population growth rate in each of Mexico's border cities was greater than the corresponding national level (37 per cent).

Table 6–2 Population Change in Major Mexican Cities Bordering the U.S., 1970–80

|  | 1970 ('000) | 1980 ('000) | 1970–80 (%) |
|---|---|---|---|
| Tijuana | 277 | 542 | 96 |
| Mexicali | 267 | 495 | 85 |
| Ciudad Juarez | 407 | 680 | 67 |
| Nuevo Laredo | 149 | 272 | 83 |
| Reynosa | 137 | 240 | 75 |
| Matamores | 138 | 258 | 87 |
| Mexico | 53,292 | 73,010 | 37 |

Sources: (1) Consejo Nacional de Población (1982): *México Demográfico: Breviario 1980– 81*, pp. 62–3, Mexico, D.F.: Consejo Nacional de Población; (2) Niles Hansan (1985): "The Nature and Significance of Border Development Patterns", p. 5, Table 2.

The BIP has promoted Mexico and the United States to become more and more interdependent in many respects across their common border, and Joel Garrean (1981) has cogently argued that Mexamerica – a relatively distinct region comprising much of the south-western United States and northern part of Mexico – would replace the Northeast Great Lakes industrial area as the economically dominant and most populous region of North America.[9]

---

[9] J. Garrean (1981): "*The Nine Nations of North America*, New York: Avon Books.

## 6.3 China's Frontier Development Programme

Territorially with about 9.6 million sq. km of land area, China is bordering on East China Sea, Korea Bay, Yellow Sea, and South China Sea, between North Korea and Vietnam. Besides a 14,500 km coastline which enables it to conveniently connect with most of the developed economies, the country has a total length of 22,143.34 km land boundaries with Afhanistan (76 km), Bhutan (470 km), Myanmer (2,185 km), Hong Kong (30 km), India (3,380 km), Kazakhstan (1,533 km), North Korea (1,416 km), Kyrgyzstan (858 km), Laos (423 km), Maccau (0.34 km), Mongolia (4,673 km), Nepal (1,236 km), Pakistan (523 km), Russia (3,605 km in northeast and 40 km in northwest), Tajikstan (414 km), and Vietnam (1,281 km) respectively.[10] Mainland China has nine frontier provinces and autonomous regions (see Table 6–3) of which 128 counties are directly exposed to the outside world through the international borders.[11]

Inspired by the open-door policy in the south-eastern coastal areas which was started in the early 1980s, mainland China embarked on another outward-looking policy in an attempt to promote the development in the frontier regions of four provinces of Heilongjiang, Yunnan, Jilin, and Liaoning and four autonomous regions of Inner Mongolia, Xinjiang Ugyur, Tibet, and Guangxi Zhuang in the early 1990s. Up to 1992, a series of policies, measures and regulations concerning the frontier development in those provinces and autonomous regions had been carried out by the central and provincial governments (see Table 6–4). The main objective of these policies, measures, and regulations is aimed at the decentralization of the planned economic system and promotion of the cross-border trade and frontier economic developments.

The economic co-operation and trade between the border residents are naturally facilitated by the fact that people on both sides of the border often belong to the same minority group and share the same language and customs across the border. But the fast border development has mainly benefited from China's open-door policy and the improvement of the diplomatic relations with the neighbouring countries since the mid-1980s, when the Chinese government approved the "Provisional Regulations for the Management of 'Small-volume' Border Trade" in 1984 and opened hundreds

---

[10]Data source: http:/www.odci.gov/publications/95fact/ch.html

[11]Based on *The Map of China* (1993), Beijing: China Maps Publishing House.

Table 6–3 Natural and Geographic Conditions of China's Nine Frontier Regions

| Frontier region | Land area ('000 km²) | Geographic location | Neighbouring countries | Length of int'l border (km) | Major opening frontier cities and towns approved by the state |
|---|---|---|---|---|---|
| Heilongjiang | 454.0 | Northeast | Russia | 3,045 | Heihe, Shuifenhe, Tonjiang, Qike, Jiayin, Shunwu, Mengbei, Mehe. |
| Inner Mongolia | 1183.0 | North | Mongolia Russia | 4,200 | Manzhouli, Erlianhaote, Heishantou, Shiwei, Arihashate, Zhu'engadabuqi, Ganqimaodao, Erbuduge, Ceke, Hulietu. |
| Xinjiang Ugyur | 1660.0 | Northwest | Russia, Mongolia, Pakistan, Kazakhstan, Kyrgyzstan, Tajikistan, Afghanistan, India | 5,400 | Yining, Boluo, Tacheng, Huoerguosi, Alashankou, Takeshenken, Laoyemiao, Wulasitai, Honshankou, Hongqilapu. |
| Tibet | 1200.0 | Southwest | India, Nepal, Bhutan, Sikkim, Myanmer | 3,800 | Zhangmu, Yadong, Pulan, Zhada. |
| Yunnan | 394.0 | Southwest | Myanmer, Laos, Vietnam | 4,060 | Kunming, Ruilin, Wanding, Hekou. |
| Guangxi Zhuang | 236.7 | South | Vietnam | 1,020 | Nanning, Beihai, Fangcheng, Pingxiang. |
| Liaoning | 145.9 | Northeast | North Korea | n.a | Dandong. |
| Jilin | 18'.4 | Northeast | North Korea, Russia | 1,430 | Hunchun. |
| Gansu | 390.0 | Northwest | Mongolia | n.a | none |

Source: (1) Liu Baorong and Liao Jiasheng (eds): *China's Frontier Opening and the Neighbouring Countries*, pp. 3–152, Beijing: Falu Press, 1993; (2) *Zhongguo Ditu Ce* (China Atlas).

of frontier cities and towns to the outside world. Contrast to the Southeast (coastal) areas development which was mainly promoted by joint ventures, most of China's inland frontier development programmes have been characterized by border trade with their respective outside neighbours. Below gives some cases in points.

Among the fast growing frontier areas, Wanding and Ruili of Dehong prefecture in Southwest China's Yunnan province, are two state-level ports. The border trade with Myanmer via Wanding and Ruili ports increased drastically from 10 million yuan and 22 million yuan in 1984 to 279 million yuan and 770 million yuan in 1992 respectively.[12] Moreover, these two areas also absorbed a certain number of foreign capitals which, as reported by Ingrid d'Honghe (1994), came from Myanmer, Singapore, the Philippines, Thailand, Hong Kong, and Taiwan, bearing testimony to the extent of Asian interests. Ruili and Wanding each obtained the approval from the State Council in 1992 to set up a national-level "co-operation zone". In addition, Ruili is developing the Jiegao Border Trade and Economic Experimental Zone (JBTEEZ), which is expected to become a major channel for exchanges between Yunnan and Myanmer. The Zone, which has a surface of 3.4 square kilometers, is surrounded by Myanmer on three sides. Jiegao is an experimental zone and focuses on bounded warehousing and the service sector, whereas in co-operation zones, industries will be developed.[13]

The Lancang–Mekong border-region is another case in Southwest China. This area includes Xishuangbanna Dai autonomous prefecture and Simao prefecture of Yunnan province in China, Upper Laos, Jingdong district in Myanmer, and the States of Chiang Rai and Chiang Mai in Thailand. In this area, mountainous environment is abundant in water, mineral, and biological resources. However, the Golden Triangle area is also a major international drug producer. Across borders, there exist similarities in agricultural practices and languages, but there are also a number of different cultural minorities. The Chinese part of the border area is located in the basin of the

---

[12]Data source: Wanding Administration for Domestic and Foreign Trade and Ruili municipal government, Yunnan, China.

[13]For more evidence, see I. d'Honghe (1994): "Regional Economic Integration in Yunnan", in D. S. G. Goodman and G. Gegal (eds.): *China Deconstructs: Politics, Trade and Regionalism*, p. 307, London and New York: Routledge, 1994.

Lancang River. The economy is rather primitive and the transportation and education are especially poor.

Table 6–4 China's Policies, Measures, and Regulations Concerning the Frontier Development, 1984–92

| Date | Policy, measure or regulation | Issued or approved by |
|---|---|---|
| Dec. 15, 1984 | Provisional Regulations of the Management of 'Small-volume' Border Trade | State Council |
| Mar. 7, 1985* | Regulations of Import and Export Tariff of the P. R. China | State Council |
| Oct. 11, 1986 | Regulations Concerning the Promotion of Foreign Investment | State Council |
| Jan. 25, 1992 | Measures Concerning the Supervision and Favourable Taxation for the People-to-People Trade in Sino–Myanmer Border | Office of Custom, P. R. C. |
| 1992 | Notification Concerning the Further Opening up of the Four Frontier Cities (Heihe, Shuifenhe, Hunchun and Manzhouli) | State Council |
| June 1992 | Notification Concerning the Further Opening up of the Five Frontier Cities and Towns (Nanning, Kunming, Pingxiang, Ruili, and Hekou) | State Council |
| May 3, 1992 | Resolutions Concerning the Extensive Opening up and Accelerating the Outward-oriented Development | Heilongjiang province |
| June 1992 | Some Favourable Policies and Economic Autonomy Authorised to the Frontier Cities (Heihe, Shuifenhe) | |
| Jun. 29, 1992 | Regulations Concerning the Promotion of Foreign Investment | Inner Mongolia autonomous region |
| Apr. 20, 1991 | Resolution of Some Issues Concerning the Extension of Open-door and Promotion of Economic Development | |
| Apr., 1992 | Eight Articles of Favourable Policies Concerning the Absorption of Both Foreign and Domestic Investments | |
| Jun. 8, 1992 | Measures and Favourable Policies Concerning the Further Opening and Promotion of Investment | Xinjiang Ugyur autonomous region |
| Feb. 9, 1992 | Notification of Promoting the Trade and Economic Co-operation with the Neighbouring and Eastern European Countries | |
| July, 14, 1992 | Resolutions Concerning the Further Reform and Opening up to the Outside World | Tibet autonomous region |
| Jul. 14, 1992 | Some Measures Concerning the Promotion of Foreign and Domestic Investments | |
| Sept. 4, 1992 | Regulations Concerning the Promotion of Foreign Investment | Yunnan province |
| Mar. 27, 1985# | Provisional Regulations Concerning the Border Trade | |
| 1991 | Favourable Measures and Policies Concerning the Promotion of Foreign Investment | Guangxi Zhuang autonomous region |
| 1991 | Favourable Measures Concerning the Promotion of Foreign Investment | Jilin province |

*Revised on Sept. 12, 1987 and March 18, 1992 respectively; #Complemented in 1991.
Sources: Bulletins of the State Council, People's Republic of China, related issues, 1984–92.

Since the 1980s, both the Chinese and international investigations have been conducted in the border area by, among others, the Canadian funded Lancang–Mekong research network, the French Mekong River research plan, the joint Chinese–Australian study, as well as the Thai, Laos, and Myanmarese governments. Some construction projects have laid the foundation for further development. International economic and co-operation has also spurred rapidly. The Asian Development Bank (ADB) has invested four million US dollars for the early stage study in Indochina which includes the Chinese Lancang River border area.

In 1994, the Chinese government prepared a priority programme in its Agenda XXI for the development of the Chinese portion in the lower reaches of the Lancang River basin and to further international co-operation across its international borders. The main projects in this programme are:[14] (1) to initiate pilot projects for sustainable development in poor cultural minority areas (including the construction of three towns for different cultural minorities); (2) to conduct a demonstration project for planning and processing tropical fruits and tropical industrial crops; (3) to conceive a plan for sustainable management for the tropical rain forest which includes a method of balancing the interests of the rubber plantations with the interests of the environment; (4) to establish an education and training center for the cultural minorities; (5) to establish international trade zones (including Daluo border trade zone, a mutual trade zone under state administration at Mohan in Mengla, and two or three zones for inhabitants of the border towns).

The demonstration plan for the Chinese area of the Lancang River (see Table 6–5), according to the official estimation, requires a total investment of 6.5 million US dollars and, once completed, will have an annual output value of 5 million US dollars for planting and processing tropical fruits and industrial crops, by eliminating poverty for twenty thousand local cultivators. About 100,000 cultivators in the adjacent areas will benefit as well. Moreover, this development plan will also become a basis for both local development and international co-operation in the border-region between China, Laos, Myanmar, and Thailand.[15]

---

[14]More details may be found in Administrative Committee of China Agenda XXI (1994): *Priority Programmes for China's Agenda XXI*, Chapter 7, State Planning Commission and State Science and Technology Commission, Beijing, China.

[15]Ibid.

Table 6–5 Budget for the Development Plan of Lancang–Mekong Border Area (in million US$)

| Items | Chinese inputs | Int'l grants | Int'l soft-loan | Total |
|---|---|---|---|---|
| Expert | 0.8 | 1.0 | | 1.8 |
| Equipment | 1.5 | 1.5 | | 3.0 |
| Demonstration | 2.0 | 2.3 | 2.2 | 6.5 |
| Miscellaneous | 0.6 | | | 0.6 |
| TOTAL | 4.9 | 4.8 | 2.2 | 11.9 |

Source: ACCAXXI (1994), Chapter 7.

## 6.4 Shenzhen Special Economic Zone (SEZ)

Shenzhen municipality, Guangdong province, is located along China's southern coast, bordering on Hong Kong's New Territories. It extends from 113°45' to 114°35' east longitude and from 22°26' to 22°52' north latitude. The total area of Shenzhen is 2,020 square kilometers with more than 800 thousands of population in 1992.

Shenzhen was initially included in Bao'an county, while the latter administered nowadays Dongwan county, Shenzhen municipality of Guangdong province and Hong Kong in ancient China. Xin'an county was established in 1573 and had covered the areas of Shenzhen and Hong Kong for as long as 268 years before Hong Kong and Kowloon peninsula were ceded to the Great Britain according to Nanjing Treaty in 1842 and Peking Treaty in 1860 respectively. In 1898, the British government rented a portion of Bao'an county as its New Territories from the Chinese government of Qing Dynasty (1644–1910).[16] Xin'an county was renamed as Bao'an in 1914, and the capital of which was moved to Shenzhen township in 1953. Shenzhen municipality was established in 1979 and has administered Bao'an county since 1981.

Even though the Chinese character, Shenzhen, means a deep gutter, no one would have expected that the "gutter" had served as a forbidden frontier fo several decades between the socialist mainland China and the capitalist

---

[16]See *Cihai*, p. 969, Shanghai: Shanghai Cishu Press, 1981.

Britain in the mid-20th century, and also have created an economic miracle in its commitment to the industrialisation since December 26, 1979, when the People's Congress of Guangdong province approved the provincial government's proposal that a part of Shenzhen area *vis-à-vis* the Britain's Hong Kong be selected to experiment as a market-oriented economy with the Chinese characteristic, namely, "special economic zone". This proposal was finally approved by the National People's Congress of China on August 26, 1980.[17]

Shenzhen Special Economic Zone (SEZ) is located in the southern part of Shenzhen municipality, covering an area of 49 kilometers long from east to west and seven kilometers wide from north to south, which is about two times Guangzhou's urban area and one and a half times larger than that of Hong Kong and Kowloon as a whole. Next to the Dapeng Bay of South China Sea in the east, the SEZ connects Zhujiang (Pearl) River in the west, shares a 28 kilometer long border with Hong Kong's New Territories in the south, and adjoins the Bao'an county in the north. The Zone is administively composed of five divisions of Luohu, Shangbu, Nantou, Shekou, and Shatoujiao. According to the overall development program of Shenzhen, the Special Economic Zone is developed in three parts in the east, middle, and west, with 18 different functional districts specializing in tourism, industry, agriculture, fishery, commerce, residence, education, scientific research, etc. (see Table 6–6)

As a fist step to improve the economic environments, Shenzhen invested as many as 20 times that of the past 30 years so as to modernize the infrastructures (including the networks of water supply, electricity, gas, drainage, telecommunication and transportation, etc.) in its SEZ during the first four years. By the end of 1983, there had nearly completed the infrastructure construction in Shenzhen's SEZ, where a wasteland in the past had been replaced by more than 800 modern buildings.[18]

---

[17]The main legal documents concerning the establishment and operations of Shenzhen Special Economic Zone (SEZ) can be found in NPC (1980): "The Regulations Concerning the Special Economic Zones of Guangdong Province, the People's Republic of China", Beijing: National People's Congress of China, August 26.

[18]See Wang Wenxiang (ed.) (1986): *China's Special Economic Zones and 14 Open Cities*, p. 51, Beijing: China Zhanwang Press.

Table 6–6 The Development Program of Shenzhen Special Economic Zone

| Part | Section | District | Main function(s) | Land area (ha) |
|---|---|---|---|---|
| East | | Dayiaomeishan | Tourism | 172 |
| | | Yantian | Fishery, agriculture, industry | 578 |
| | | Shatoujiao | Commerce, residence | 260 |
| | East | Lianlang | Industry | 300 |
| | | Luohucheng | Commerce, residence, industry | 200 |
| | | Jiucheng-qu | Commerce, residence, industry | 400 |
| | | Shuiku-qu | Tourism, residence | 440 |
| Middle | Middle | Shangshe-qu | Industry, residence, storehouse | 1,000 |
| | West | Futian xin-qu | Synthesis | 3,000 |
| | | Chegongmiao-qu | Synthesis | 600 |
| | | Xiangmihu-qu | Tourism | 210 |
| | | Agronomic academy & research garden | Scientific research | 400 |
| West | | Shahe-qu | Mainly in industry | 1,200 |
| | | Shekou gongye-qu | Mainly in industry | 230 |
| | | Houhai-qu | Synthesis, education | 600 |
| | | West lihu-qu | Tourism | 300 |
| | | Chiwan gang-qu & petroleum base | Industry, shipping port, synthesis | 500 |
| | | Nantou, Bao'an town | Industry, synthesis | 610 |

Source: Programming Office for Municipal Development, Shenzhen, Guangdong province, China, 1982.

Since the enactment of the legislation for the Special Economic Zones of Guangdong province by the National People's Congress of China in 1980, a series of "special" laws, regulations, and favourable measures relating to the industrial and commercial registration, economic contract, technology import, labour and personnel, real estate, etc.[19] have been established for Shenzhen's SEZ. Among other factors contributing to the rapid economic growth of Shenzhen, three major aspects are analysed below:

(1) Abundant natural resources. The Rivers of Dasha-he, Guanglan-he, Pindi-he, and Buji-he in Shenzhen's SEZ produce endless high-quality sand. Mts. Wutong-shan, Yantai-shan, and Nan-shan have excellent-grade granite. The plentiful marble and lime ore in the areas of Henggang, Longgang, Kuicheng, etc. near the SEZ may provide enough industrial materials for the SEZ's economic construction. Nearby Shenzhen there has a plenty of agricultural and aquatic resources. In addition, Shenzhen has also a moderate natural environment with an average annual temperature of 22.4°C and less harassing attacks by typhoons. Located at the coast of Dapeng Bay with clean, soft, and plain beach, the places of Damei-shan , Xiamei-shan, and Xicheng with beautiful hills plus the Sea in the front are the ideal scenic pots for the touristic attractions. The hot spring in Mt. Wutong range, Shiyan as well as the mineral water in the area of Mt. Bijia may serve as the natural resources for building sanatoriums.

(2) Proximity to the most dynamic economies in the world. As a coastal frontier town, Shenzhen has about 350,000 natives and their descendants scattered in more than 50 countries and regions, particularly in Hong Kong (about 230,000 natives) and other Southeast Asian economies.[20] The development of Hong Kong inevitably influences that of Shenzhen. What is more, there are many mutual complementarities between Shenzhen and Hong Kong in terms of natural resource, technology, and industrial structure. For example, Hong Kong has been one of the four "small dragons" and trade, finance and shipping centers in Asia, but lacks of natural resources (especially drinking water, energy, agricultural products, etc.) and endures the increasing pressure of high manufacturing costs in land, housing, labour, raw materials, etc. During the 1980s, Hong Kong's factory buildings were sold at 5,000 or more HK$ per square kilometers which was dozens of times higher than that in mainland China during the same period. The average labour costs in Hong Kong were more than five times higher than that in Shenzhen, even though the latter were still ten times higher than

---

[19]These policies, regulations and laws may by found in Wang Wenxiang (ed.) (1986), Appendix, pp. 177–217.

[20]See *Zhongguo Chengshi Jingji Shehui Nanjian* (The Almanac of China's Urban Economy and Society), Beijing: China Social Science Press, 1986.

else where in Guangdong province, South China. In addition, the income tax was different between Hong Kong (25 per cent) and Shenzhen (17 per cent).[21] Through cross-border co-operation, the above comparative advantages will be benefited by both Shenzhen and Hong Kong substantially.

(3) Broad hinterland with abundant natural resources and a huge market as well. Mainland China has about 9.6 million square kilometers of land area with almost all types of natural and geographical conditions that can be found in the rest of the world. Furthermore, mainland China's huge population (1.2 billions in 1995) not only serves as a great potential of consumers' market but also provides a low-cost supply of eager, and hard working labour force by which Shenzhen's economy will be greatly facilitated.

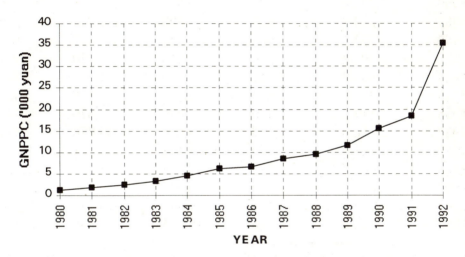

Figure 6–1 Shenzhen's Per Capita GNP, 1980–92

The establishment and operation of the Special Economic Zone (SEZ) has promoted Shenzhen's economy to a fast growing era since the early 1980s. Table 6–7 shows that Shenzhen increased from 1980 to 1992 only one and a half times of population but as many as 68.84 times of gross national product! In 1980, for example, Shenzhen's per capita gross national

[21]Source: (1) *The Economists* (1991): "The South China Miracle", October 5, pp. 19 and 44; (2) Wang Wenxiang (ed.) (1986), p. 35.

product (GNP), national income (NI), gross value of industrial output (GVIO), total public revenue (TPR) were only 1,271, 1,038, 263, and 171 yuan respectively. But these indicators drastically increased to 35,531, 23,697, 48,502, and 5,357 yuan respectively in 1992. The average annual growth rates for the four indicators during 1980–92 were 31.99 per cent (GNP), 29.78 per cent (NI), 54.46 per cent (GVIO), and 33.25 per cent (TPR) respectively.

Table 6–7 Major Indicators for Shenzhen's Economy, 1979–92

| YEAR | POP | GNP | NI | GVIO | TPR |
|------|------|------|------|------|------|
| 1979 | 312.6 | NA | NA | 61 | 36 |
| 1980 | 320.9 | 408 | 333 | 84 | 55 |
| 1981 | 333.9 | 608 | 498 | 244 | 130 |
| 1982 | 354.5 | 906 | 746 | 362 | 163 |
| 1983 | 405.2 | 1,350 | 1,116 | 720 | 304 |
| 1984 | 435.2 | 2,012 | 1,670 | 1,815 | 513 |
| 1985 | 478.6 | 3,000 | 2,500 | 2,756 | 629 |
| 1986 | 514.5 | 3,400 | 2,670 | 3,670 | 740 |
| 1987 | 556.0 | 4,749 | 3,626 | 5,870 | 880 |
| 1988 | 601.4 | 5,709 | 4,173 | 9,071 | 1,244 |
| 1989 | 648.2 | 7,543 | 5,233 | 11,964 | 1,877 |
| 1990 | 686.5 | 10,720 | 6,972 | 16,598 | 1,949 |
| 1991 | 732.2 | 13,550 | 9,543 | 23,735 | 2,556 |
| 1992 | 802.0 | 28,496 | 19,005 | 38,899 | 4,296 |

Note: POP=population ('000 person), GNP=gross national products (million yuan); NI= national income (million yuan); GVIO=gross value of industrial output (million yuan); TPR=total public revenue (million yuan).

Sources: (1) *Shenzhen Tongji Nianjian* (Shenzhen Statistical Yearbook), each issue; (2) *Zhongguo Chengshi Jingji Shehui Nianjian* (The Almanac of China's Urban Economy and Society), various issues.

# CHAPTER 7

# TRANSBORDER CO-OPERATION: CASE STUDIES

The independence in any border-region which has potentially joined a cross-border co-operation agreement implies at least two problems: on one hand, no participating side can be forced into the cross-border co-operation coalition but participation must be voluntary; on the other hand, the participating sides can always opt for leaving the cross-border co-operation agreement even if they had initially decided in favour of participation. Even though there are both advantages and costs in the process of cross-border co-operation between different political authorities, as the cross-border relationships in border-regions have been, and still often are, relationships of conflicts for various reasons, such as the existence of different ethnic minorities, fear of immigration, fear of unfair competition, negative environmental spillover effects, and so on, more and more border-regions have been transformed from conflictual relationships into relationships of co-operation, whenever bilateral relationships are economically interpreted in a larger space perspective. In this chapter, we will briefly introduce, *inter alia*, four major ongoing transborder co-operation programmes, which include: (i) the European cross-border co-operation programmes; (ii) the US–Mexican border environment co-operation; (iii) China's transprovincial border economic zones (BEZs); and (iv) the Tumen River area development programme (TRADP).

## 7.1 The European Cross-border Co-operation Programmes

Even though cross-border relationships in border-regions have still been relationships of conflicts for various reasons in some areas of Europe[1], a series of cross-border co-operation programmes have been effectively promoted in most of the border-regions between the western European nations since the Single European Act (SEA) was implemented. These programmes currently involve as many as 31 border-regions (see Table 7–1)

---

[1]For more details, see D. Maillat (1990): "Transborder Regions Between Members of EC and the Non-member Countries", *Built Environment*, Vol. 16, pp. 38–51.

of the 16 European countries. In this section, we will briefly introduce four programmes.

Table 7–1 The European Border-Regions under Co-operation

| No. | Border-region |
| --- | --- |
| 1 | Spain–Portugal |
| 2 | Greece |
| 3 | Ireland–United Kingdom (Northern Ireland) |
| 4 | France–Spain |
| 5 | Chores–Sardinia |
| 6 | France–Italy |
| 7 | Belgium (West Flanders)–France (Nord–Pas-de-Calais) |
| 8 | Belgium (Wallonia)–France (Nord–Pas-de-Calais) |
| 9 | France (Champagne–Ardennes)–Belgium (Wallonia) |
| 10 | France–Belgium–Luxembourg |
| 11 | Germany–France–Switzerland |
| 12 | France–Germany (Pamina) |
| 13 | France–Germany |
| 14 | France–United Kingdom |
| 15 | France–Switzerland (Rhone–Alps) |
| 16 | France–Switzerland (Franche–Comte) |
| 17 | Belgium–Netherlands (Middengebied) |
| 18 | Belgium–Netherlands (Scheldemond) |
| 19 | Germany–Belgium–Netherlands (Meuse–Rhine) |
| 20 | Germany–Netherlands (Ems–Dollard) |
| 21 | Netherlands–Germany (Rhine–Waal) |
| 22 | Netherlands–Germany (Rhine–Northern Meuse) |
| 23 | Netherlands–Germany (Euregio) |
| 24 | Denmark–Germany |
| 25 | Denmark |
| 26 | Italy–Slovenia |
| 27 | Italy–Austria |
| 28 | Italy–Switzerland |
| 29 | Germany (Bavaria) |
| 30 | Germany–Switzerland (Hochrhein–Bodensee) |
| 31 | Germany–Luxembourg |

Source: *INTERREG PROGRAMMES*, Association of European Border Regions, Enscheder Strabe 362, D–4432 Gronau.

## 7.11 The European Development Pole

Launched on July 19, 1985, through the joint political determination on the part of the three member states concerned and the initiative of the regions associated with the project, the European Development Pole (EDP) takes in the steel-making areas close to the French, Belgian, and Luxembourg borders. Actually, these three adjacent areas already had close ties as they faced the same problems of industrial reconversion. The initiative was chiefly centred on the French city of Longwy (about 60 km from Metz, the capital of the Lorraine region), the Luxembourg town of Rodange (20 km from Luxembourg, the capital of the Grand Duchy of Luxembourg, an important financial centre with an international airport), and the Belgian town of Aubange (Athus – 20 km from Arlon, the provincial capital of Belgium). In December 1986, the Commission of the European Community decided to provide this cross-border project with major support by awarding special status to the International Activity Park thus created and by offering considerable financial backing through the European Regional Development Fund (ERDF).

The main thrust of the EDP, according to M. Quévit and S. Bodson (1993), is the creation of an International Activity Park covering a continuous area beyond the borders of some 400 hectares which were left unused after the demise of the steel-making industry. This cross-border project has involved six interrelated and integrated initiatives: (1) to improve the appeal of the environment to offer new investors the incentive to locate in these regions; (2) to set up a system of financial intervention to encourage companies to locate; (3) to offer a specific customs regime to the EDP; (4) to improve road and rail links; (5) to create joint enterprise services, information desk, advice services, telecommunications; and (6) to offer joint training courses to meet the training needs expressed by the companies locating locally and to enhance the level of training of the local population.[2]

---

[2]See M. Quévit and S. Bodson (1993): "Transborder Co-operation and European Integration: The Case of Wallonia", pp. 194–5, in R. Cappelline and P. W. J. Batey (eds.): *Regional Networks, Border Regions and European Integration*, European Research in Regional Science Series No. 3, London: Pion Limited, 1993.

## 7.12 The Cross-border Co-operation Between Galicia and Norte

Eixo Atlântico (Atlantic Axis) is the name of the network formed by the seven most important cities of Galicia of Spain and the six most important cities of the North of Portugal. The creation of a new development space in the territory occupied by those thirteen cities calls for a co-operation process in which relations of economic complementary and cultural neighbourliness tend to be the key dynamic factors. The interregional co-operation between Galicia and Norte is a good empirical example in which different stages of regional political autonomy have not been a major obstacle to a co-operation strategy, given that autonomy in Galicia is very high compared with that in Norte, while the latter lacks administrative and political autonomy.

The cross-border co-operation between the Galicia–Norte region has been already conducted on eight projects:[3] (1) "Study on Galicia and Norte wines" (including global characterisation and identification of all types of wines production supply); (2) "Study on vineyard diseases" (including common research and development projects of some vineyard diseases in order to improve the quality of wines and the profitability of investments); (3) "Development potential of indigenous cattle breeds" (including exchanges of experiences, research projects, and reproduction techniques, aiming to conserve and to improve indigenous races); (4) "Development perspectives of agriculture and complementary activities in transborder areas" (including global study of transborder agricultural areas in order to identify the most important production systems, their profitability, and the impacts of price changes); (5) "Interregional co-operation as regards Development Agents Training programmes" (including global meeting between local development agents working in both regions, development of common training actions for local development agents); (6) "GALLAECIA 92–93" (including a vast programme of cultural initiatives between the transborder areas of Ourense and Chaves in the fields of urban animation, art, painting, theatre, etc.); (7) "Santiago de Compostela roads" (including inventory of historical roads to Santiago de Compostela as a factor of cultural animation of transborder areas and of promotion of cities integrated in those historical itineraries for pilgrimage); (8) "Exchanges of pupils,

---

[3]See A. M. Figueiredo (1993): "Theory and Practice of International Co-operation and Urban Networks in Economically Lagging Regions: The Experience of Galicia and the North of Portugal", in R. Cappelline and P. W. J. Batey (eds.), pp. 96–115, 1993.

teachers, and experiences between professional schools (intermediate schools) for young people of 15–18 years old" (including the exchanges concern the fields of tourism, agricultural, and communication).

## 7.13 The European Cross-border Action and Co-operation Programme

Launched in 1988 in the form of feasibility studies, the European Cross-border Action and Co-operation Programme (PACTE) is based from a legal point of view on the signing on May 30, 1989 of a joint declaration between the French government, the Nord–Pas-de-Calais region, the Department of Nord, and the Walloon region, with the participation of the French-speaking community of Belgium. This declaration, which was signed by the representatives of the French and Belgian official bodies concerned, formalized the process of cross-border co-operation and laid down specific objectives, modes of operation, and working practices. According to R. Rider (1988), an organizational instrument for cross-border co-operation was established on the basis of the preparatory work carried out by the French and Walloon authorities concerned, which brought together the operational bodies representing the signatories of the joint declaration by providing an opportunity to: (1) establish seven thematic working and three territorial groups which were entrusted with the task of defining and finalizing cross-border co-operation projects will be submitted to the arbitration of the Permanent Commission; and (2) define for each group a precise mission laid down in specific work schedules serving as the task description of the working party.[4]

As a result of the co-operative efforts by both sides of the border, a wider variety of programmes have been jointly set up on the ground in subjects as diverse as: (1) technological research and development – consolidation and amplification of the scope of action of the CETT–CERAM (Centre Européen Transfrontalier de Transfert Technologique en Néocéramique – European Cross-border Neoceramic Technology Transfer Centre) and the implementation of a project involving experimentation and demonstration with wood; (2) support for the economic and technological development of SMEs – the creation of an enterprise liaison bureau, a cross-border venture

---

[4]See A. Rider (1988): "Growth Potential of the Pacte Region and Cross-border Co-operation with the Nord–Pas-de-Calais", Research Report of Interdisciplinary Research Group on Regional Development (IRGRD), University College, London.

capital institution, and a joint structure to provide advice and assistance to young entrepreneurs; (3) the environment – joint management of a cross-border park, cleaning of waste water, management of cross-border taints, and so on; (4) tourism – integrated development plans for the promotion of tourism and cultural heritage; (5) urban problems – implementation of a joint town and country planning study; and (6) training in the field of human resources – creating joint training initiatives to provide qualifications in fields as diverse as new materials, jobs in the textile industry and the graphic arts; creation of an interregional co-ordination structure to harden the training potential on either side of the border.[5]

## 7.14 The Meuse–Rhine EUREGIO

Including as many as 106 municipalities, the EUREGIO is one of the oldest border-regions in West Europe. It extends across the south of the Dutch Limburg, the provinces of Liege and Limburg in Belgium, and the districts of Aix–la-Chapelle, Duren, Euskirchen of the Rhineland Region, and North Westphalia in Germany. The cross-border consultants on common problems led to the establishment of the so-called EUREGIO council in 1978, which founded the first cross-border parliamentary assembly (not elected by citizens, but by the representatives of the municipalities) in Europe. This kind of cross-border co-operation on the level of parliament is the main feature of the EUREGIO in which all municipalities are organized via Regional Associations.[6] The EUREGIO Council, through its Board and Administration, organizes the cross-border co-operation in the following nine fields of activities: (i) economics, (ii) transportation infrastructure, (iii) social affairs, (iv) environment, (v) technology, (vi) culture, (vii) education and training, (viii) tourism, and (ix) agriculture.[7]

---

[5]See M. Quévit and S. Bodson (1993): "Transborder Co-operation and European Integration: The Case of Wallonia", pp. 198–9, in R. Cappelline and P. W. J. Batey (eds.) (1993).

[6]More details about the institutional aspects of the cross-border co-operation may be found in EUREGIO (1991): "Cross-border Co-operation in Practice: Institutional Aspects of Cross-border Co-operation", EUREGIO, Enschede, the Netherlands.

[7]A. van der Veen (1993): "Theory and Practice of Cross-border Co-operation of Local Governments: The Case of the EUREGIO Between Germany and the Netherlands", p. 191, in R. Cappelline and P. W. J. Batey (eds.), 1993.

## 7.2 The US–Mexican Border Environment Co-operation

In the vicinity of the U.S.–Mexico border, there is a great deal of variation in dependency on the natural environment being subject to open access to the two nations. The Colorado River, for example, flows over a distance of 1,440 miles, and form a drainage basin of 244,000 square miles. For 17 miles, the River serves as the border between Arizona of the U.S. and Mexico; it then flows 80 miles through Mexico to the Gulf of California. Issues concerning groundwater quantity and quality particularly take on even more complex dimensions along the U.S.–Mexico border. Waters in underground basins located partly in the United States and partly in Mexico have never been apportioned between the two countries. At least twelve U.S. border municipalities are completely dependent on groundwater, and another four partially so. Agricultural production in Arizona and New Mexico and along the upper Rio Grande in Texas is also heavily dependent on groundwater. With the exception of the lower Rio Grande valley, Mexican agriculture relies just as much on this resource. The Mexican cities of Nogales, San Luis Rio Colorado, Agua Prieta, Ciudad Juarez, Presido, and Ciudad Acuna are nearly totally dependent on groundwater, while Mexicali, Tijuana, Reynosa, and Matamoros are variously dependent on it for up to half of the water. Along the entire border area there are at least twenty locations where groundwater is at present or may become a source of binational conflict.[8]

Besides the international issues associated with Colorado and Rio Grande Rivers, there remain other locally significant surface issues along the U.S.–Mexico border. For example, the waters of a number of international streams have yet to be apportioned. These include the Tijuana River in the Tijuana–San Diego area; and the Santa Cruz River, San Pedro River, and Whitewater Creek, which all cross the Arizona–Sonora border. The San Pedro River carries contaminants from the large copper works at Cananer, Sonoran into Arizona, and the New River, which rises south of Mexicali and flows northward to the Salton Sea in California, is perhaps the most polluted

---

[8]For more details, refer to S. P. Mumme (1982): "The Politics of Water Apportionment and Pollution Problems in United States–Mexico Relations", pp. 3–4, U.S.–Mexico Project Series No. 5, Overseas Department Council, Washington, D. C.

stream in the United States.[9] In addition to water pollution in those cross-border rivers, principal solid waste, air pollution resulting from fast industrialization and population growth (as demonstrated in Tables 4–3 and 4–4 of Chapter 4) in both sides next to the border have also posed challenges to the governments of the United States and Mexico.

Even though many difficulties still exist between the United States and Mexico because independent countries usually have different preferences and cannot agree on a rigorously common standard, the two countries have attempted to develop international co-operation concerning environmental protection in their common border-region, as can be found in the two agreements which were already signed by the two national presidents of the United Sates and Mexico in August 1983 in La Paz, Mexico, and later in February 1994 in Washington D. C., U.S.A., respectively.

The La Paz Agreement states that "the two governments will adopt appropriate measures, to prevent, reduce, and eliminate sources of air, land, and water pollution in the border area", which is defined to cover 100 kilometers on both sides of the border. The Washington Agreement, wishing to follow upon the goals and objectives of the North American Free Trade Agreement, is purposed to "help preserve, protect, and enhance the environment of the border-region ...."[10] As joint ventures, the Border Environment Co-operation Commission (BECC) and the North America Development Bank (NADB) will be established with other national and international institutions, and private sources supplying investment capital, and environmental infrastructure projects in the border-region.

In carrying out this purposes of cross-border water co-operation and environmental protection implemented by the United States and Mexico, the BECC may do any or all of the following focuses:[11]

– to assist states and localities and other public entities and private investors in (A) co-ordinating environmental infrastructure projects in the

---

[9]N. Hansen (1989): "Environmental Impacts of Human Settlement System Growth in the U.S. Southwest", in L. J. Gibson and A. C. Renteria (eds.): *Regional Structural Change in Two Mature Nations*, pp. 137–8, Regional Science Research Institute, Peace Dale, Rhade Island, 1989.

[10]US–Mexico (1994): "Agreement Between the Government of the United States of America and the Government of the United Mexican States Concerning the Establishment of a Border Environment Co-operation Commission and a North America Development Bank", Washington D. C., USA, February 3, Section I, Article I, Chapter I.

[11]Ibid., Section 2, Article I, Chapter I.

border region; (B) preparing, developing, implementing, and overseeing environmental infrastructure projects in the border region, including the design, siting and other technical aspects of such projects; (C) analyzing the financial feasibility or the environmental aspects, or both, of environmental infrastructure projects in the border region; (D) evaluating social and economic benefits of environmental infrastructure projects in the border region; and (E) organizing, developing and arranging public and private financing for environmental infrastructure and projects in the border region;

– to certify applications for financing to be submitted to the North American Development Bank, or to other sources of financing that request such certification, for environmental infrastructure projects in the border region.

Furthermore, according to Article III of Washington Agreement, the Commission shall have a Board of Directors, a General Manager, a Deputy General Manager, an Advisory Council and such other officers and staff which are based on the border region to perform such duties as the Commission may determine.

The purposes of the North American Development Bank (NADB) as a joint venture established by the United States and Mexico have also been determined: (a) to provide financing for projects certified by the Border Environment Co-operation Commission, as appropriate, and, at the request of the Commission, to otherwise assist the Commission in fulfilling its purposes and functions; (b) to provide financing endorsed by the United Sates, as appropriate, for community adjustment and investment in support of the purposes of the North American Free Trade Agreement; and (c) to provide financing endorsed by Mexico, as appropriate, for community adjustment and investment in support of the purposes of the North American Free Trade Agreement.

To implement its purposes, the Bank has planned to utilize its own capital, funds raised by it in financial markets, and other available resources and shall fulfil the following functions: (a) to promote the investment of public and private capital contributing to its purposes; (b) to encourage private investment in projects, enterprises, and activities contributing to its purposes, and to supplement private investment when private capital is not available on reasonable terms and conditions; and (c) to provide technical and other assistance for the financing and, in co-ordination with the Commission, the implementation of plans and projects.[12]

## 7.3 China's Transprovincial Border Economic Zones (BEZs)

China's vast size has at least two clear implications: firstly, with mainland China's 30 provinces (autonomous regions, autonomous cities) averaging about one-third million square kilometers of land area and more than 40 millions of population, each province is equivalent to a country in the rest of the world; secondly, China's great diversities in terms of physical geography, resource endowment, political economy, and ethnical identity[13] have given rise to great regional divergence and even inter-regional conflicts. For instance, China has 66 inter-provincial border lines, while 65 of which have been discordantly portrayed by the related provincial and local authorities.[14] Consequently, border-regions usually become a source of inter-provincial disputes. By 1988, there had been more than 800 cases of border disputes in 333 of the 849 inter-provincial border counties of almost all provinces, autonomous regions, and autonomous cities. The total disputed areas (about 140,000 square kilometers) include grassland (about 95,000 square kilometers), mining field (about 4,000 square kilometers), arable land (about 3,000 square kilometers), forestry (about 2,000 square kilometers), water area (about 1,000 square kilometers), and mixed grass-mining-forestry area (about 30,000 square kilometers).[15] Many inter-provincial disputes even led to armed fights and seriously affected the social security and sustainability of economic development in those border-regions regardless of the administrative regulations concerning the resolution of inter-provincial disputes issued by the central government.[16]

Since the advent of administrative decentralisation stemming from the economic reform in the early 1980s, China's national economy has become effectively "cellularized" into a plethora of semi-autarkic regional enclaves.

---

[12]Ibid., Section 2, Article I, Chapter II.

[13]There currently exists 56 different ethnical identities in mainland China.

[14]Zhang Honghuan (1990): "The Importance of Regulating the Transprovincial Borders in China", *Journal of East China Normal University*, No. 1.

[15]More details may be found in *Baokan Wenzhai* (The Digest of Newspapers and Magazines) (1989), p. 4, June 13.

[16]See State Council (1990): "Contemporary Regulations Concerning the Resolutions of the Border Disputes of the Administrative Divisions of the P. R China", Beijing, China.

In order to protect local market and revenue sources, it became common in China that provinces restrict import (export) from (to) other provinces by levying high, if informal, taxes on commodities and by creating non-tariff barriers. Xinjiang autonomous region, for example, effectively banned the import of forty-eight commodities on the grounds that they would harm its domestic economy. Jilin refused to market beer produced in its neighbouring provinces of Heilongjiang and Liaoning. Hunan province prohibited to export grain to its neighbour, Guangdong province. ... In some provinces, local authorities established, and provided finance for, a variety of schemes so as to promote the sales of local products. Enterprises from other provinces, however, often had difficulties in finding office spaces, accommodation, or land for their business activities. These protectionist measures, which were often in violation of central directives, were enforced through a patchwork system of roadblocks, cargo seizures, ad hoc taxes, commercial surcharges, and licensing fees, and in a number of well-publicised cases, outfight highway robbery across the inter-provincial borders.[17] It is inevitably that this unfair competition between provinces could be fierce in the "battlegrounds" of the border-regions, and there were numerous tales of "trade embargoes" or "border commodity wars" between provinces over, amongst other items, rice, wool, tobacco, soy beans, and mineral products.[18]

Notwithstanding the above difficulties, transprovincial co-operation in some border-regions has spurred rapidly since the mid-1980s when the central government began to implement its regional economic strategy in an

---

[17]This phenomenon has been described as *Zhuhou Jingji* (feudal prince economy) or *Duli Wangguo* (independent kingdom). See, for example, (1) Shen Liren and Dai Yuanchen (1990): "Chinese Zhuhou Jingji: Mechanisms, Impacts, and Sources", *Jingji Yanjiu* (Economic Research Journal), No. 3, p. 12; (2) Li Zhengyi (1993): "In-Depth Exploration of the Question of Regional Blockades", *Chinese Economic Studies*, Vol. 26, No. 5, pp. 23–36; and (3) A. H. Wedeman (1993): "Editor's Introduction to Chinese Economic Studies", *Chinese Economic Studies*, Vol. 26, No. 5 (special issue on regional protection).

[18]More details about the "border commodity wars" and their impacts on border-regions may be found in Guo Rongxing (1993b): *Economic analysis of Border-Regions: Theory and Practice of China*, Beijing: China Ocean Press, pp. 201–5.

Table 7–2 Natural and Social Conditions of China's Transprovincial BEZs

| Transprovincial border economic zone (BEZ) | Participating provinces | Land area (000 km²) | Population (million) | Main mineral resources |
|---|---|---|---|---|
| The Yellow River Delta Economic Zone | Shanxi, Shaanxi, Henan | 36.6 | 10.00 | Coal, bauxite; copper; hydraulic power |
| H–H–S–S Border Zone for Economic Co-operation | Hubei, Henan, Sichuan, Shaanxi | 153.8 | 32.91 | Petroleum; coal; phosphor; iron ore; natural alkali; crystal; mercury |
| S–G–S Border Economic Zone | Shaanxi, Gansu, Sichuan | 162.0 | 22.60 | Lead; zinc; petroleum; natural gas; pottery |
| F–G–J Border Zone for Economic and Technological Cooperation | Fujian, Guangdong, Jiangxi | 74.6 | 11.39 | Coal; manganese; hydraulic power; copper; gold; silver |
| Dabieshan Area Joint Congress for Promotion of Economic Development | Anhui, Henen, Hubei | 123.0 | 25.69 | Few mineral resources |

Sources: (1) Zhang Wanqing (1987): *Regional Co-operation and Economic Networks*, Beijing: Economic Academic Press; (2) Yang Shuzhen (1990): *Studies of Chinese Economic Zones*, Beijing: China Zhanwang Press.

attempt to tear down the transprovincial border barriers.[19] For example, China established only one border economic zone before 1983 and five in 1985 in its transprovincial border-regions. According to an incomplete statistics, the total number of the transprovincial border economic zones (BEZs) reached to 41 by the end of 1989, which are distributed in the eastern (13 BEZs), central (15 BEZs), and western (13 BEZs) areas of China

---

[19]State Council (1986): "The Regulations of Issues Concerning the Extensive Regional Economic Co-operation", *Renmin Ribao* (People's Daily), March 26.

respectively.[20] Table 7–2 gives some basic natural and social conditions for five transprovincial border economic zones.

China's transprovincial border economic zones were usually established in voluntary and jointly administered by adjacent local governments under two, three, four, or five provincial governments. Many of them also have permanent bodies (i.e., the liaison offices which are jointly operated by representatives from the participating sides) and convene regular (annual) meetings co-chaired by the government officials from the participating sides. To investigate the mechanisms and functions of the transprovincial border economic zones, let us take Zhongyuan Association for Economic and Technological Co-ordination as an example.

The border-region of Shanxi, Hebei, Shandong, and Henan provinces in Central China plays a leading role in the economic interdependence between China's East and West regions. Wishing to promote the transprovincial economic co-operation, the nine municipal mayors of Changzhi, Xinxiang, Anyang, Handan, Jincheng, Jiaozuo, Xingtai, Hebi, and Puyang and five prefectural governors of Xinxiang, Xingtai, Handan, Liucheng and Hezhe of the border-region met in Handan, Hebei province, September 27, 1985 to establish a multi-governmental association, namely, Zhongyuan Association for Economic and Technological Co-ordination (ZYAETC).[21]

As a permanent body housed in Handan city, Hebei province, the ZYETC's Liaison Office is operated jointly by representatives from the participating municipalities and prefectures under the leadership of the ZYAETC. The ZYAETC has been convening its annually regular meetings co-chaired by the municipal mayors and prefectural governors, with the participation of heads of the Economic Committee, Planning Committee, Office of Economic Co-operation, and Center for Economic Research from each municipality or prefecture, while the chairpersons of which shall be appointed to the mayors (governors) of the participating municipalities (prefectures) by turn from 1986 in the following order: Changzhi municipality, Xingtai (municipality and prefecture respectively), Anyang

---

[20]More information about China's 41 transprovincial border economic zones can be found in Guo Rongxing (1993b), Appendix A4.

[21]For more information, see Zhongyuan Association of Economic and Technological Co-ordination (1985): "Agreement on Transborder Economic and Technological Co-ordination Among 14 Municipalities and Prefectures in the Border-Region of Shanxi, Hebei, Shandong, and Henan Provinces", Handan, Hebei province, China, September 27.

municipality, Handan (municipality and prefecture respectively), Jincheng municipality, Liucheng prefecture, Jiaozuo municipality, Xinxiang (municipality and prefecture respectively), Hebi municipality, Puyang municipality and Hezhe prefecture. The main topics of the annual meetings have included: (1) to discuss the key issues relating to the economic developments of all parts in the border area; (2) to formulate the regulations and measures concerning the promotion of the socio-economic development in the border area; (3) to develop the bilateral and multilateral co-operation; and (4) to formulate the reciprocal measures for transborder trade.[22] According to their working schedule, 11 fields of cross-border co-operation have been agreed to start between the 14 municipalities and prefectures in the border-region:

1.  joint exploitation and utilization of underground resources so as to develop coal, petroleum, power and metallurgic industries;
2.  joint exploitation and synthetic utilization of agricultural resources so as to promote the development of aquatic, forestry, and livestock products;
3.  promotion of co-operation and transborder combination in the sectors of textile, chemistry, machinery, electrics, building materials, etc.;
4.  reinforcement of urban-rural combination in terms of the joint development of feed-processing plants, food-processing industry and the production of meat, egg, chicken, milk, etc.;
5.  joint establishment of trading centers and setting up liaison offices in each other's side;
6.  co-operation in science and technology by establishing joint research projects;
7.  co-operation in capital, technology, and equipment so as to develop cross-border railway, highway, and air transports;
8.  co-operation in education and exchange of personnel;
9.  mutual assistance to each other's unbanization;
10. establishment of cross-border information network; and
11. promotion of cross-border financial and labour markets.[23]

---

[22]Ibid., Article III.
[23] Source: The Liaison Office of ZYAETC, 1990, Handan, China.

## 7.4 The Tumen River Area Development Programme (TRADP)

*"... If the region is to develop its expected potential over a span of approximately 20 years, there will be a need for as many as 10 or 11 modern marine terminals, and housing and related facilities for upwards of 500,000 people in new communities. The related total costs may run as high as 30 billion U.S. dollars ... All of the above ideas and factors reinforce the concept of Tumen delta area as a future Hong Kong, Singapore or Rotterdam with the potential for entropy trade and related industrial development akin to theirs."* (Quoted from UNDP (1991): *Tumen River Area Development: Mission Report*, by M. Miller, A. Holon, and T. Kelleher, Pyongyang: Consultation with Participant Governments, October 11–18.)

### 7.41 Background

Few people knew of the Tumen River delta before July of 1990, when an International Conference on the Economic and Technological Co-operation in Northeast Asia was held in Changchun, Jilin province, Northeast China. The conference firstly focused on the possibility and feasibility of Tumen River delta development and received considerable attentions from regional scientists and policy-makers of the Northeast Asian countries and the world as well.

On July 6–7, 1991, involving representatives from China, North Korea, South Korea, and Mongolia, a Northeast Asian sub-regional program meeting was convened by the UNDP in Ulan Bator, Mongolia. In this meeting, all participating countries accorded a top priority to start the Tumen River area development project.

In late August and early September of 1991, the UNDP met again with representatives from the above four countries plus observers from Japan and Russia at the Second International Conference on the Economic and Technological Development in Northeast Asia, held in Changchun, China. After the conference, a UNDP-sponsored mission paid a fact-finding visit to the three dimensional area bordering China, North Korea, and Russia and reported to the relevant countries that the strategical location of the Tumen River delta has enormous potentials of both natural resources and global trade.

On October 11–18, 1991, the six countries of Northeast Asia unanimously agreed to start the Tumen River Area Development Program (TRADP) in the UNDP-convening conference on the Tumen River area development, held in Pyongyang, North Korea. In this conference, the TRADP management Committee, Experts Office, TRADP Office, National Project Offices were established in order to reinforce the co-ordination and promotion of the program. At the meantime, the UNDP decided to support the pre-feasibility studies of the program with 3.5 million U.S. dollars. Since then, the TRADP has become a remarkable project in world.

Until 1993, the UNDP had convened or co-sponsored four inter-governmental meetings and 12 expert conferences on the development of Tumen River area. On May 30, 1995, trade officials from China, Russia, South and North Korea and Mongolia met in Beijing and initialed three agreements aimed at revitalizing a faltering UN-sponsored scheme to develop the delta area. In addition to a commitment of establishing the Tumen River Area Development Co-ordination Committee (TRADCC) whose task will be to boost trade and investment in this area, the three Tumen River riparian states (China, Russia and North Korea), plus South Korea and Mongolia, also agreed to set up a consultative commission with broader responsibilities for developing trade, infrastructure, finance and banking in the under-developed but resource-rich Asian Northeast.[24]

According to a News Conference in the UN headquater on October 24, 1991, Tumen River area will eventually become a new Hong Kong, Singapore or Rotterdam with 30 billion U.S. dollar investment in the next 20 years, from which the 300 million people in Northeast Asia will benefit greatly.

## 7.42 Northeast Asia and Tumen River area

The Northeast Asia, as generally defined, includes North and South Korea, Japan, Mongolia, Northeast part of China, and Siberia and the Far East part of Russia. The area covers more than 9.6 million square kilometers and comprises 300 million population. Northeast Asia has plentiful natural resources, including minerals, energy, waters, farmlands, and forests, and

---

[24]For more details, see Northeast Asian Nations (1995): "Agreement of the Tumen River Area Development Programme among China, Mongolia, Russia, North and South Korea", signed in Beijing, China, May 30.

particularly, has great mutual complementarities in terms of natural resource, labour force, and industrial structure by region: Japan and South Korea, with the most dense population and developed manufacturing industry as well as abundant capital, technology, and information sectors in one aspect, have relatively limited land area and scant natural resources in the other aspect; the vast and resource-rich Siberia and Far East of Russia has a sparse population and is far away from its European core; Northeast China, with relatively appropriate land area, population density, and physical environment, faces the lack of resources, especially capital and technology (see Table 7–3). From an economic prospect, the uneven distribution of natural resources and industrial sectors also implies a great potential of cross-border co-operation among these countries.

Even though Northeast Asian countries have still different economic and political systems, most of them are more or less culturally interdependent,[25] which were or still are influenced by the Confucian ideology. What is more important, the increasingly political *détente* has greatly contributed to the multi-national economic co-operation in Northeast Asia.

The end of the Cold War has softened the bilateral hostilities and nurtured the bilateral relations, including between China and South Korea, China and Japan, and Russia and its Northeast Asian neighbours. The collapse of the Soviet Union abruptly cut off the supply line to the Far East region from Russia's European core. Since establishing formal diplomatic relations with South Korea and China, the Russian government has become more concerned about the economic issues of its Far East area. The progress of China's open-door policy especially its rapid economic growth not only provides a huge potential of investments and consumers markets for the industrial economies, but also shows an example for North Korea's

---

[25]Hunchun city, Jilin province, China, for example, has a total population of more than 175 thousands, of which 47.3 per cent, 42.2 per cent, and 10.22 per cent are Korean, Han-Chinese, and Manchu respectively. Furthermore, 1,000 and 1,500 people of this city have marriage relations with Japan, North and South Korea, 5,000 people have relatives in Russia, the United States, Canada, Brazil, etc. (Source: Jin Tie (1993): "The Openness and Development of Hunchun City: Situation and Perspectives", *Northeast Asia Forum*, No. 1, pp. 12–3.)

Table 7–3 The Mutual Complementary Conditions of Northeast Asian Countries

| Nation | Advantages | Disadvantages |
|---|---|---|
| Japan | Capital saving, advanced technology, plenty of superior equipment ready to move out, vanguard industrial products and management experiences. | Severe shortage of energy and industrial resources, insufficient grain for animal husbandry and some agricultural products, comparative deficiency of labour. |
| Russia (Far East) | Plenty of forest, non-ferrous metal ore, aquatic resources, oil, gas, coal and some products of heavy and chemical industries (such as steel, fertilizers, etc.) | Severe shortage of agricultural and light industrial products, lack of labour and capital, backward industrial equipment and management experience. |
| China (Northeast) | Favourable agricultural conditions, adequate and various agricultural products (such as corn, soybean, meat, fruit), some textile industrial products, oil, coal, building materials, Chinese medicinal herbs, and excess labour. | Lack of capital, advanced equipment, technology and management experience, comparative shortage of some mineral resources, conditioned infrastructure. |
| DPRK | Rich mineral resources, metal ore and simple processed products, aquatic products, some industrial commodities and plentiful labour. | Shortage of capital, insufficiency of farm, sideline and light industrial commodities, backward equipment and technology. |
| ROK | Surplus capital, advanced technology and equipment ready to move out, vanguard industrial products. | Shortage of energy and industrial resources, lack of grains for stock raising, insufficiency of labour. |
| Mongolia | Plentiful products of animal husbandry and of mineral ores, especially fluorspar. | No convenient way to communicate directly with other Northeast Asian nations, lack of capital, technology, equipment, farm products and light industrial commodities. |

Source: Chen Cai, Yuan Shuren, Wang Li and Ding Shibao (1991): "Regional Co-operation in Northeast Asia and the Exploitation of Triangle Area of Lower Tumen River", paper presented at the Second International Conference on the Economic and Technological Development of Northeast Asia, Changchun, August.

industrialzation and internationalization given their traditional ties[26]; Japan, being subject to its internal resource and market potentials, may be more than happy to economically (even though not politically) co-operate with those once known as her "co-prosperity" sphere where, apart from the cultural homogeneity at some extent, at least demonstrates considerably locational advantages and industrial complementarities over the rest of the world, given the increasingly improved political environment in Northeast Asia; South Korea, perhaps has an exceptional interest in the Tumen River delta. Having mighty national identity and social, cultural, and linguistic homogeneities, the people of the two Koreas have been separated by the 38th Parallel since the World War II. Recently, especially since South Korea established formal diplomatic relation with China in 1992, the two Koreas have found an intermediator in the mainland, due to the later's political access to both of the two starkly rival regimes. In conclusion, the increasing interdependence among the Northeast Asia will inevitably result in a mutual co-operation across their adjacent land – the lower Tumen River delta.

With a total length of more than 500 kilometres, Tumen River originates from Mt. Changbai-shan (Paektu san) between North Korea and China's Jilin province, which is said to be the mythic birthplace of the Korean ethnic. The River flows north-eastward at first and then south-westward along the Sino–North Korea border and, before running into the Sea of Japan, forms an about 18 kilomenter-long international border between North Korea and Russia. The Tumen River area is generally known as the delta area bordering China, North Korea, and Russia while in close proximity to Mongolia, South Korea, and Japan. Broadly, the area extends triangularly to China's Yanji, North Korea's Chongin, and Russia's Vladivostok; A narrow scope of the area covers China's Hunchun, North Korea's Najin, and Russia's Posyet (see Table 7–4).

The Tumen River area has been the dwelling place of Manchu, Korean, and Han-Chinese for a long history. In 1860, the China's Qing Dynasty (1644–1911) ceded as large as 400 thousand square kilometers of territory to the tsarist Russia under Sino–Russian Treaty of Peking. In 1862, the duty-free trade within 100 kilometers from both sides of the border was permitted in accordance with Sino–Russian Trade Treaty. Since then, China's

---

[26]Notice that Northeast China has about two million minorities which have ethnical relations with both North and South Korea in 1990. (Source: Office of 1990's Census of P. R. of China, Beijing, China.)

Hunchun city became an international trade center. In 1909, Vladivostok became a naval port. In 1913, Sino–Russian Trade Treaty was abolished.[27]

Table 7–4 The Tumen River Delta under China, North Korea and Russia

| | Small delta | | | | Great delta | | | |
|---|---|---|---|---|---|---|---|---|
| | China | N.Korea | Russia | Total | China | N.Korea | Russia | Total |
| Key city (own) | Hunchun | Najin | Posyet | | Yanji | Chongjin | Vladivostok | |
| Location: | | | | | | | | |
| East longitude | 130°35' | 130°30' | 130°84' | | 129°58' | 129°76' | 131°92' | |
| North latitude | 42°88' | 42°25' | 42°67' | | 42°90' | 41°80' | 43°14' | |
| Population in '90 ('000 person) | 126.5 | 32.5 | 132.5 | 291.5 | 886.5 | 842.5 | 1302.5 | 3031.5 |
| Land area (km²) | | | | 1000 | | | | 10000 |

Sources (1) *Northeast Asia Forum*, No. 2, 1993, p. 58; (2) The map of each country. Calculations by the author.

Before the mid-1980s, part of the Tumen River delta served as the defensive bases for China and the former USSR, between which the confrontation created a military "core" and a socio-economic periphery. In China's side, few infrastructures (such as railway, highway, ports, etc.) were built. While in Russia's side, the Far East area remained as an economic virgin. As the outpost for the Asian and Pacific strategy of the former USSR, Vladivostok had been closed for several decades and served as a military base. In addition, Sino–North Korea border-region has been still a backward area because of its difficult physical environment as well as the geographic peripheries far away from their respective economic and political cores.

7.43 The strategical role of TRADP

As a triangle border area, the Tumen River delta strategically plays an important role in the Northeast Asian economic development and co-operation, which may be found through three aspects:

---

[27]See Ding Shisheng (1993): "The Development of the Ports in the Tumen River: Suggestions", *Northeast Asia Forum*, p. 1, No. 1.

First of all, the Tumen River delta area has a huge and resource-rich hinterland, including Northeast China, North Korea, and Russia's Far East region. For example, Northeast China abounds in iron and steel, timber, coal, grain, and mechanical products; North Korea has already established Songbong industrial zone of mining, non-ferrous metals, forest and aquatic production from the Tumen River, Najin, to Chongjin; Russia specializes in coal, natural gas, forest, and aquatic production within the area from Tumen River, Posyet, Vladivostok, to Sovestskaya Gavan'.

Secondly, through the Sea of Japan, the Tumen River delta area is expected to create a closer connection between the ports of the Northeast Asian mainland and the coastal cities of South Korea (such as Pusan, Pyonghae, etc.) and Japan (such as Hakodate, Akita, Sakata, Niigata, Kanazawa, Fukui, Shimonoseki, etc.). After the shipping routes are established across the Sea of Japan, mutual complementarities can be more effectively developed between the South (Japan and South Korea) and the North (Northeast part of China, North Korea, and Russia's Far East region) economies. What is more, the Tumen River port near the exit of Tumen River to the Sea of Japan has the geographical advantages in terms of both deep water, proximity to Far East port of  Russia in the North, and connection with the main ports of the Korean peninsula in the South.

Thirdly, the Tumen River delta may serve as a new Europe–Asia land bridgehead. There have already two land bridges between Europe and Asia, which are (1) Siberia Land bridge (from Russia's Eastern port via the Siberia railway to Europe) and (2) China's Land bridge (from East China's Liangyunang port via Longxi–Haizhou and Lanzhou–Xinjiang railway networks to Europe). The establishment of the new land bridge will generate many benefits to most parts of the Northeast Asia. For example, Mongolia used to transport its commodities through Siberia Land bridge to the Sea of Japan, the total distance of which is 3,645 kilometers. After the Sino–Mongolia border railway lines are connected, it will take only 1,430 kilometers for Mongolia's goods to enter the Sea of Japan via the Tumen River delta.[28]

To summarize up, the UNDP-sponsored plan for the joint development of the Tumen River area may offer a pilot project for the industrialization and

---

[28]Zhang Xiuyuan (1994): "The Functions of the Inner Ports in Tumen River Delta", *Northeast Asia Forum,* pp. 7–8, No. 2.

sustainable development in the delta area. The TRADP will generate diffusive effects to the nations in Northeast Asia:

**China**: Through the TRADP, China may either build its own  ports in Tumen River or use the ports of North Korea and Russia as the entrance to the Sea of Japan. The positive effects may be produced by international co-operation between the prominent advantages of capital and technology in Japan and South Korea and the abundant labour force and natural resources in Northeast China.

**South Korea**: South Korea will obtain a relatively low-cost source of energy, industrial materials, agricultural products, and labour force with its surplus capital, advanced technology and equipment. In addition, the process of the TRADP may also provide a unique chance for South Korea to co-operate with its ethnically homogeneous but still ideologically antagonistic counterpart in northern Korea.

**Russia**: The development of the Far East region may, at a certain extent, benefit from both the surplus capital and technology of South Korea and Japan and the surplus labour force and agricultural products of China and North Korea.

**North Korea**: The development of Chongjin and Najin areas in North Korea will benefit substantially from the export of its mineral products and the imports of agricultural products from China and the absorption of capital, advanced technology and equipment from Japan and South Korea.

**Mongolia**: Mongolia will obtain a more convenient and cheaper route to export its copper, coal, and herd products to the countries and regions along the Sea of Japan and the Pacific Basin and benefit from the surplus agricultural products in China and capital and advanced technology in Japan and South Korea.

**Japan**: Japan, even though not currently a TRADP member but an observer, will find a relatively low-cost source of energy, industrial materials, and agricultural products, and labour force with its comparative advantages such as surplus capital, advanced technology, and equipment through co-operation with China, North Korea, Russia, and Mongolia, especially in the area of the Tumen River. In addition, the development of Japan's western coastal areas which is still far less-developed than its eastern core areas will be accelerate by the TRADP.

The input-output effects of the TRADP on Northeast Asian countries may be illustrated as Table 7–5.

Table 7–5 The TRADP's Input-output Effects on Northeast Asian Countries

| Country | Input | Output |
|---------|-------|--------|
| China (Northeast) | Labour force, grain, building materials, industrial finished products, applied technology, mechanical equipment. | High-technology, capital, industrial finished products, aquatic products. |
| North Korea | Labour force, mineral products, agricultural, forest products. | Light industrial products, industrial equipments, technology, capital, qualified personnel. |
| Russia (Far East) | Raw materials, forest products, science and technology. | Light industrial products, foods, agricultural products, capital, technology. |
| Mongolia | Livestock and herb products, mineral products. | Industrial products, capital, technology (especially in agricultural production). |
| Japan and South Korea | Capital, advanced technology, industrial equipment, tourism products. | Industrial raw materials, energy, building materials. |

## 7.44 Conclusions

Since the early 1990s, much progress has been made in the Tumen River area development. In November of 1991, Hunchun city was approved by the Chinese government to open to foreigners; One month latter, North Korea declared Chongjin port as a Free Port and established Najin–Songbong Free Trade Zone (FTZ) in December; the Russian government decided to open Vladivostok in January of 1992; Hunchun became one of the first open frontier cities in China in March of 1992 and was approved to establish Hunchun Economic Co-operation Zone which may use the same economic mechanism as that has been successfully pursued by other Special Economic Zones (SEZs) in China's southern coastal area next to Hong Kong, Taiwan and other newly industrialized economies (NIEs).

Indeed, the positive implications of the Tumen River area development have been far beyond the program itself, as TRADP has been attracting the Northeast Asian regimes with different political ideologies to shake hands and discuss the mutual co-operation and development. According to Tony Walker (1995), the UNDP has provided US$4.5 millions to advance the scheme and been promoting to provide Mongolia and China's landlocked northern provinces with transport routes to the Sea of Japan through the Tumen River (about 18 km section) between Russia and North Korea; China has already spent Chinese Y4.5 billions (about US$542 millions) on infrastructure and industrial development and made considerable progress in developing road and rail systems to ease cross-border trade with its Russian and North Korean neighbours; Russia and North Korea have been upgrading ports on the Sea of Japan to handle extra traffic from China; the Russians have installed new handling facilities at Zarubino; and the North Korean have been modernizing Chongyin, Sonbong and Rajin ports and indicated that they will facilitate visa-free access to a free trade zone being set up on the border with China.[29]

It is much close to an orthodoxy among practitioners and theorists of international relations that cross-border conflicts frequently arise between the narrowly individual interests and protectionisms of different states, on the one hand, and an orderly cross-border interdependent system, on the other hand. Notwithstanding the political, economic, and cultural differences between the participating countries, it looks more and more possible, under the growing mutual complementarities as well as the tendency towards the unanimity of political, social, especially economic points of views among the participants, to find an appropriate approach that can maximize the benefits for all the parties concerned, while also taking into account their respective articulated objectives in the future even though not immediately.

---

[29]T. Walker (1995): "Five Nations in Pact to Develop NE Asian Region", *Financial Times* (News: Asia – Pacific), May 31.

# CHAPTER 8
# BORDER-REGIONAL DYNAMICS

In general, border-regional economics has dealt with different types of spatial problems from that of regional economics. These problems, therefore, cannot be effectively studied by the existing theories and methodologies in regional economics. As indicated in the previous chapters, many border-regional economic problems stem from the fact that each border-region as a multi-dimensional spatial system is separated by two or more independent sub-regions (or sub-systems). Obviously, only a portion of the natural and social resources in the border-region falls under the jurisdiction of one sub-region, so do the other portions by the rest sub-regions. This circumstance actually implies a spatial issue related to economies (diseconomies) of regional sizes. In the last chapter of the book, we try to develop a regional cost-benefit analysis (RCBA) framework which is based on a number of theoretical assumptions for an isolated economy and apply it to analyse the optimal sizes for political regions under different conditions. Based on the RCBA approach, the spatial mechanisms of border-regions formed by political regimes with different kinds of spatial status will be also investigated. The results obtained in this chapter are at least helpful for us to understand the rational expectations and dynamic patterns for those political regions differing in spatial size to develop cross-border co-operation and economic integration.

## 8.1 An Isolated Country: Some Assumptions

The world never stops changing its economic and political structures. In one aspect, some adjacent political regimes have emerged as a new and larger political union or formed a single economic community of their own, in the desire of an increased return from the economies of scale, while in the other aspect, the artificial barriers are still existing between neighbouring communities to serve as a protection of the political and economic interests for each of their own. Moreover, even the sub-political barriers are separating the internal economic connection and co-operation within some countries. All these phenomena have resulted in different patterns of spatial mechanisms and dynamics for border-regions and, furthermore, posed different challenges and opportunities for the respective governments concerned to develop cross-border co-operation.

In a research supported by Ford Foundation, I used the micro-economic method to compare the dynamic effects of spatial size on the national competitiveness among the United States, Japan, former West Germany, and former USSR.[1] As a simplified cost-benefit approach was suggested in this paper for the analytical interpretation of the effects of spatial sizes on the structures of the rapid changing economies, Jia Shaofeng and Meng Xiangjing (1994) responded a commentary paper in which the possibility of the application of the cost-benefit analysis approach in the national studies was denied.[2] Of course, there were some mathematical and theoretical problems needed to be further clarified in details in my paper as both of us have agreed that it would not be an easy task to construct such a complex cost-benefit model as to cope with those economies differing in natural, geographical, and social conditions before a number of crucial assumptions and simplifications are made.

In order to clarify the above problems and establish a general cost-benefit model for the regional economic analysis, let us start with the simplest case by stipulating our target political region as an isolated country which

1. has not any form of economic and technological exchange and co-operation with the outside world;
2. is homogeneously distributed by production factors (such as labour force, capital, technology, natural resource, information, etc.) throughout its territory;
3. has an isotropic communication and transport network and the quality (efficiency) of which is positively related to the economic level of the country;
4. is to aim at the maximisation of total benefit and the minimisation of total cost of its own economy; and

------

[1]See Guo Rongxing (1993c): "The Effects of Spatial Size on the World's Economies", in Xiao Lian (ed.): *Dynamics of the World's Economic Structure – Discussions of the Role of USA*, Chapter 3, pp. 40–55, Beijing: The World Knowledge Press, 1993.

[2]See Jia Shaofeng and Meng X. (1994): "Is U.S. Territory Too Large to Sustain a Good Economy? – Comments on Dr. Guo Rongxing's Theory of the Optimal Size of a Country", *American Studies*, Vol. 8, pp. 114–25.

5. can increase and decrease its size freely with a range between zero and a large figure.

## 8.2 Does the Isolated Country Exist Any Optimal Size?

### 8.21 Some concepts

Before constructing a regional cost-benefit model, we should define some concepts for political regions which are related to the cost-benefit analysis in micro-economics.

*Regional size.* There are different approaches to measure the size of a political region. Regional size may be expressed by territorial area or population size. In general, territorial area reflects the size of natural resources under which the isolated economy is necessarily operated. Population size usually reflects the size of social resources under which the isolated economy is necessarily operated. Sometimes, territorial area and population size change in the same direction, i.e., when a political region's territorial area increases (decreases), so does its population size, and *vice versa*. However, given the complexities of the real world, this is not always the case with some political regions. Therefore, the third approach to measure the regional sizes may be approximately introduced by the geometric mean of territorial area and population size.

*Regional cost.* Regional cost is the whole expenses that a political region needs so as to manage its internal society. It involves the expenditures in socio-economic affairs, public service and administration, and other costs relating to the management of risks for the political region. Sometimes, regional cost may also be approximately expressed by government expenditure. Usually, regional cost can be classified into fixed cost, variable cost, average cost, and marginal cost. Firstly, variable cost, as a portion of regional cost, is positively related to the regional size. Theoretically, if the size of the political region is zero, the variable cost should be also zero. Fixed cost does not change with respect to the regional size. More plausibly, it still exists even though the size of the political region becomes zero. As two typical cases, the number of state head (here its expense constitutes a portion of fixed cost) of the former USSR (the largest country in the 20th century) would not in any case exceed that of San Marino, the smallest republic with a tiny land area of 24 square miles and only 2,300 population.[3] Secondly, average cost, or the total cost used in one unit of regional size, is the division of regional cost by regional size. Thirdly, marginal cost, also called newly increased cost, is the change in total cost when one more unit of size is increased.

*Regional benefit.* Regional benefit is the total economic output generated within a certain size of a political region. Marginal benefit refers to the rate at which total benefit changes with respect to the increase of an additional unit of regional size.

8.22 Cost-benefit curves for the isolated country with a set of sizes

Marginal cost of regional size (expressed by territorial area, population size or the geometric mean of territorial area and population size) is the ratio of change in cost per period to change in regional size by the political region per period. When the regional size administered by a political authority is small, the increased total cost will decrease with respect to the increase of regional size because the fixed cost remains as a constant. However, when the regional size administered by the political authority exceeds a certain quantity, the government will no longer efficiently manage the socio-economic affairs and, as a result of the managing difficulties of the additional quantity of regional size, will eventually bear a relatively higher increased rate of administrative expenditure (cost) with respect to the increase of regional size.

For a given set of regional sizes, there is an expansion that defines the least-cost combinations of regional size inputs and thus specifies the lowest total variable cost attainable at each rate of administered size. Variable cost functions illustrated by a *S*-shaped curve are often found in practical cases: near the point of origin, variable cost is increasing at a decreasing rate; whereas near the point in which the input size is in maximum, variable cost is increasing at an increasing rate.[4] By adding fixed cost per period to variable cost, one may obtain a function that relates total cost per period to the regional size administered by the political regime.

The assumptions in the beginning of Chapter 3 completely accord with the isolated country defined in the beginning of Chapter 8. Therefore, the

---

[3]Data source: *World Atlas,* Rand Mc. Nally & Company, USA, 1994.
[4]This has been generally confirmed in micro-economics.

result in Figure 3–2 can help us to understand the isolated country's benefit curve that shows a decreased marginal return with respect to the increase of regional size (shown in Figure 8–1), which generalises that as the quantity of the size is increased, holding other factors constant, the marginal benefit and average benefit must eventually decrease.

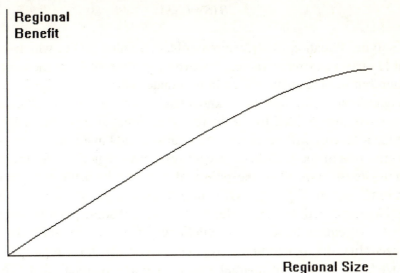

Figure 8–1 The Benefit Curve with respect to Territorial Size
for an Isolated Country

## 8.23 How to seek the isolated country's optimal size?

If the performances of the regional cost (*RC*) and regional benefit (*RB*) with respect to regional size (*S*) in the isolated country are known, we can derive the most efficient level of the regional size by maximising its regional benefit and minimising its regional cost. Let the regional cost be formulated by *RC*=*C*(*S*) and the regional benefit by *RB*=*B*(*S*). Consider that *RC* and *RB* are continuous functions of regional size (*S*).[5] Subtracting *RC* from *RB*, we obtain the net benefit for the isolated country:

$$Y=RB–RC=B(S)–C(S) \tag{8–1}$$

---

[5]The continuity of these two functions is rigidly propped by Assumptions (1)–(5) in the beginning of Chapter 8.

By deriving the first order differential of the net benefit ($Y$) with respect to regional size ($S$) and letting it be zero, we obtain

$$dY/dS=B'(S)-C'(S)=0$$

i.e.,

$$B'(S)=C'(S) \tag{8--2}$$

By solving Equation (8–2), we may obtain a value ($S^*$) at which the net benefit ($Y$) has an extreme value. However, Equation (8–2) is the necessary condition but not the sufficient condition under which the optimal regional size is determined. Because, as we know that, marginal cost, which equals to the increased cost divided by the increased regional size, is the differential rate of the total cost with respect to regional size, and marginal benefit is the differential rate of the total benefit with respect to regional size, there may sometimes exist more than one points of size at which the marginal cost equals to the marginal benefit. Of course, only one point can make the net benefit be maximized. For example, the total cost at some point at which the marginal cost equals to marginal benefit might be maximized rather than minimized. In order to determine a regional size at which the regional cost is minimized, we let the differential rate of average regional cost (i.e., the division of regional cost by regional size) with respect to regional size ($S$) equal to zero,

$$\frac{d(RC(S)/S)}{dS}=\frac{RC'(S)}{S}-\frac{RC(S)}{S^2}=0$$

i.e.,

$$RC'(S)=RC(S)/S \tag{8--3}$$

By combining Equations (8–2) and (8–3) together, we may easily determine an optimal size for any isolated political region which is characterized by Assumptions (1)–(5).

Generally, the sources for the return of economies of scale for political regions are many and diversified, but may be generally grouped into four categories as below:

1. Technical economies. The political regions with larger sizes can make relatively sufficient uses of their fixed costs which do not almost change with respect to the increase of territorial sizes and hence give themselves considerable advantages over small political regions in size.
2. Marketing economies. Marketing in a larger size of economy embraces many benefits, but the main economies of scale from marketing include the bulk purchases and distribution potentialities.
3. Financial economies. Relatively larger economies are frequently able to obtain finance more easily.
4. Risk-bearing economies. A number of advantages can lead to larger political regions experiencing risk-bearing economies. The underlying factor is that large political regions frequently engage in a range of diverse activities, so that a fall in the return from any one unit of regional economy does not threaten the stability of the whole economy.

While increases in size frequently confer advantages on a political region, in many cases there is a limit to the gains from growth. In other words, there is an optimal level of spatial capacity and increases in size beyond this level will lead to a loss of economies of sizes which manifest themselves in rising average cost of the political region. Diseconomies of sizes have several sources, but the main one of which is the managerial difficulties. There is no doubt that the increased complexity of managing a large political region in size is a major source of administrative inefficiencies when the political region grows beyond a certain size. It becomes increasingly difficult for a government to control and manage the various socio-economic affairs and risks as the political region grows in size. Using a numerical general equilibrium model, for example, Markusen and Wigle analyse the roles of a country's size on the country's "optimal" (Nash equilibrium) tariffs and obtain a higher optimal rate of protection for a larger country rather than a smaller country.[6] This result simply confirms that the scale diseconomies exist in the relatively larger countries in size which have to pursue higher cost to protect their internal socio-economic benefits.

---

[6]For more details, see J. R. Markusen and R. M. Wigle (1989): "Nash Equilibrium Tariffs for the United States and Canada: The Roles of Country Size, Scale Economies, and Capital Mobility", *Journal of Political Economy,* Vol. 97, pp. 368–86.

## 8.3 Extensions

The above cost-benefit analysis framework may also be extensively applied to analyse the optimal sizes for, besides the isolated economy as defined above, other economies with different internal and external conditions.

### 8.31 From isolated to open economies

Now, let us eliminate the Assumption (1) and consider an open economy which is characterized by Assumptions (2)–(5) in Section 8.1 and has freer trade with its outside neighbouring countries. Notice that, because the peripheral area in the open economy can additionally benefit from the co-operation with the outside world, the regional benefit curve will not possess such a decreased marginal rate[7] with respect to the regional size as that in the isolated country shown in Figure 3–2, even though it still follows the same internal trade benefit law. Therefore, compared to the regional benefit curve ($B_0$) for the isolated country, the open country's benefit curve will move up and be shaped as $B_1$ (see Figure 8–2). Given the same regional cost curve (i.e., $C_0$), the possible optimal size for the open country will be able to move from $S_0^*$ to $S_1^*$ (see Figure 8–2).

### 8.32 From less to well developed economies

Suppose that the isolated economy is now transformed from the backward stage to a developed one. The most different consequence might be that the latter has a higher economic level and, therefore, more advanced facilities of transportation and communication network with, in particular, a correspondingly higher average efficiency of public administration throughout the whole country. Along with these changes, the regional cost curve will not yield such an increased marginal rate with respect to the regional size as that in the backward stage. Therefore, the regional cost curve will move down (here it is assumed to shape as $C_1$) compared with the regional cost curve for the less developed economies (here it is expressed as $C_0$ in Figure 8–2). Given the regional benefit curve as $B_0$, the possible

---

[7]If its neighbouring countries are also characterised by Assumptions (2)–(4), the trade benefit difference between the open country's core and peripheral regions will be only decided by its tariff and non-tariff barriers.

optimal size for the developed country will be able to move from $S_0^*$ to $S_2^*$ correspondingly (see Figure 8–2).

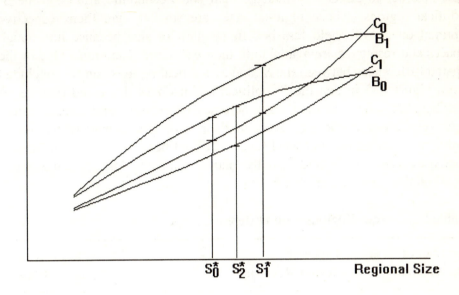

Figure 8–2 The Optimal Sizes under Different Conditions

## 8.33 An extension to border-regions

After the above efforts, the optimal sizes for political regions which are characterized by Assumptions (2)–(5) in Section 8.1 can be determined by the regional cost-benefit analysis (RCBA) model constructed as above. Briefly, political regions can be classified into three kinds in spatial status: (I) the actual size of a political region equals to its optimal size, we label this political region by $S^*$; (II) the actual size of a political region is smaller than its optimal size, we label this political region by $S^-$; (III) the actual size of a political region is larger than its optimal size, we label this political region by $S^+$. Given that all the political regions concerned have been identified with their respective spatial status: (i.e., $S^*$, $S^-$ or $S^+$), the border-regions formed by those political regions can also be classified into several types in terms of spatial compositions. Table 8–1 gives different types of border-regions with 2-d, 3-d, and 4-d compositions of $S^*$, $S^-$ and $S^+$.

There is no doubt that the $S^+$ political regions (whose regional sizes are larger than their respective optimal ones) will shoulder more cost per unit of size in order to effectively manage their socio-economic affairs; while $S^-$ political regions (whose regional sizes are smaller than their respective optimal ones) will yield less benefit per unit of size because no enough spaces and resources are available to their economic operations. One of the spatial differences between the $S^+$ and $S^-$ political regions can be concluded from Figure 8–3 in that the $S^+$ political regions have decreased (increased) net benefits when regional size increases (decreases) and usually show relatively lower economic levels in their peripheral areas, while the $S^-$ political regions have increased (decreased) net benefits when regional size increases (decreases) and usually show relatively less heterogeneities between the core and peripheral areas.

Table 8–1 Border-Regions with Different Compositions

| Number of Dimensions | Types of Border-Regions | Number of Compositions |
|---|---|---|
| 2-d | (\*\*), (\*-), (\*+), (--), (++), (+-) | 6 |
| 3-d | (\*\*\*), (\*--), (\*++), (+++), (---), ... | 10 |
| 4-d | (\*\*\*\*), (\*\*-+), (\*--+), (--++), ... | 15 |

Note: * denotes that the political region's size equals to its optimal size; - denotes that the political region's size is less than its optimal size; + denotes that the political region's size is larger than its optimal size.

After having made the above deductions, we may return back to Table 8–1 to understand the economic mechanisms of different border-regions. For the sake of expositional ease, let's take the case of 2-d border-regions as an example. $S^*S^*$, $S^-S^-$ and $S^+S^+$ border-regions are all homogeneous but different from each other: (1) $S^*S^*$ border-regions are usually well-developed and stable; (2) $S^+S^+$ border-regions are usually less developed compared with their respective political cores; (3) $S^-S^-$ border-regions are usually well developed but have strong desire to develop transborder co-operation so as to benefit from the economies of scale. Under certain internal and external conditions, this kind of border-regions may form economic communities and/or political unions of their own. $S^*S^-$, $S^*S^+$ and $S^-S^+$ border-regions are all heterogeneous: (1) $S^*S^+$ border-regions are stable because each side does not have a stronger desire to develop transborder interaction; (2) $S^*S^-$ and $S^-S^+$ border-regions are not stable because $S^-$ side needs to develop transborder interaction in order to extend its economic space, while neither $S^*$ nor $S^+$ side has so stronger desire as to develop its transborder interaction with the outside economies because an extra marginal increase in economic space cannot contribute more to the economic benefit while, at the meantime, has to bear a higher marginal regional cost in $S^*$ and $S^+$ political regions than $S^-$ political regions.

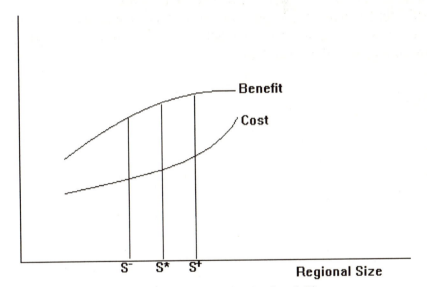

Figure 8–3 Beyond the Optimal Size

The above patterns of mechanisms of the cross-border economic co-operation and trade in border-regions under different political regions in size may also be effectively illustrated by the mathematical outcomes in Ychanan Shachmurove and Uriel Spiegel (1995). Their paper in which a model of non-cooperative Nash equilibrium between countries differing in size is constructed plausibly demonstrates the following results: the non-cooperative free-trade Nash (NCFTN) equilibrium price in the small country is higher than the corresponding price in the large country. The producer in the small country exploits the fact that, as borders are opened, some foreigners in large neighbouring countries find it cheaper to cross-shop than to travel to their respective core areas. The producer in the large country, therefore, loses customers, some cross-shopping and some not buying the product at all, and thus charges a higher price relative to the autarky case. So, for the large country, and in some cases for the small country as well, more competition does not lead to lower prices. This is a case where free trade causes an increase in the prices in the two countries relative to the autarky regimes.[8]

Briefly, the above discussions have explained the cross-border conflicts that countries differing in size face when opening their borders for economic co-operation or lifting their border-related barriers for trade. The diversification of political regions in terms of their spatial status of optimal sizes will always determine the fundamental characteristics and dynamic patterns of border-regional economics.

---

[8]In addition, a comparison between the small and large economies before and after international trade is also done via four propositions by Y. Shachmurove and U. Spiegel (1995): "On Nation's Size and Transportation Costs", *Review of International Economics*, Vol. 3(2), pp. 235–43.

# BIBLIOGRAPHY

Administrative Committee of China Agenda XXI (1994): *Priority Programmes for China's Agenda XXI*, State Planning Commission and State Science and Technology Commission, Beijing, China.

Alker, Hageward R. (1974): "Analysing Global Interdependence", Center for International Studies, Massachusetts Institute of Technology, USA.

*Baokan Wenzhai* (The Digest of Newspapers and Magazines) (1989), p. 4, June 13.

Barrett, Scott (1992): "International Environmental Agreement as Games", pp. 11–36, in Rüdger Pethig (ed.).

Bayerische, Grenzpolizei (1981): *Bayerns Landesgrenze Zur DDR*, Bayerisches Staatsregierung, Munich.

Braun, K.-H. and J. Maier (1983): *Industrie im Peripheren Raum unter dem Einfluss der Grenze Zur DDR und CSSR*, Institut für Geowissenschaften, Bayreuth.

Brown, Lesley (ed.): *The New Shorter Oxford English Dictionary on Historical Principles*, p. 2274 and p. 2527, Oxford: Clarendon Press, Vol. 2 (N–Z), 1993.

Bruinsma, F. and P. Rietveld (1992): "De Structurerende Werking van Insfrastructuur", Economische Faculteit, Vrije Universiteit, Amsterdam.

Cappellin, R. and P. W. J. Batey (eds.): *Regional Networks, Border Regions and European Integration*, European Research in Regional Science Series No. 3, London: Pion Limited, 1993.

Carraro, C. and D. Siniscalco (1993): "Strategies for the International Protection of the Environment", *Journal of Public Economics*, Vol. 52, pp. 309–28.

Carraro, C. and D. Siniscalco (1995): "Policy Co-ordination for Sustainability: Commitments, Transfers and Linked Negotiations", in I. Goldin and Winter L. Alan (eds.).

Cattan, N. and C. Grasland (1993): "Migratization of Population in Czechoslovakia: A Comparison of Political and Spatial Determinants of Migration and the Measurement of Barriers", *Trinity Papers in Geography*, forthcoming.

Cecchini, P. (1988): *The European Challenge 1992: The Benefit of a Single Market*, Hants Wildwood House.

Chen Cai, Yuan Shuren, Wang Li and Ding Shibao (1991): "Regional Co-operation in Northeast Asia and the Exploitation of Triangle Area of Lower Tumen River", paper presented at the Second International Conference on the Economic and Technological Development of Northeast Asia, Changchun, 1991.

Choy, Bong-youn (1984): *A History of the Korean Unification Movement: Its Issues and Prospects*, Ill: Bradley University.

Christaller, W. (1933): *Die Zentrallen Orte in Suddeutschland* (The Central Locations in Southern Germany), Darmstadt: Wissenschaftliche Buchgesellschaft, reprinted in 1980.

*Cihai*, Shanghai: Shanghai Cishu Press, 1988.

Consejo Nacional de Población (1982): *México Demográfico: Breviario 1980–81*, Mexico, D.F.: Consejo Nacional de Población

Council of Europe (1982): *European Outline Convention on Transfrontier Co-operation between Territorial Communities or Authorities*, Strabourg, France: Council of Europe.

d'Honghe, Ingrid (1994): "Regional Economic Integration in Yunnan", in Daivid S. G. Goodman and Gerald Gegal (eds.).

Damasevich, Alla (1993): "Problems Concerning Cultural and Educational Development at the Transboundary Territories of the Ukraine and Russia", unpublished paper, Kharkov State University, Ukraine.

Dempsy, Judy (1995): "Berliners Pay Prices for Wall around Utilities", *Financial Times*, p. 3, September 6.

Ding Shisheng (1993): "The Development of the Ports in the Tumen River: Suggestions", *Northeast Asia Forum*, p. 1, No. 1.

Eatwell, John, and Murray Milgate and Peter Newman (eds.): *The New Palgrave: A Dictionary of Economics*, Vol. 4, London: The Macmillan Press Limited, 1987.

Eichengreen, B. and D. A. Irwin (1995); "Trade Blocs, Currency Blocs and the Reorientation of World Trade in the 1930s", *Journal of International Economics*, Vol. 38, pp. 1–24.

Environment Monitoring Station (*Huanjing Jiance Zhan*) (1991): "A Mission Report of the Environmental Quality in Yanbian Area (1986-1991)", Yanbian Korean autonomous prefecture, Jilin province, China.

EUREGIO (1991): "Cross-border Co-operation in Practice: Institutional Aspects of Cross-border Co-operation", EUREGIO, Enschede, the Netherlands.

FAMY Organizing Committee (ed.): *Proceedings of the First Academic Meeting of Youths (FAMY), Chinese Association for Science and Technology*, Beijing: China Science and Technology Press, 1992.

Figueiredo, A. M. (1993): "Theory and Practice of International Co-operation and Urban Networks in Economically Lagging Regions: The Experience of Galicia and the North of Portugal", in R. Cappelline and P. W. J. Batey (eds.), pp. 96–115, 1993.

*Financial Times*, p. 4, September 29, 1995.

Forester, Jay W. (1965): *Principles of Systems*, Cambridge, MA: MIT Press.

Frankel, J., S.-J. Wei and E. Stein (1994): "APEC and Regional Economic Agreements in the Pacific", unpublished manuscript, University of California at Berkeley, USA.

Friedmann, John (1993): "Borders, Margins, and Frontiers: Notes Towards a Political Economy of Regions", unpublished draft, University of California at Los Angeles, U.S.A.

Garrean, Joel (1981): "*The Nine Nations of North America*, New York: Avon Books.

Gibson, Lay James and Alfonso Corona Renteria (eds.): *Regional Structural Change in Two Mature Nations*, Regional Science Research Institute, Peace Dale, Rhade Island, 1989.

Gibson, Lay James and Alfonso Corona Renteria (eds.): *The U.S. and Mexico: Borderland Development and the National Economies*, Boulder: Westview Press, 1985.

Goddard, Haynes C. (1985): "Evaluating the Benefits and Costs of Mexico's Border Industrialization Program", in Lay James Gibson and Alfonso Corona Renteria (eds.), 1985.

Goldin, I and Winter L. Alan (eds.): *The Economics of Sustainable Development*, Cambridge: Cambridge University Press, 1995.

Goodman, Daivid S. G. and Gerald Gegal (eds.): *China Deconstructs: Politics, Trade and Regionalism*, London and New York: Routledge, 1994.

Gradus, Yehuda (ed.): *Frontiers in Regional Development*, Rowman and Littlefield, forthcoming.

Grunwald, Joseph (1985) "Internationlization of Industry: U.S.–Mexican Linkages", in Lay James Gibson and Alfonso Corona Renteria (eds.), 1985.

Guichonnet, P. and C. Raffestin (1974): *Géographie des Frontières* (Geography of Border Regions), Paris: Presses Universitaires de France.

Guo Rongxing (1991): "A Preliminary Study of Border-Regional Economics: Theory and Practice of Economic Development in the Provincial Border-Regions of China", Ph.D. thesis, CUMT School of Economics and Trade, Xuzhou, China.

Guo Rongxing (1992): "Some Theoretical Problems of Border-Regional Economics", in FAMY Organizing Committee (ed.), pp. 1–6.

Guo Rongxing (1993a): "The Impact of Spatial Organizational Structures on the Economic Development of the Provincial Border-Regions of China", *Scientia Geographica Sinica*, Vol. 13, pp. 196–204. Also translated and published by *Chinese Geographical Science*, Vol. 5, No. 4. pp. 204–10.

Guo Rongxing (1993b): *Economic Analysis of Border-Regions: Theory and Practice of China*, Beijing: China Ocean Press.

Guo Rongxing (1993c): "The Effects of Spatial Size on the World's Economies", in Xiao Lian (ed.), Chapter 3, pp. 40–55.

Guo Rongxing (1994): "The Economic Comparison of Border-Regions: The Case of Central China", in Lou Zhaomei et al. (eds.), pp. 417–22.

Guo Rongxing (1995a): "A Proposal on the Exploitation of Natural Resources in the Provincial Border-Regions of China", *Science and Technology Review*, No. 2, February.

Guo Rongxing (1995b): "The Impacts of Provincial Borders on the Economic Development of China: The N-dimensional Model of Spatial Economies", *Xitong Gongcheng Lilun Yu Shijian,* (Journal of China Society of System Engineering), Vol. 15, No. 4, pp. 38–43.

Guo Wenxuan (ed.) (1989): *An Introduction to Henan's Economy*, in Chinese, Zhengzhou: Henan Renmin Press.

Hansen, Niles (1977): "Border Regions: A Critique of Spatial Theory and A European Case Study", *Ann. Regional Science*, Vol. 11, pp. 1–14.

Hansen, Niles (1981): *The Border Economy: Regional Development in the Southwest*, Austin: University of Texas Press.

Hansen, Niles (1985): "The Nature and Significance of Border Development Patterns", in Lay James Gibson and Alfonso Corona Renteria (eds.), 1985.

Hansen, Niles (1989): "Environmental Impacts of Human Settlement System Growth in the U.S. Southwest", in Lay James Gibson and Alfonso Corona Renteria (eds.), pp. 137–8, 1989.

Harris, William H. and Tudith S. Levey (eds.): *The New Columbia Encyclopaedia*, New York/London: Columbia University Press, 1975

Hartshorne, R. (1933): "Geographical and Political Boundaries in Upper Silesia", *Ann. Association of American Geography*, Vol. 23, pp. 195–228.

Hecter, M. (1975): *Internal Colonialism: The Celtic Fringe in British National Development, 1576–1966*, London: Routledge and Kegan.

Heffernan, Shelagh and Peter Sinclair (1990): *Modern International Economics*, Oxford/Cambridge: Basil Blackwell.

Herzog, Lawrence A. (1990): *Where North Meets South: Cities, Space, and Politics on the U.S.–Mexico Border*, Austin, Tx: Center for Mexican American Studies, University of Texas.

Hughes, David W. and David W. Holland (1994): "Core-periphery Economic Linkage: A Measure of Spread and Possible Backwash Effects for the Washington Economy", *Land Economics*, Vol. 70, pp. 364–77.

Hwang, Eui-Gak (1993): *The Korean Economies: A Comparison of North and South*, Oxford: Clarendon Press.

Ilbery, Brain W. (1984): "Core-periphery Contrasts in European Social Well-being", *Geography*, Vol. 69(4), pp. 289–302.

*Information Times*, p. 2, August 2, 1992.

*INTERREG PROGRAMMES*, Association of European Border Regions, Enscheder Strabe 362, D–4432 Gronau.

Israel–PLO (1993): "Protocol on Israeli–Palestinian Co-operation in Economic and Development Programs", Washington D. C., USA, November 13.

Israel–PLO (1995): "Agreement on Establishing the Palestinian Self-Rule in Most of the West Bank", Washington D. C., USA, September 28.

Jia Shaofeng and Meng Xiangjing (1994): "Is U.S. Territory Too Large to Sustain A Good Economy? – Comments on Dr. Guo Rongxing's Theory of the Optimal Size of A Country", *American Studies*, Vol. 8, pp. 114–25.

Jin Tie (1993): "The Openness and Development of Hunchun City: Situation and Perspectives", *Northeast Asia Forum*, No. 1, pp. 12–3.

Jones, Philip N. and Trevor Wild (1994): "Opening the Frontier: Recent Spatial Impacts in the Former Inner-German Border Zone", *Regional Studies*, Vol. 28, pp. 259–73.

Kaldor, N. (1934): "A Classificatory Note on the Determinateness of Equilibrium", *Review of Economic Studies*, Vol. 1, February, pp. 122–36.

Keeble, David (1989): "Core-periphery Disparities, Recession and New Regional Dynamisms in European Community", *Geography*, Vol. 74(1), pp. 1–11.

Krumm, Ronald J. and George S. Tolley (1987): "Regional Economics", in John Eatwell and Murray Milgate and Peter Newman (eds.), p. 117.

Li Qing (1991): "Pay More Attention to Border-Regions", p. 5, *Zhongguo Jingji Wenti* (Chinese Economic Issues), No. 4.

Li Zhengyi (1993): "In-Depth Exploration of the Question of Regional Blockades", *Chinese Economic Studies*, Vol. 26, No. 5, pp. 23–36.

Li Zhisheng (1988): "Influences, Disadvantages and Suggestions", in Zhang Ping (ed.), pp. 338–9.

Liu Baorong and Liao Jiasheng (eds.): *China's Frontier Opening and the Neighbouring Countries,* Beijing: Falu Press, 1993.

Lösch, A. (1954): *The Economics of Location*, New Haven: Yale University Press.

Lou Zhaomei et al. (eds.): *Advances in Management Science*, Beijing: International Academic Publishers, 1994.

Luk, Chiu-Ming (1985): "Core-periphery Contrasts in China's Development During the Early Eighties", *Socio-economic Planning Sciences*, Vol. 19(6), pp. 407–16.

Mailla, D. (1990): "Transborder Regions Between Members of EC and the Non-member Countries", *Built Environment*, Vol. 16, pp. 38–51.

Mao Zedong (1929): "Why Has the Red Political Power Still Been Existing?", in *Mao's Selected Works*, pp. 47–84, Vol. 1, Beijing: Remin Press, 1977.

Marcuse, Peter (1992): "The Goal of the Wall-less City: New York, Los Angeles and Berlin", Harvey S. Perloff Lecture, UCLA Graduate School of Architecture and Urban Planning.

Markusen, James R. and Randall M. Wigle (1989): "Nash Equilibrium Tariffs for the United States and Canada: The Roles of Country Size, Scale Economies, and Capital Mobility", *Journal of Political Economy*, Vol. 97, pp. 368–86.

Mexico Statistical Yearbook, related issues.

Mouafo, Dieudonne and Javier Herrera (1993): "The Challenge of the Frontier in Central Africa: The Cameroon–Nigeria Border Case", unpublished paper, Univerite Laval, Canada.

Mumme, S. P. (1982): "The Politics of Water Apportionment and Pollution Problems in United States–Mexico Relations", *U.S.–Mexico Project Series No. 5*, Overseas Department Council, Washington, D. C, USA.

Northeast Asian Nations (1995): "Agreement of the Tumen River Area Development Programme among China, Mongolia, Russia, North and South Korea", Beijing, China, May 30.

NPC (1980): "The Regulations Concerning the Special Economic Zones of Guangdong Province, the People's Republic of China", Beijing: National People's Congress of China, August 26.

Oudis, Gilles and Jeffrey Sachs (1984): "Macroeconomic Co-ordination among the Industrial Economies", *Brookings Paper*, No. 1, Washington, D. C., USA.

Pan Naigu and Ma Rong (eds.): *Papers on the Frontier Areas Development,* Beijing: Peking University Press, 1993.

Peach, James T. (1985): "Income Distribution in the U.S.–Mexico Borderlands", in Lay James Gibson and Alfonso Corona Renteria (eds.), 1989.

Pethig, Rüdger (ed.): *Conflicts and Co-operation in Managing Environmental Resources*, Berlin: Springer-Verlag, 1992.

Plane, D. (1989): "The Interregional Impacts of U.S. Core-periphery Net Migration", in Gibson et al. (eds.), 1989.

Pond, Elizabeth (1990): *After the Wall: American Policy Toward Germany*, A 20th Century Fund Paper, New York: Priority Press Publication.

Quévit, M. and S. Bodson (1993): "Transborder Co-operation and European Integration: The Case of Wallonia", in R. Cappellin and P. W. J. Batey (eds.), pp. 194–5, 1993.

Ratti, R. (1990): "The Study of the Spatial Effects of the Borders: An Overview of Different Approaches", NETCOM, Vol. 4, pp. 37–50.

Ratti, R. (1993): "How Can Existing Barriers and Border Effects Be Overcomed? A Theoretical Approach", in R. Cappellin and W. J. Batey (eds.), pp. 60–69.

Ratti, R. and S. Reichman (eds.): *Theory and Strategy of Border Areas Development*, Bellinzona: IRE, 1993.

Rider, A. (1988): "Growth Potential of the Pacte Region and Cross-border Co-operation with the Nord–Pas-de-Calais", Research Report of Interdisciplinary Research Group on Regional Development (IRGRD), University College, London.

Rietveld, P. (1993): "Transport and Communication Barriers in Europe", in Riccard Cappellin and Peter W. J. Batey (eds.), pp. 47–59.

Ross, Stanley R. (ed.): *Views Across the Border: The United States and Mexico*, Albuquerque: University of New Mexico Press, 1978.

Rumley, D. and J. Minghi (1991): *The Geography of Border Landscapes*, London/New York: Routledge.

Schank, H. (1993): "The Rurban Fringe: A Central Area Between Region and City: the Case of Bangalore, India", University of Amsterdam, The Netherlands.

Secretariat of the United Nations Commission for Europe (1994): "Protection and Use of Transboundary Watercourses and International Lakes in Europe", *Natural Resources Forum*, Vol. 18(3), pp. 171–80.

Shachmurove, Ychanan and Uriel Spiegel (1995): "On Nation's Size and Transportation Costs", *Review of International Economics*, Vol. 3(2), pp. 235–43.

Shen Liren and Dai Yuanchen (1990): "Chinese Zhuhou Jingji: Mechanisms, Impacts, and Sources", *Jingji Yanjiu* (Economic Research Journal), No. 3, p. 12.

*Shenzhen Tongji Nianjian* (Shenzhen Statistical Yearbook), each issue.

State Council (1986): "The Regulations of Issues Concerning the Extensive Regional Economic Co-operation", *Renmin Ribao* (People's Daily), March 26.

State Council (1990): "Contemporary Regulations Concerning the Resolutions of the Border Disputes of the Administrative Divisions of the P. R China".

The Aquatic Products Station (*Shui Chan Zhan*): *Statistical Report*, each year, Hunchun Municipality, Jilin Province, China.

*The Economists*, p. 17, September 30, 1995.

*The Economists:* "The South China Miracle", October 5, 1991, pp. 19 and 44.

*The Map of China* (1993), Beijing: China Maps Publishing House

*The World Yearbook of Economic Statistics*, 1983–84.

U.S. Bureau of the Census (1983): *Summary Characteristrics for Governmental Units and Standard Metropolitan Statistical Areas* (*PHC 80–3-33*), Appendix B, Washington, D. C., USA.

U.S. Department of Commerce, Bureau of Census: *Statistical Abstract of the United States*, Washington D. C.: U.S. Government Printing Office, 1981.

Ugalde, Antonio (1978): "Regional Political Process and Mexican Politics on the Border", in Stanley R. Ross (ed.).

UNDP (1991): *Tumen River Area Development: Mission Report*, by M. Miller, A. Holon, and T. Kelleher, Pyongyang: Consultation with Participant Governments, October 11–8.

United Nations Economic Commission for Europe (1988): *Water Pollution Control and Flood Management in Transboundary Waters*, Geneva: ECE/ENVWA/7.

US–Mexico (1994): "Agreement Between the Government of the United States of America and the Government of the United Mexican States Concerning the Establishment of a Border Environment Co-operation Commission and a North America Development Bank", Washington D. C., USA, February 3.

van Den Berg, L. M. (1984): *Anticipating Urban Growth in Africa, Land Use and Land Values in Rurban Fringe of Luska, Zambia*, Zambia Geographical Association, Occasional Study No. 13, Lusaka, Zambia.

van der Veen, A. (1993): "Theory and Practice of Cross-border Co-operation of Local Governments: The Case of the EUREGIO Between Germany and the Netherlands, in R. Cappelline and P. W. J. Batey (eds.), 1993.

van Waas, Michael (1981): "The Multinationals' Strategy for Labour: Foreign Assembly Plants in Mexico's Border Industrialization Program", unpublished Ph. D. thesis, Standford University (University Microfilms International).

Vining, D. R. (1982): "Migration Between Core and Periphery", *Scientific American*, Vol. 247, pp. 45–53 (December).

von Thünen, J. H. (1826): *The Isolated State*, Translated by C. M. Wartenburg, London: Pergamon Press, 1966.

Walker, Tony (1995): "Five Nations in Pact to Develop NE Asian Region", *Financial Times* (News: Asia – Pacific), May 31.

Wang Wenxiang (ed.) (1986): *China's Special Economic Zones and 14 Open Cities*, Beijing: China Zhanwang Press.

Wedeman, A. H. (1993): "Editor's Introduction to Chinese Economic Studies", *Chinese Economic Studies*, Vol. 26, No. 5 (special issue on regional protection).

Wild, Trevor and Philip N. Jones (1993): "From Periphery to New Centrality? The Transformation of Germany's Zonenrandgebiet", *Geography*, Vol. 78, pp. 281–94.

*World Altals,* Rand Mc. Nally & Company, USA, 1994.

*World Resources 1992–93,* Oxford: Oxford University Press, 1992.

Xiao Lian (ed.): *Dynamics of the World's Economic Structure – Discussions of the Role of USA*, Beijing: The World Knowledge Press, 1993.

Yanbian Agricultural Institute (1980): "The Impacts of San Tail Pollution in Tumen River on the Farmland and Rice Production", Yanbian Korean Prefecture, Jilin Province, China.

Yang Shuzhen (1990): *Studies of Chinese Economic Zones*, Beijing: China Zhanwang Press.

*Yearbook of Provincial Statistics* (Zhejiang, Fujian, Jiangxi, Guangdong and Hunan provinces), each issue.

Yergin, Daniel (1992): *The Prize: the Epic Quest for Oil, Money and Power,* New York: A Touchstone Book, Published by Simou & Schuster.

Zhang Honghuan (1990): "The Importance of Regulating the Transprovincial Borders in China", *Journal of East China Normal University*, No. 1.

Zhang Ping (ed.): *Studies of the Economic Relations Between Hunan and Guangdong Provinces*, Changsha: Hunan Renmin Press, 1988.

Zhang Wanqing (1987): *Regional Co-operation and Economic Networks*, Beijing: Economic Academic Press;

Zhang Wenkui (ed.) (1991): *An Introduction to Human Geography*, second edition, Changchun: Northeast Normal University Press.

Zhang Xiuyuan (1994): "The Functions of the Inner Ports in Tumen River Delta", *Northeast Asia Forum,* pp. 7–8, No. 2.

Zhang Yunling (1989): *The Interdependence in the World's Economies*, Beijing: The Economic Science Press.

*Zhongguo Chengshi Jingji Shehui Nianjian* (The Almanac of China's Urban Economy and Society), each issue.

*Zhongguo Ditu Ce* (China Atlas), Beijing: China Map Publishing House, 1983.

*Zhongguo Tongji Nianjian* (China Statistical Yearbook), each issue.

Zhongyuan Association of Economic and Technological Co-ordination (1985): "Agreement on Transborder Economic and Technological Co-ordination Among 14 Municipalities and Prefectures in the Border-Region of Shanxi, Hebei, Shandong, and Henan Provinces", Handan, Hebei province, China, September 27.

Zhu Chunme, Ren Huanying and Shen Hengzhe (1993): "The Environment Pollution in Tumen River and Its Impacts on the Tumen River Area", *Northeast Asia Forum*, pp. 64–7, No. 2.

# INDEX OF BORDER-REGIONS